Sonja Koppensteiner

Process Mapping and Simulation for Software Projects

Sonja Koppensteiner

Process Mapping and Simulation for Software Projects

Bridging the Project Management and Software Development Gap

VDM Verlag Dr. Müller

Imprint

Bibliographic information by the German National Library: The German National Library lists this publication at the German National Bibliography; detailed bibliographic information is available on the Internet at http://dnb.d-nb.de.

Any brand names and product names mentioned in this book are subject to trademark, brand or patent protection and are trademarks or registered trademarks of their respective holders. The use of brand names, product names, common names, trade names, product descriptions etc. even without a particular marking in this works is in no way to be construed to mean that such names may be regarded as unrestricted in respect of trademark and brand protection legislation and could thus be used by anyone.

Cover image: www.purestockx.com

Publisher:
VDM Verlag Dr. Müller Aktiengesellschaft & Co. KG , Dudweiler Landstr. 125 a, 66123 Saarbrücken, Germany,
Phone +49 681 9100-698, Fax +49 681 9100-988,
Email: info@vdm-verlag.de

Zugl.: Linz, JKU, Diss., 2007

Produced in USA and UK by:
Lightning Source Inc., La Vergne, Tennessee, USA
Lightning Source UK Ltd., Milton Keynes, UK
BookSurge LLC, 5341 Dorchester Road, Suite 16, North Charleston, SC 29418, USA

ISBN: 978-3-8364-7433-7

Kurzfassung

Projekt Management hat in den letzten Jahren in der Software-Industrie immer mehr an Bedeutung gewonnen. Die Globalisierung und der damit verbundende Anstieg des Wettbewerbes, erfordern es, Software Produkte so schnell als möglich auf den Markt zu bringen. Entscheidend für eine erfolgreiche Entwicklung von Softwareprodukten ist die Prozesssicht. Diese unterscheidet drei mehrschrittige Prozesse: Prozesse für das Produktmanagment, für das Projektmanagement und für die Softwareentwicklung im engeren Sinn (Software Methologie).

Die Softwareindustrie unterscheidet sich von der klassischen Produktionsindustrie vor allem dadurch, dass es eine große Auswahl an verschiedenen Prozessen und Softwareentwicklungsmethoden gibt, die angewendet werden können.

Sehr oft werden Projektmanagement-Prozesse isoliert von den produkt-erzeugenden Prozessen betrachtet, wobei es sich um keine Produktionsprozesse im Sinne von Hardwareerzeugung handelt.

Um einen erfolgreichen Ablauf der Produktentwicklung zu gewährleisten, müssen wesentliche Abstimmungen zwischen den Phasen und den Meilensteinen der drei Prozesstypen durchgeführt werden. Diese Arbeit zeigt den Prozessabgleich aus dem Blickwinkel von Projekt Mangement auf.

Diese Arbeit identifiziert die Zusammenhänge und Überschneidungen von Projekt Management mit Produkt Management und Software-Entwicklungsmethoden. Es werden die Meilensteine der drei Prozesse definiert. Jeder Meilenstein charakterisiert entweder den Abschluss einer Produktentwicklungs-, einer Projekt- oder Softwareentwicklungsphase und ist mit einer Review verbunden. Zu jedem Meilenstein stehen gewisse Informationen zur Verfügung, die das Management mit den „richtigen" Fragen und Anworten im Rahmen einer Review erkunden kann.

In dieser Arbeit werden allgemein gültige Fragen definiert, die für jedem Meilenstein angewendet werden sowie die notwendigen/verfügbaren Informationen identifiziert. Um die Variabilität der Softwareentwicklungsmethoden zu erfassen werden drei prototypische Entwicklungmethoden („Wasserfallmodel, Spiralmodel und Agile

I

Softwareentwicklung") herangezogen um aufzuzeigen, welchen Einfluss diese Methoden auf die Verfügbarkeit von Informationen, als auch auf die Abstimmung des Produktlebenszyklus mit dem Projektlebenszyklus haben.

Die Arbeit stellt ferner für jede der Softwareentwicklungsmethoden ein Systems Dynamics Modell zur Verfügung, welches es ermöglicht das zeitliche Verhalten jeder der Produktentwicklungsmethoden aufzuzeigen und Parameter zu identifizieren, die einen Einfluss auf den Verlauf des Projektes haben können. Diese Modelle werden an realistischen Entwicklungsszenarien angewendet. Als Ergebnis zeigen die Simulationsläufe das Verhalten dieser Softwareentwicklungsmethoden bei Auftreten von Fehlern im Code und Fehlern im Design.

Diese Systems Dynamics Modelle können als Vorlage für die Simulationen anderer individueller Projekte herangezogen werden. Zusätzlich können diese Modelle als Grundlage für die Weiterentwicklung von Projektspezifischen Modellen dienen.

Abstract

Within the last ten years project management has become more important in the software industry. Globalization and increased competition require that software products are introduced to the market as early as possible. For the successful development of software products it is crucial to take the process view. The process view distinguishes between three processes that consist of multiple steps: product management processes, project management processes and software methodologies.

The software industry differentiates itself from the classical production industry by having a great variety of software methodologies available that can be applied to software development. Often project management processes are perceived isolated from the product development processes for software products.

In order to guarantee a successful product development the phases and milestones between these three process types need to be aligned. This thesis shows the process alignment from the project management view.

It further identifies the relationships between project management, product management and software development methodologies. We define the milestones of these three processes. Each milestone characterizes the end of a product development phase, a project phase or a software development phase and is associated with a review. Information is available at each milestone. Asking the right review questions at the time information is available becomes key not only to amend misperceptions in management but also to enable management to react to the available information.

A set of basic generic review questions is established and can be applied at project reviews throughout the life cycle of a product development.

The relationship between product life cycle, project life cycle and software development methodology are defined in order to identify their interaction and the right timing for project reviews.

As prototypical development examples the waterfall model, agile development methodologies, and the spiral model are used to show the influence of these methodologies on the availability of information as well as the alignment of the product life cycle with the project life cycle

This thesis also provides systems dynamics models for each of these software methodologies to show the effect of these software methodologies over time and to identify the parameters that can influence the progress of a project. These models are applied to real scenarios of software development exhibiting both code and design errors. These models can be used as a template for individual project simulations. In addition they can be advanced to project specific models.

Dank

Die vorliegende Arbeit, wäre ohne die Unterstützung vieler Menschen nicht möglich gewesen. All jenen, die zum Gelingen dieser Arbeit beigetragen haben, möchte ich meinen Dank aussprechen.

Allen voran danke ich meinem Doktorvater, *Herrn Professor Dr. Gerhard Chroust*, der die Arbeit in ihrem Entstehungsprozess begleitet hat. Ich danke ihm vorallem für die zahlreichen Diskussionen und für sein erstklassiges Feedback. Beides hat dazu beigetragen meinen Horizont wesentlich zu erweitern. Weiters möchte ich mich für seine Flexibilität bedanken mit der er mich, eine Auslandsösterreicherin, betreut hat.

Herrn Professor Dr. Friedrich Roithmayr möchte ich für die Zweitbegutachtung ebenfalls meinen besonderen Dank aussprechen.

Fuer zusaetzlichen Diskussionen, ueber die Anwendung von Software Methoden in der Instustrie, möchte ich mich bei *Herrn Dipl.-Ing. Dr. Gerhard Eschelbeck* bedanken.

Mein Dank gilt auch *Frau Dagmar Reinmann*, für Ihre spontane und schnelle Hilfeleistungen beim Prozess zum Einreichen dieser Arbeit.

Last but not least möchte ich mich bei meinen Eltern *Christine* und *Heinz Koppensteiner*, meinem Mann *Dipl.-Ing. Dr. Helmut Puchner*, meiner Schwester *Mag. Susanne Koppensteiner*, als auch meinen österreichischen und in Amerika lebenden Freunden dafür bedanken, dass sie mich immer ermutigt haben meinen eigenen Weg zu verfolgen.

Ich moechte diese Arbeit meinen Patenkindern *Carina Timmel* und *Sandra Langer* widmen, um sie zu ermutigen Ihre eigenen Träume in Ihrem Leben zu verwirklichen.

"Everyone has inside of him a piece of good news. The good news is that you don't know how great you can be! How much you can love! What you can accomplish! And what your potential is!"

--Anne Frank

Table of Content

VII

List of Tables

List of Figures

XI

XIII

XIV

Chapter 1: Introduction and Motivation

Due to the unpredictable nature of software development and the increasing complex business environment structural approaches are required to manage software projects. Actually software companies have to operate and deal with more difficult situations than ever before caused by the trend of outsourcing, increased pressure of time-to-market [Chroust-Koppensteiner, 2006]. Outsourcing and the related complexity of problems will continue to grow as a consequence of globalization [ACM, 2006].

The challenges arising from the increasing complexity of outsourcing have to be managed on the top of the unpredictable nature of software projects. Consequently project management has become a key skill in managing software projects. In order to address project challenges such as cultural diversity, different time zones, and dislocated teams project management processes and their interaction with software methodologies have to be in place and understood. This thesis analyses and discusses how the project management processes relate to key software methodologies and how software methodologies influence the project duration and the availability of project information.

Another main motivator for this thesis is based on a personal observation and experience of the author. After working in the software industry as a project manager for several years the author realized that extensive knowledge about software project management has been available for a long time but was not applied and/or not well understood. Often the author was called for help as a project manager when it was almost too late to turn a project around. Some of the results of no or improper applied project management the author has seen included ill-defined project goals, extreme delays of product delivery and high turn-around of staff. Some of these were caused by product development processes that were not linked to project management processes. On the other hand the author has also realized and experienced how solid project management practices can have an impact on the success of a software project. Some of the success factors are summarized in Table 1.1.

1

Top 10 Success Factors
Executive Support
User Involvement
Experienced Project Manager
Clear Business Objectives
Minimized Scope
Standard Software Infrastructure
Firm Basic Requirements
Formal Methodology
Reliability Estimator
Other

Table 1.1: Top ten project success factors [Standish, 2001].

1.1 Influence of Project Management on Project Success

The Standish Chaos report of 2004 demonstrates some facts related to the success of projects [SoftwareMag, 2004]. The Standish group is a professional research company that has been publishing the results of their research on software projects since 1994 [Standish, 1994]. So far they have evaluated over 50,000 projects mainly performed in the US and Europe. See illustration in Figure 1.1 for the demographics of the Chaos Report projects [Standish, 2004]. The majority of companies that participate in this study are located in the US (58 percent), some are located in Europe (27 percent) and only a low number participate from the rest of the world. *It can be concluded that the findings of the Chaos reports are strongly influenced by the cultural specifics of Europe and the US.* The evaluation consists of a mixture of various types of projects including pure software development, a combination of development with purchased components and the roll-out of purchased software products. (See Figure 1.2)

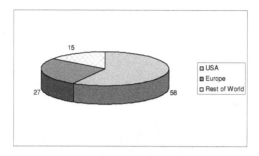

Figure 1.1: Demographics of 2004 Standish report [Standish, 2004].

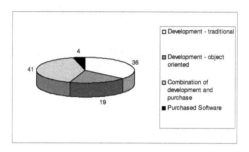

Figure 1.2: Project Mix of projects evaluated by Standish group [Standish, 2004].

Figure 1.2 shows that most companies participating in this study are actively creating software. Only four percent use purchased software products.

The latest CHOAS report published in 2004 states that the project success rate increased to 34 percent of all projects compared to the success rate of about half of this value published in 1994 [SoftwareMag, 2004].

Although this shows some improvement it still means that more than half of all projects fall into the categories of challenged and failed projects. See the illustration in Figure 1.3 for the results of the Chaos Report of 2004. Challenged projects are those that do not fulfill the success criteria defined by the Chaos Research Group. Projects that finish on time, within budget and with all the features originally specified are considered successful. Projects that are cancelled or never implemented are considered as failed. Therefore challenged projects run late and/or exceed their budget and/or changed their

3

scope during project execution. The reasons most of projects are failing are a lack of skilled project management and executive support as well as lack of user involvement [Standish, 2001].

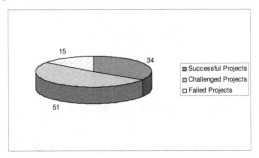

Figure 1.3: Results of 2004 Standish report [SoftwareMag, 2004].

The lack of project management skills can mean that the costs can double or triple for the project [Philips-Bothell, 2002]. Project management provides a pro-active approach to manage cost, time, and resources (see Chapter 2).

1.2 Claims

For some time software development was considered part of hardware development [Raccoon, 1997]. Over time companies decided to separate these two domains and to create software that can run on different computer models [Chroust, 2006]. Today applications or so called software products or software-intensive products work also on different platforms. The independence of software from hardware created a whole new industry, the software industry that produced revenue of $155 billions in 1998. The biggest market share had the US with 47% and Western-Europe with 34% [Wilson, 2001]. One of the differences between software and hardware production is flexibility of changes that occur during product development. Any errors or changes in hardware production can create significant costs as a physical product has to be revised. These changes are usually related to material expenses. Changes in software applications relate to code changes and cost mainly additional effort (labor costs). As a result changes in hardware projects will be avoided. Changes in software project cannot be avoided to a certain degree. Project management processes can help to facility change management for

4

software developments and make sure that information is communicated between management and development. Management is responsible for the overall product development. What is often missing in organizations is an understanding of the alignment of project management processes with related management processes. [Chroust, 1996] states that *industrial maturity demonstrates itself in the ability to separate the product from its development process*, that is *separating the WHAT from the HOW*. In case of an organization that creates software products the project management processes have interaction with product management processes and a software methodology and if done properly can link the WHAT (product) to the HOW (development process). Based on experience we assume that product, project and software development are related to each other as shown in Figure 1.4.

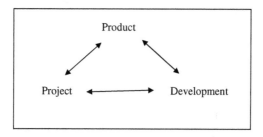

Figure 1.4: Relationship between project, product and development.

Projects apply project management processes to manage development efforts and guarantee that the product becomes available at a certain given time. Product-related processes help to manage the product from the onset of the product idea through the development and maintenance until the retirement of the product. Development applies software methodologies to create a new software product.

Projects, products and development processes need to be integrated or compatible with each other in order to work together. The relationship and interfaces between these three "key elements" must be defined consciously by the organization. They do not just exist or come into existence by chance. Some organizations develop their processes on the go which does not allow enough time to assess any impacts of a newly defined process on other existing processes. Therefore little attention is paid to the compatibility of processes. Imagine a link between two key elements is broken or not existing, because it never was correctly defined. As a result necessary information might not be available when needed and/or projects run late and/or go in the wrong direction.

Working in small to large companies I have noticed that one of the main problems to manage software projects successfully is a missing link between the product development related processes and the software methodologies. My overall goal for this work is to provide information that can help organizations to better understand the influence of product, project and development processes on each other and their impact on the project success. There is a strong relationship between product, project and software development life cycle.

This leads to the first claim of this work:

Claim #1:

Alignment of the relationship between product, project and software development life cycle can be done in an organization

Project and development processes exchange information throughout the duration of the project. Project management processes track the development activities. Therefore development reports its status to the project manager on a regular basis. The milestones for the development activities are defined by the applied software development methodology. The progress information from development helps to determine if the project is on time and within budget. This builds the basics for claim 2 and 3.

Claim #2:

The software development method determines at what key points of a project and in what form information becomes available.

In several organizations I also noticed that little attention is paid to the nature of the chosen software methodology for the specific project and its impact on the project. Many organizations choose their software development methodology at the beginning of their existence. They often select the method based on the preferences of the individuals working there as well as the nature of the projects at that time. Both can change over time. In the meantime these methods have become routine and often turned into a standard that is required to be applied for all development efforts. The reasons for selecting the methods are forgotten and changing the way development is done becomes extremely hard. Organizations hold on to concepts and methodologies that were defined long time ago. Software development methodologies that do not correspond well with the nature of its overall project potentially jeopardize the project success.

In recent years several software development organizations started to move from traditional software methodologies to more iterative or agile development methods. A number of benefits have been stated for the iterative and agile development methods such as quality improvements [Larman, 2004], and a better responsiveness to requirements changes throughout the project duration.

The Standish group published also the top ten success factors for a software project. The more factors are present in a given project the higher the chances for success [Standish, 2001]. See Table 1.1.

Only few of these success factors favor a specific development methodology. User involvement and minimized scope are typical attributes of iterative development methods. Firm basic requirements are more falling into the traditional category. All of the success factor must be taken under consideration for the project management methodology.

One of the success factors states the use of a formal methodology. The question is what difference does it make to the project which software development methodology is used? How much different is the effect of using one over the other? In today's market for most businesses time is the most critical success criteria. This thesis will assess the effect of different software methodologies on the timeline of a software development. Therefore the next claim is stated below.

Claim #3:

Different software methodologies generate different project durations and effort.

7

There are many aspects that influence the project duration. Specifically international projects with dislocated and divers teams introduce a lot of additional complexity to a project. When applying project management to international projects the alignment of product, project and software methodologies have to be understood. We focus on how project management relates to a software methodology that is used for developing a software product. Other project and organizational specific aspects can be added when the basic relationship between project, product and software methodology is understood.

Focus of Research

Many different types of software projects exist. We focus our analysis and evaluations on software product developments. We refer to software products as software functionality or features that can be bundled and sold as one entity (Chapter 2).

We limit our assessment to the prototypical methods: waterfall, spiral and agile type software methodologies. [ComputerZeit, 2005] states that *"nevertheless experts recommend iterative software models, software development is still done sequentially. This proofs the high use of the waterfall model. However companies use this model* [waterfall model, added by author] *in conjunction with the spiral model."* Waterfall, Spiral and incremental methods are amongst the most used methodologies in companies these days [ComputerZeit,2005].

We selected the assessment of the waterfall model as it is a well-known representation of a sequential software methodology. To the contrary the so called agile methodologies have in common to develop software in iterations with strong user interaction. Each iteration creates a product increment. We select agile methodologies as a representation of incremental development. The spiral model combines iterative development with sequential development and emphasizes risk containment. We select a spiral type model to assess if there is a benefit of using this combination of methodologies.

Other software methodologies like component based development and software product lines are not addressed in this thesis. Component based development refers to the fact that

8

large software components can be assembled to form a system [Ning, 1997]. Each component has a defined interface that allows it to be added to any system that requires the component's specific functionality.

Software product lines configure and compose a collection of software assets –such as requirements, source code components, architecture and documentation to create all products in a product line [Donohoe,2006] [Softwareproductlines, 2007] [Clements, 2002] [Bosch, 2000] [Parnas, 1976] [Hoyer, 2007].

In both cases components and software assets have to be created at one time before they can be reused. The reuse of software and its artifacts leads to decreased development times. For the initial development also software methodologies apply.

In this thesis we focus on software creation from requirements to the implementation and test.

1.3 Goals and Methodic

Various research options exist to evaluate the relationship of product, project and software methodology as well as the influence of the software methodology on the project.

One research option could be an empirical approach. As an example three project teams could be established that create the same software product in parallel using a different methodology. This approach would be rather costly. The results of one empirical trial would also not be very representative.

Another option could be a survey that would provide some project data. One of the challenges is that not necessarily all companies track and store the required information well [Hunger, 2005]. Other aspects such as the influence of the organizational structure and culture would influence the data. The focus of this thesis lies on gaining some insight of the influence of a software methodology on a project without considering other influential factors.

The overall goal of this thesis is to apply concepts that allow a manager to correlate a software project with the software methodology it uses. In order to either fortify or falsify the stated claims we apply process mapping and systems dynamics modeling. The emphasis of applying systems dynamics modeling in this thesis lies on showing how systems dynamics models for software development methodologies can be created und used.

We use the concept of "process mapping", to take a static view of the alignment between the processes related to a project, a product and development (Chapter 3). The "process mapping" aligns a project with a product and development (see Figure 1.4).

Then we apply systems dynamics modeling to simulate the behavior of a methodology over time (Chapters 4, 5, 6, 7). Both of these approaches should enable a manager to identify parameters that can influence the effect of a methodology on a project.

Overall Goal:

To develop concepts and system models that can help a manager to assess the impact of a software methodology on a project at different phases of a project.

This goal is broken down into a number of sub-goals that help to achieve the overall objective.

Sub-Goal #1:

To create "process maps for software methodologies" by using process mapping, a concept that demonstrates the relationship between project management, product management, and software development.

Further we will use "process mapping" to identify the right points of time during a project for management and project reviews (see Chapter 2). In addition the "process mapping" can be used to identify the information exchange between project, product and development.

10

Sub-Goal #2:

To identify the key review milestones and information for a software methodology using "process mapping".

The "process mapping" can be applied before the start, during execution or after completion of a project.

In order to asses the behavior of a software methodology over time we create systems dynamics models for three software methodologies as described in Chapter 4. We show in Chapters 5, 6 and 7 how these models can be developed. We apply values that are derived from [Jones, 1996] and some are based on industry experiences of the author. The applied values will help to show the variability of the systems dynamics models and provide reasonable but not statistical representative results.

Sub-Goal #3:

Create a simulation model that helps to analyze the behavior of a software development methodology over time.

Simulating these systems models can allow a manager to identify parameters that have an influence on the duration and cost of a project and can be used outside of this thesis.

Sub-Goal#4:

Identify parameters of a simulation model for a software development methodology that have influence on the project duration and cost.

Understanding the parameters of a software methodology that can influence the project duration, allows managers set the right actions.

1.4 Overview of Thesis.

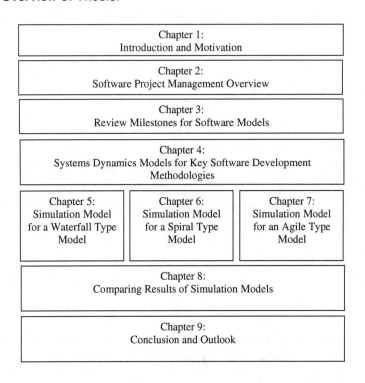

Figure 1.5: Chapter overview of this thesis.

This chapter (*Chapter 1*) provides an overview of the problem, claims and goals of this thesis.

Chapter 2 defines the basic terminology of project management. It introduces the basic principles of managing a software project. Further it describes the basic lifecycle processes for a product and project. It creates the understanding of the relationship between product, project and software methodology. We also identify the need for project reviews and define general questions that can be applied at each review.

Chapter 3 explains the characteristics of three software methodologies: a waterfall type, a spiral type and an agile type methodology. It defines the relationship of project, product and software methodology by applying process mapping for each software methodology. Process mapping allows to identify the individual review milestones for each software methodology. The basic review questions will be applied to each milestone in order to identify the information and artifacts available at each milestone.

Chapter 4 introduces the basics of systems dynamics. It includes systems definitions, and how to use a causal loop diagram to asses the behavior of a system over time. Then we explain how to transfer the systems behavior into a systems diagram and introduce an approach on how to asses a systems model. We also define the problem (four different scenarios of software development of increasing impact of errors appearing in the development process) and basic assumptions for the systems dynamic models we will develop for a waterfall type model (Chapter 5), a spiral type model (Chapter 6) and an agile type model (Chapter 7).

Chapter 5 describes the creation and simulation of a systems dynamics model for a waterfall type methodology in order to investigate the impact of this methodology on the duration of a software development project. We identify and explain the parameters for this model. We create this model in four sequential steps, starting with an idealistic scenario and increasingly adding complexity.

Chapter 6 and *Chapter 7* do the same for a spiral type and an agile type methodology.

Chapter 8 summarizes and compares the results of Chapter 5, 6, and 7.

Chapter 9 summarizes the outcome of this thesis and draws the conclusions. It also provides an outlook for how the work of this thesis can be further applied.

Chapter 2: Software Project Management Overview

This chapter supplies the basic understanding about project management. It describes project management as considered in this work. Many ideas of this thesis are based on the project management definitions of the Project Management Body of Knowledge. The Project Management Body of Knowledge is an accepted standard of the American National Standards Institute (ANSI 99-001-2004). This standard was defined by the Project Management Institute (PMI), an non-profit organization operating world wide.

2.1 The Need to Manage Product, Project, and Development

Software development has been going through an enormous evolvement in the past 50 years. [Raccoon, 1997] describes how new "*hardware generations have always driven the software economics*". At the time mainframes were developed (in the 1950s and 60s), software was considered to be part of hardware development. Raccoon also points out that in the late 70s "*software development staff could no longer be hidden in the hardware budget*" [Raccoon, 1997]. As a result separation of software and hardware costs occurred. Since then the gap between the production of hardware and software has increased. In today's world software and hardware production have only little in common. Once a hardware product is developed and transferred to production, the production process will hardly change as it creates many copies of the same parts. The process is essentially finished when one copy is produced. Reproduction is almost effortless. In comparison software development is a creative process that can apply different software methodologies. In addition the flexibility of software development allows changes even after the software product was delivered to the customer. The software product can be adapted to new user or customer needs and hides hardware changes. Errors in software products become more visible to the customer and can be fixed as long as the software product is supported by the company that produced it. Software products ("applications") need maintenance. Development of software products and their adaptation to new customer needs is often managed in projects. Like any other product, software products also go through different life phases. Chapter 2.2 provides an overview of the product life cycle.

2.2 Product Life Cycle Overview

For each product organizations follow a product life cycle to define, create, modify and terminate their products.

Definition: "The **Product Life Cycle** is the concept that a product goes through several stages in the course of its life: market introduction, market growth, market maturity and sales reduction. At each stage, a product's marketing mix might change, as will its revenue and profit profile" [Perrault-McCarthy, 1997].

The market view of the product life cycle is often demonstrated as a function of the revenue over the stages of the product life cycle: market introduction, market growth, market maturity and sales decline. [Perreault-McCarthy, 1997] (see Figure 2.1).

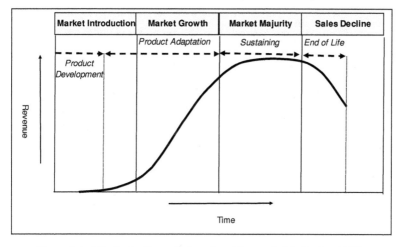

Figure 2.1: Life Cycle of a typical product [Perreault-McCarthy, 1997].

Figure 2.1 shows the revenue of a product over time. This figure also shows how the market view relates to various phases (product development, product adaptation, sustaining, end of life) of the product life cycle from a development perspective. The overview of the market perspective is described below.

15

Figure 2.2 shows the product life cycle from a development perspective. For details about several phases of the development perspective refer to Chapter 2.2.1.

Figure 2.2: Product Lifecycle for a product from a development perspective.

Market Introduction:

During the market introduction phase the innovators are the first to buy the product followed by the early adopters who are opinion leaders influencing other buyers.

Market Growth:

As a result the demand for the product increases and more customers buy the product during the market growth phase. New requirements are identified for the product in order to reach a broader customer base and / or satisfy customer needs better. The product gets adapted to these new requirements and becomes more attractive for buyers.

Market Maturity:

During the market maturity phase the product reaches the majority of buyers. At this "stable" stage the company makes only little or no investment in the modification of the product. The emphasis lies on making revenue for the product.

Sales Decline:

After a while sales starts to decline. Price cuts influence the latest type of buyer, the "laggards" or non-adopters [Perrault-McCarthy, 1997], to buy the product. Soon thereafter the product reaches the end of its life and it is taken off the market. The curve of the typical product (Figure 2.1) is idealized and can be but must not necessarily be smoothly increasing over time.

Figure 2.3 shows an overview of the product life cycle from a market and a development perspective. Note that in Figure 2.3 the product life cycle starts long time before the product is introduced to the market.

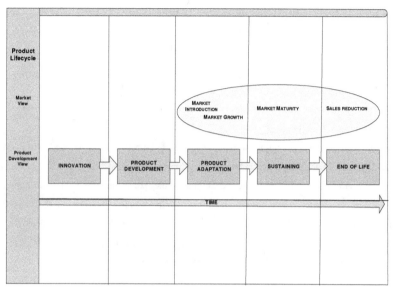

Figure 2.3: Overview of a product life cycle.

The market dynamics influence also the duration of the product development. A product that is released too late to the market has lost its window of opportunity.

Chapter 2.3 explains the product life cycle from a development view in more detail.

2.3 Development Perspective of a Product Life Cycle

Every product lifecycle follows very similar phases as shown in Figure 2.2. The product lifecycle starts with the idea of a new product in an organization that gets evaluated during the innovation phase. It is followed by the product development phase. After the initial market introduction the product is adapted and then sustained and finally reaches its end of life.

We explain the individual phases of the product life cycle in more detail below:

Innovation:

It starts with the idea of a new product that addresses a market need or creates a new market need (innovation). At the end of the innovation phase management needs to make

17

the decision to proceed with the product implementation or, either continues with research, or cancels the effort for this product idea. If they decide to move to the product development phase they choose the specific product out of multiple product options.

Product Development:

The product development phase starts with the decision to initiate a project that manages the development activities.

During the product development phase the selected product is developed based on identified market needs. Market needs can change over time and result in changed product requirements. If the product development takes some time it is likely that market needs might change while the organization is implementing their product. Changed market needs might get ignored during this phase and the product might be released as originally specified. At the end of the product development phase the product is delivered to the market. Typically product developments need to be managed in projects.

Product Adaptation:

Once the product is shipped to the market the company is most interested in how the product is perceived by its customers and what changes would make it more successful. As new requirements develop, the product is adapted to newly identified, changed and existing user needs. With each change to the product, the organization tries to make the product meet a new or changed requirement it was not designed for. At a certain point the existing design cannot accommodate the new needs and the rework would take as many resources as needed for a new product design. Usually the efforts of adapting a product are managed in projects.

Sustaining

When the product has reached its capability for expansion or fulfills the market needs it moves into the sustaining phase.

During the sustaining phase the product is maintained. Product errors and minor changes will be corrected.

For software products maintenance can be defined the following way:

Definition:	"**Maintenance** is the modification of a software product after its delivery to correct faults, improve performance and other attributes, or to adapt the product to a changed environment"[Young-Mookerjee, 2005] [Heinrich-Roithmayr, 2004].

As the efforts are usually minor maintenance becomes part of daily responsibilities of Engineering. Therefore no formal projects will be defined for this effort.

The releases are called maintenance releases in this phase. Typically maintenance releases follow a predefined company schedule and contain code fixes for previously identified errors.

"An important difference between maintenance and new development is that maintenance must inherit and start with the software generated by development" [Young-Mookerjee, 2005]. Typically maintenance takes about 50 percent of the cost spent for the product throughout its life cycle [Young-Mookerjee, 2005] [Lakhotia, 1999] or more. Whenever an organization has not a defined maintenance process in place it needs to define and prepare for maintenance during the product development phase of the product life cycle.

In case a maintenance process exists the software will be handed off as defined by this process.

Typically software maintenance not only includes the correction of errors in the software but also the adjustments of the software product to new demands. As an example a security software product that protects the computer against viruses has to adjust their products to new virus as they occur. Consequently they provide an update, a so called software patch, of their software product to their customers.

In comparison maintenance of hardware products includes a functional verification of the hardware components and service tasks that guarantee or increase the product's lifetime. In case a part reached the end of his lifetime or is identified as defective it will be replaced e.g. a car's oil filter, a computer's hard drive, or a battery exchange of an electronic device.

At the end of the sustaining phase management needs to understand whether the customer base / revenue is big enough to quantify the support. New enhancements may become too expensive to implement into the existing product. One possibility is to start a new product development in order to address the new user needs [Davis-Bersoff-Comer, 1988].

The existing product stays in the sustaining mode until it is announced End of Life. Development activities during sustaining do not need a project.

End of Life

At the "End of Life" phase it is of extreme importance for a company to keep the existing customer base tied to its products and keep its market share.

During End of Life customers get transferred from the old product to the new released product. After the customer transfer the product is taken off the market.

2.4 Definition of a Project

The way an organizations manages its work is often based on the nature of work the company performs. Some of the work might be organized in projects and other can be considered part of ongoing operations.

Often projects are utilized as a means of achieving an organization's strategic plan [PMI, 2004]. *"Projects are typically authorized as a result of one or more of the following strategic considerations:*

- *A market demand*
- *An organizational need*
- *A customer request*
- *A technological advance*
- *A legal requirement"*

[PMI,2004]. All of these considerations apply to software products.

Definition:	"A **Project** is a temporary endeavor undertaken to create a unique product, service or result" [PMI, 2004].

A project is fundamentally different to ongoing operations of a company. The purpose of ongoing operations is to sustain the business [PMI, 2004]. The difference between a project and ongoing operations can be best described in an example. Keeping accounting books up to date is considered a daily responsibility of a firm that has to be done on an ongoing basis. Implementing an accounting application to move a manual paper based accounting system to an automated software based accounting system can be considered to be a project.

Definition:	"An **Objective** is something toward which work is to be directed, a strategic position to be attained, or a purpose to be achieved. A result to be obtained, a product to be produced, or a service to be performed" [PMI, 2004].

Moving the accounting system from a manual paper process to an automated software based process will be done only one time for one organization. This project creates a unique product, the software based accounting system. Many accounting systems might have been created for companies but each individual accounting system is unique in regards to meeting the company's specific needs. When the product is implemented and proven to work the project will be terminated. The purpose of a project is to attain its objective and then terminate [PMI, 2004].

A project is temporary. This means that it has a definite beginning and a definite end [PMI, 2004]. The project is in place as long the objectives have not been met or the objectives become obsolete or it becomes clear that the objectives cannot be met and the project is terminated [PMI, 2004]. The word "temporary" does not indicate a specific duration of the project. Projects are different in duration. The duration of a project is dependent on the project objective.

At the beginning of a project usually little information is know about the work that need to be accomplished. As the project progresses over time more details about the project objective is identified. Projects follow the concept of progressive elaboration. Progressive elaboration means developing in steps and continuing in increments [PMI, 2004].

2.5 Project Management Concepts

We apply the project management definition from PMBoK to this thesis (see definition below).

Definition:	"**Project management** is the application of knowledge, skills, tools and techniques to project activities to meet the project requirements" [PMI 2004].

Each of the terms used in the definition of project management is defined below. Every project requires a certain skill set that has to be applied to the project tasks.

Definition:	"**Skill:** Ability to use knowledge to effectively and readily execute or perform an activity" [PMI 2004].

Tools and techniques are specific to the industry. The use of tools and techniques can help to increase performance and organize the work for a task.

Definition:	"**Tool**: something tangible, such as a template or software program, used in performing an activity to produce a product or result" [PMI 2004].

Definition:	"**Technique:** a defined systematic procedure employed by a human resource to perform an activity to produce a product or result or deliver a service, and that may employ one or more tools" [PMI 2004].

Requirements help to define what has to be achieved in the project. Usually requirements are high level at the beginning of a project. As the project progresses the requirements will be broken down in more detail.

Definition:	"**Requirement:** a condition or capability that must be met or possessed by a system, product, service, result, or component to satisfy a contract, standard, specification or other formally imposed document " [PMI 2004].

We limit our perspective to the overall definition of project management above and the project life cycle (see Chapter 2.8) and do not discuss project management tools of [PMI, 2004].

Project Management correlates to different types of processes (project, product and development processes) that facilitate identifying and executing of all activities that are required to achieve the project objective.

Definition:	"A **Process** is a structure whose elements are tasks, task owner, material and information and are tied together by logical relationships…A process has a definite start event (Input) and result (Output) whose purpose is to create a value for customer" (based on [Fischermanns, 2006]). "It is a set of interrelated activities, which transform Inputs into Outputs" [ISO 15504].

The purpose of project management is to help with the realization of strategic goals by defining projects that create products or services with benefit for the organization and customer (see Figure 2.4). It takes the definition of goals and objectives, the expenditure of resources, time, effort, risks, knowledge, standards (Input factors) to turn them into a product that creates benefits, probably revenue and customer reception (Output factors). Processes and methodologies are applied to transform Input factors to Output factors.

All of the Input factors, Output factors and transformation are specific to every organization. Some of the Input factors, Output factors and transformation can be project, product and method specific.

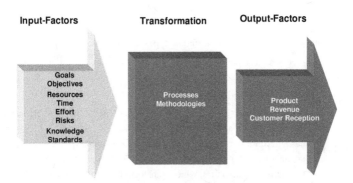

Figure 2.4: Relationship of Input and Output Factors with Project Management.

The elements Input, Output and transformation are defined below.

2.5.1 Input-Factors

Goals are typically long-range aims for a specific period. [Montana-Charnov, 2000]. Organizations define their goals often in terms of yearly or three year business plans or even for a longer period of time. Objectives are results that have to be achieved within a shorter time e.g. three to twelve months. Objectives help to meet the goals of an organization.

Resources are assigned to the project. Resources include material as well as employees that perform the project tasks.

Definition: "**Resource**: Skilled human resources, equipment, services, supplies, commodities, material, budgets or funds [PMI, 2004].

Time stands for the calendar time available for the project. Usually the time project activities take are planned and tracked in a schedule. Time is critical and therefore project success is often expressed in terms of delivering the project "on" time.

Definition:	"**Time**: a dimension in which events occur in sequence" [Wikipedia-time, 2006].

In projects often the term "timeline" is used.

Definition:	"A **timeline** is the presentation of a chronological sequence of events along a drawn line that enables a viewer to understand temporal relationships quickly"[SearchSMB, 2003].

An effort estimate of a project task includes the time it takes to accomplish the task without any interruptions. Effort can be transformed into so called elapsed time, by dividing the effort over the available time per day for working on that task.

Definition:	"**Effort**: the number of labor units requires to complete the project work" [PMI, 2004].

Project risks have to be identified, addressed and monitored throughout the duration of the project. A positive risk is referred to as an opportunity and a negative one as a threat in [PMI, 2004] (see especially Chapter 3.3).

Definition:	"**Risk**: an uncertain event or condition that, if it occurs, has a positive or negative effect on a project's objectives" [PMI, 2004].

Knowledge corresponds to the required skilled set that is needed to accomplish the project tasks. Only over time knowledge can be gained. A project that applies resources with the required knowledge is more likely to succeed. Often the project team develops knowledge throughout the duration of a project.

Definition:	"**Knowledge**: Knowing something with the familiarity gained through experience, education, observation, or investigation [PMI, 2004].

Standards are applied in a project because the organization chose to use it. There are different organizations that create and / or approve standards.

Some of the best known organizations in the software domain are:

- International Standards Organization (ISO)
- Institute of Electrical and Electronic Engineers (IEEE)
- American National Standard Institute (ANSI)

Definition:	"**Standard:** a document established by consensus and approved by a recognized body that provides, for common and repeated use, rules, guidelines or characteristics for activities or their results, aimed at the achievement of the optimum degree of order in a given context." [PMI, 2004].

2.5.2 Transformation

Every organization selects specified methodologies and processes (see Chapter 2.4) that apply to the industry they operate in and will adapt them to their specific needs over time.

Definition:	"**Methodology:** a system of practices, techniques, procedures, and rules used by those who work in a discipline. (**Discipline** is a field work requiring specific knowledge)" [PMI, 2004].

2.5.3 Output-Factors

The outcome of a project is either a product or service. The ultimate goal of an organization is to sell and usually to make money from their products or services. When a company starts to sell a new product they may make revenue but not necessarily profit. This means that the money they earn does not cover all the expenses of product development. Only over time when the product sales increases the company makes profit off product sales.

Definition:	"**Revenue** is a U.S. business term for the amount of money that a company earns from its activities in a given period, mostly from sales of products and/or services to customers [Wikipedia-revenue, 2006].

Customers have three main roles in new product developments. In case they have a need that a new product can address, they may provide requirements for the product. Once the product is ready they may test the product. Later on when the product becomes available on the market they may purchase it. *"Customers usually purchase or use a firm's products or services"* [PDMA, 2006]. The products and services of a company create a customer's perception of the company. The customer reception will increase with the level a product serves their needs.

In this thesis we focus on software products only.

Definition:	**"Product**: Term used to describe all goods, services, and knowledge sold. Products are bundles of attributes (features, functions, benefits, and uses) and can be either tangible, as in the case of physical goods, or intangible, as in the case of those associated with service benefits, or can be a combination of the two [PDMA, 2006].

We refer to software products as software functionality or features that can be bundled and sold as one entity.

We take the point of view that project management processes and practices help with the transformation process from the Input factor to the Output factors as explained above.

2.5.4 Triple Constraint Management

In order to deliver a product to the market that meets defined requirements, it becomes critical to assess truthful project information throughout the duration of the project and manage the project accordingly to the received project data. Figure 2.5 shows the triple constraints (scope, time, cost) for a project. Not all three constraints can be chosen at will as they are strongly depending on each other.

Definition:	**"Quality:** the degree to which a set of inherent characteristics fulfills requirements." [PMI 2004].

Projects have to be managed within certain constraints which are a complex mix of time, cost, scope, also called triple constraint model (Figure 2.5 based on [Baker, 1992]). We assume fixed quality. Due to time pressure many projects sacrifice the quality of their development in order to stay within their time and budget constraints. We presume that a project does not compromise in the quality of the product as a result of a change of one of the constraints.

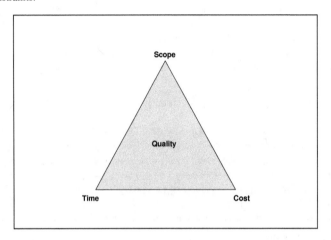

Figure 2.5: Project Key Constraints based on [Baker, 1992].

Scope relates to the product that will be created by the project. Cost is based on the resources and effort needed to carry out the project. Time is related to the schedule that is created based on the resources and efforts needed for the project. The schedule is the planned dates for performing the project activities [PMI, 2004].

Definition:	"**Scope** is the sum of the products, services, and results to be provides as a project" [PMI 2004].

The scope of a software project can be measured in function points [Coombs, 2003].
Cost of a software project is mostly related to labor costs.

Definition:	"**Cost** is the monitory value or price of a project activity or component that includes the monetary worth of the resources required to perform and complete the activity or component, or to produce the component" [PMI 2004].

Understanding how to manage a project within these constraints can be responsible for project success or failure. The constraints are related to and dependent on each other. A change in one has an impact on one or more constraints that cannot be chosen freely. Theses impacts are a result of the change. Often changes are related to scope changes or alteration of deadlines. Adding functionality to the scope would require increasing the budget to fund additional resources in order to keep the deadline and satisfy the quality criteria. If both budget and deadline cannot be changed, scope has to stay constant too.

There can only be certain flexibility for each project's constraints. It is unrealistic to think that the time, cost and quality stay the same when the scope increases. Project Management can only manage the possible, the impossible remains unfeasible. Project priorities can be set at the beginning of the project. Table 2.1 shows an example of a project priority matrix assuming fixed quality for the project. It helps to make the right decision when the project faces challenges.

	Time	Scope	Cost
Priority	1	2	3

Table 2.1: Example for a Project Priority Matrix based on [Perreault-McCarthy, 1997].

Each of the triple constraints has to be a priority assigned. The constraint with the highest (1) priority has the least flexibility. In the example of Table 2.1 the time for the project cannot change. The second highest priority means that there is some flexibility to changing this constraint. The constraint with the lowest priority (3) has the most freedom to change.

2.5.5 Process Orientation

Leadership, organizational culture and structure also have an influence on the success of a project. We speak of organizational culture.

Definition: **Culture:** Values, customs, heritage, legal codes, educational traditions, social attitudes, political institutions, processes and economic system [Montana-Charnov, 2000].

29

Organizational culture is characterized by values and norms, rituals and stories communicated by management to employees. It establishes the framework for how people work together and whether they are encouraged to air conflict and criticisms openly. An environment that does not allow raising issues will create challenges for a project when it runs into problems. The existing structure of an organization can support the organizational culture. A change in the structure can help to create a certain work culture.

Definition: "**Structure** is an organizational framework that provides reporting relationships and flow of information [Montana-Charnov, 2000].

See [Montana-Charnov, 2000] [PMI, 2004], [PMI, 2000] for different types of organizational frameworks.

Process orientation plays an important factor in an organizational culture.

Most organizations are positioned somewhere between two extremes: a chaotic or a bureaucratic work culture. Figure 2.6 shows the scale for cultural dynamism in an organization.

Organizations that like to create a process oriented culture are likely to implement a structure that defines clear reporting relationships to allow fast information exchange.

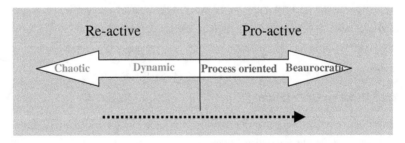

Figure 2.6: Scale of cultural dynamism in organizations based on [Boehm-Turner, 2005].

Project Management processes fit better in a process oriented culture. They also can help organizations to move from a dynamic environment to a process oriented one. Typically a

30

cultural environment has the tendency to move from a re-active work environment to a process oriented culture when implementing project management practices.

Projects that take place in a chaotic environment are likely not to have clear milestones defined. Management does not actively manage the outcome of the project and its impact on the overall success of the business. What does not get measured does not get managed. Projects that are unattended have a higher chance to become self-dynamic over time and drift away from its original purpose. As a result non-compliances of the project's product to the requirements stay undetected throughout the duration of the project. Therefore the outcome does not meet the projects objectives and the project can be considered a failure.

2.6 Questions and Project Review

In order to analyse the progress of a project and support the decision process of managers, management reviews are needed at appropriate times (milestones) of the project.

Definition:	**Review:** An inspection or examination for the purpose of evaluation [Farlex, 2007].

Reviews are associated with milestones.

Definition:	"**Milestone** is a significant point or event in the project." [PMI 2004].

Reviews are part of the project management processes as well as of a process oriented culture. They are an essential means to evaluate the status of a project to identify how well the project is doing. To identify the project information two views must be taken: the product and the process view.

The right questions for the product view have the goal to identify more detailed product attributes. The process view questions help to understand what work flow and approaches are taken to create and roll-out the product. Managers use their personal standards as well as the organizations value system to evaluate projects progress and success. Conducting regular project reviews helps management and the project team to make the right decisions.

31

A project review at a milestone helps to identify if the milestone has been met and provides key information. Project reviews focus take place involving key project stakeholders who ask questions (like listed in Table 2.2) to understand the progress of the project.

Project reviews differentiate significantly from the reviews of deliverables such as design reviews or code reviews that verify the correctness of specific work products.

It has to be recognized that reviewing a product costs time and resources at the time when it is done, see [Chroust-Lexen, 1999]. Not asking questions about the product and project will usually cost more time later. As it has to be acknowledged that time is critical for the success of a company the time focus also creates a big distraction for asking the right questions. The focus of the review questions is on obtaining information that can help to validate that the project is heading in the right direction and the approach taken is feasible. In this case we focus on project reviews that are conducted throughout the project duration by the key project stakeholder including the sponsor, project team and representatives of all affected organizations.

Definition:	"**Sponsor** is the person or group that provides the financial resources, in cash or in kind, for the project" [PMI, 2004].

Definition:	"**Stakeholder** are persons and organizations such as customers, sponsors, performing organization and the public, that are actively involved in the project, or whose interests may be positively or negatively affected by execution or completion of the project" [PMI, 2004].

Project reviews are done internally to the projects. In comparison project audits are conducted by independent audit groups who are external to the project [Gray-Larsen, 2006] [Heinrich-Roithmayr, 2004]. We are focusing on the internal project reviews only. The intention for proposing basic questions for the project reviews is to keep the project in line with its goal and the organization's purpose. Asking essentially the same questions at milestones throughout the project duration will lead to more granularity, detail and precision of the information as the project progresses.

We identified six basic questions for acquiring the right project information in Table 2.2.

Perspective	Question	Purpose
Product View	Q1. What is the product we are building and why?	Identify the final goal for the project.
		At the beginning of a product life cycle the product can only be vaguely described. With each review more product details are discovered and identified if they meet the stakeholders expectations.
		The answer to this question builds the basis of the scope of work and therefore triggers the understanding what resources, knowledge, time, effort and investment are associated with this product development.
	Q2. Is this product feasible as well as achievable and why?	Identify how realistic it is to be successful with the selection of the product and the project plan. The responses to these questions will be associated with the additional risk that needs to be taken to develop and deliver this new product.
		The answer to this question needs to provide the information if the product can solve the problem it supposed to address.
	Q3. Is this product marketable and why?	Identify how realistic it is to be successful with this selection of the product. The responses to this question will help to identify if the product concept can address the customer need when it is rolled out to the market.
	Q4. Is the product functioning at the level of current abstraction and why?	Identify if the product is functional and running within the given time frame.
Process View	Q5. How are we building this product and why?	Helps to identify what technology, processes and methodologies are needed and applied for building the product. The answer to this question is an indicator to the risk and investment the organization is taking for this product implementation.
	Q6. Is the plan predictable and realistic and why?	Identify how realistic it is to be successful with the the product development methodology and the project plan. The responses to this question will help to identify gaps between the plan, reality and stakeholder expectations.

Table 2.2: Six basic review questions.

In Chapter 3 we will identify the milestones that are relevant to a software development project and apply these questions to reviews at these milestones in order to find out what level of information exists at each milestone of the project.

2.7 Software Project Definition

This thesis focuses on the software project management aspects of software development. We introduced the basic definitions of project management in Chapter 2.4 and 2.5.

In general a project is a temporary endeavor undertaken to create a unique product or service [PMI, 2004] (refer to Chapter 2.4). So how is a software project different from other projects?

Actually all the traditional project management tools and techniques apply to software projects in the same way as they do to other projects. [Humphrey, 1989] states that although software development is a unique field, traditional management methods can and should be used. There are some software project specific tools that can be used for estimating software development activities [Coombs, 2003].

What makes software projects special is the nature of software development as listed in [Humphrey, 1989]:

- *"Software is generally more complex than other Engineering products.*
- *The insignificant cost of reproducing software forces software solutions to many late-discovered system problems.*
- *In other Engineering fields, release to manufacturing provides a natural discipline that is not present with software………"*

The creation of software appears more flexible than the production of a hardware product that has to go through an expensive manufacturing process. The costs of redoing a production step for a hardware product can be very expensive and is often avoided. Changing software is less costly as no tangible components need to be reproduced when requirements change. The flexibility of software development depends on the software methodology that is used. The chosen software methodology interacts with the project management processes. We will assess this interaction in Chapter 3.

Figure 2.7 compares a project life cycle (defined in Chapter 2.8) with a software development life cycle (see Chapter 3) and shows the product life cycle (Chapter 2.2). The project life cycle exists until the software project meets the project objective of creating a software product. The software development life cycle also supports the software maintenance phase (see Chapter 2.2).

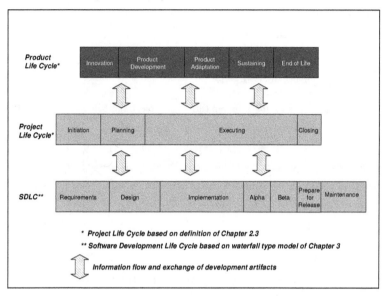

Figure 2.7: Example of overlapping product life cycle, project life cycle and SDLC as defined in Chapter 3.

In summary a software project:

- Generates a software product that has to meet specified requirements.
- Follows a software development life cycle
- Can be managed following a project life cycle (see Chapter 2.8)

2.8 Project Life Cycle

We provide an overview of the project life cycle in this chapter. A project life cycle shows typically distinct phases a project passes through as it progresses.

"Project managers or the organization can divide projects into phases to provide better management control.....Collectively these phases are known as the project life cycle" PMI, 2004].

Definition: "**Project Life Cycle**: A selection of generally sequential project phases whose name and number are determined by the control needs of the organization" [PMI 2004].

Definition: "**Phase** is a collection of logically related project activities, usually culminating [PMI, 2004].

Usually milestones mark the achievements of a project and help to track a project's progress. Often a milestone is assign to the end of project phases.

In this thesis we apply a project life cycle based on the description in the Project Management Book of Knowledge in [PMI, 2000] that consists of the following phases: Initiation, Planning, Executing and Closing (see Figure 2.8).

Figure 2.8: Project Phases based on [PMI, 2004].

Monitoring and controlling take place as part of all phases to a different degree with expected importance during the executing phase.

Table 2.3 summarizes the main activities taking place during each phase of the project life cycle. Each of these activities is assigned to an owner, the person or organization that is responsible that the activity is executed.

Project Phase	Activities	Owner
Initiation	Create Project Mandate Identify project requirements, limitations, and constraints. Assign project manager and key staff to project	Management
Planning	Identify specifications for the software product Create project schedule and project plan.	Project Team
Executing	Carry out project plan Monitor, measure and track progress of the project.	Project Team
Closing	Review product of the project for formal acceptance Achieve all project and product information	Key Stakeholder (see Chapter 2.4.2) including Customer Project Team, Sponsor.

Table 2.3: The Phases of the project life cycle based on [PMI, 2004].

36

Note that for product developments the innovation phase has to be completed before a development project is initiated (See Chapter 2.2).

At each stage of the project life cycle specific information is available that evolved from the previous phase. Usually the end of each phase is marked with a milestone [PMI, 2004]. This milestone is often related to a review in order to evaluate the state of the project. At these milestones frequently management requests information or pushes for commitments from the project team that is not available at that particular phase. In Chapter 2.6 we defined questions that will help us to identify what information is available at each defined milestone (see Chapter 3).

2.9 Relationship of Product Life Cycle, Project life cycle and Software Methodology

So far we have explained the product life cycle of a generic product. In Chapter 3 we will identify the milestones based on a software product development in order to assess what information has to be available at different milestones of the project. In order to identify the milestones we need to recognize how the software development is embedded into the overall product development of an organization. Therefore we will assess the relationship of product life cycle, project life cycle and software methodology in Chapter 3.1.

Figure 2.9 shows the principle of how product life cycle, project life cycle and software methodology relate to each other: The creation of the software product takes place within the product development phase and the product adaptation phase of a product life cycle. Note that projects are only defined for the product development and product adaptation phase. The product life cycle entails the project life cycle that defines the phases a project goes through from project initiation, then planning, followed by executing and finally project closing (see Chapter 2.8). The project life cycle manages the development of a software product and administers the software methodology. The software methodology is the approach selected to develop the software product.

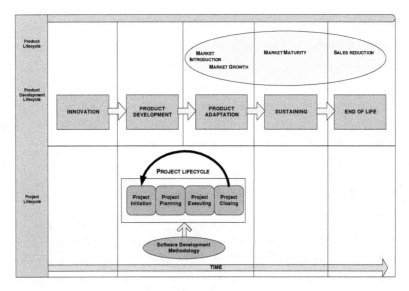

Figure 2.9: Relationship of Product Life Cycle, Product Development Life Cycle and Project Life Cycle.

Chapter 3: Review Milestones for Software Models.

Progress of software development projects has to be carefully monitored. Reviewing a project at all milestones allows assessing the "health" of a project. The milestones for reviews need to be set at times where the interaction of the product life cycle, the project life cycle and the software methodology generate the necessary information. In Chapter 2 we described the basics definitions of project management. Further we identified basic review questions that can be asked at every milestone. Chapter 2.9 describes the relationship between these life cycles. Figure 2.9 shows an overview of the relationships between these three life cycles: product life cycle, project life cycle and software development life cycle. In this section we tie all knots together and identify the interaction between these processes in order to evaluate a project at each milestone in regards to time, scope and cost. In this chapter we will link the product life cycle, the project lifecycle and the software methodology to each other. For this purpose we map these life cycles with the software development methodology in Figure 3.1 to define the relationship between product life cycle, project life cycle and the software methodology. We refer to this approach as process mapping.

We will apply process mapping to three important software methodologies (waterfall, spiral and agile) as typical representatives of current trends and approaches in order to identify the milestones on the product, project and software development level. We will also identify critical questions that can be asked at each of the identified milestones. These questions will help to identify the information that exists at each milestone and the information that is exchanged between the software methodology and the project life cycle.

3.1 Mapping of Project Life Cycle to the Product Life Cycle

Figure 3.1 shows an example of mapping the product life cycle with the project life cycle. Both processes were presented in a simplified way in the overview (Figure 2.9). Refer to Chapter 2.2 for the definition of the product life cycle and its phases. The project life cycle has to be applied to the product development phase (see solid lines marked with "1" in Figure 3.1), and the product adaptation phase (dashed lines marked with "2") of the product life cycle. The product is developed during the product development phase by following the project life cycle once. The product development phase is completed when the product is delivered to the market.

During the product adaptation phase multiple projects are carried out sequentially as an answer to adapt the product to new or additional market needs. This is indicated with the text "multiple times" above the product adaptation phase in Figure 3.1. At the end of each "adaptation" project the new development is delivered to the market. Depending on the success of the product the product can go through the entire product life cycle.

A product review needs to take place whenever the product moves from one phase to the next. Each phase end review should help management to get all needed information to make relevant decisions for the next phase. Similar to the model in [Chroust, 1992], Table 3.1 lists questions that management should ask at the phase end reviews in order to make the decision to move from the current product phase to the next phase. At the end of each "adaptation" project, management assesses if the product meets current market needs. This results in a milestone review for every adaptation (End of Product Adaptation(i) in Table 3.1).

We also relate the six general review questions (defined in Chapter 2.6) to the management review milestones questions in Table 3.1. Note that different basic questions are relevant at the different phases of the product life cycle (see column "Related Basic Review Questions" in Table 3.1).

All management reviews are marked with triangles pointing upwards (colored red) in the process mapping shown in Figure 3.1.

Figure 3.1 also shows that the project life cycle administers the software development life cycle. It should be noted that the software development life cycle depends on the chosen software methodology.

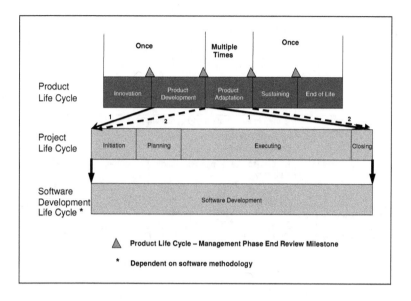

Figure 3.1: Example of mapping the project life cycle to the product life cycle.

The project life cycle is the link between product life cycle and software methodology. In each sub chapter of Chapter 3 the phases of a different software methodology are mapped to the project life cycle. For each software methodology we will explain each process step of the product life cycle in more detail. The review milestones for the product development and adaptation phase are identified based on the activities that take place during each step of the development methodology.

The figures showing applications of the process mapping in Chapter 3 indicate the management reviews with a triangle pointing upwards (red), the project reviews with a triangle pointing downwards (green), and the software development reviews with a rectangle (black).

41

Review Milestone	Milestone Questions	Related Basic Review Questions (see Table 2.2)
End of Innovation	Does a product idea exist that is ready for production? Is the available product idea a good fit for the company and its target market?	Q1, Q2, Q3, Q5
End of Product development	Is the implementation done correctly? Is the product functionality meeting customer needs? Is the software product ready for delivery? Is marketing ready to launch the product?	Q1, Q2, Q3, Q4,Q5, Q6
End of Product Adaptation(i)	Do existing product modifications meet customer demands?	Q3, Q4
End of Sustaining	How big is the existing customer base that is actively using this product? Is this customer base ready to transfer to a new product? Can resources supporting this product be shifted to other product developments?	Q3, Q4, Q5
End of Life	Have all customer been transferred to the new product? Has the infrastructure, the product and its documentation been archived?	Q3

Table 3.1: Management questions specific for each phase of the product life cycle.

Further we apply five of the six basic review questions from Table 2.2 (see Chapter 2.6) to these management reviews to see what level of information is available from the beginning (see Table 3.2). Question 6 refers to the plan for the software project. This plan is defined and carried out in the product development phase and is not applicable for other phases of the product life cycle. For that reason question 6 is not shown in Table 3.2. All other questions can be applied to each milestone.

We explain the management milestones below.

End of "Innovation"

At the "End of Innovation" milestone (see Table 3.1) the product idea has been selected. It is highly likely that the product idea is related to the core competency of a company and the technology exists or is about to exist on the market.

Definition:	"**Core Competence**: That capability at which a company does better than other firms, which provides them with a distinctive competitive advantage and contributes to acquiring and retaining customers." [PDMA, 2006].

New technology is expected to trigger a new generation of new products. One of the most recent examples is the development of the router, a computer networking device [Wikipedia:router, 2006]. The invention of the router enabled computers to connect and communicate between each other and built the foundation for the creation of the World Wide Web [Wikipedia:world wideweb, 2006].

A company's product idea is supported by a business case.

Definition:	"**Business Case**: The results of the market, technical and financial analyses, or [also called, author] up-front homework [PDMA, 2006].

The business case is dependent on the availability of information about a company's customers, competitors, or markets. A company often refers to market research firms to gain access to these data. The creation and study of prototypes supports the technical analysis of the business case. Further it provides information whether the product idea is technical feasible.

Definition:	A **prototype** is an original type, form, or instance of some thing serving as a typical example, basis, epitome, or standard for other things of the same category [Wikipedia:prototype, 2006].

The creation of prototypes can be very expensive and labor intensive.

End of "Product Development"

Looking at the available information for the "End of Product Development" review milestone in Table 3.2 shows that most of the information is known at this point of the product development life cycle. The organization chooses the technology, processes and methodologies at the beginning of the product development phase and applies them throughout this phase. It is likely that the same or similar technology, processes and methodologies will be used for the following phases (product adaptation, sustaining) of the product life cycle. The selection of technology, methodologies and processes depend on the experience with these in an organization.

In case an organization has little or no experience with any methodology it is likely to select processes and methodologies that are compatible with its culture (see Chapter 2.5.5) and can be supported by the company's environment.

Definition:	**Culture:** Values, customs, heritage, legal codes, educational traditions, social attitudes, political institutions, processes and economic system [Montana-Charnov, 2000].

Some companies have defined methodologies and processes that are applied to all projects. In this case the information about processes and methodologies is known at the beginning of the product development phase. Other companies select or tailor their approach for each project. As a result the methodologies and processes are defined and applied throughout the product development phase.

Based on the summary in Table 3.2 all relevant information is defined throughout the product development phase. It indicates that the software development methodology that is applied during this phase determines at what key points project information becomes available.

End of "Product Adaptation"

At the "End of Product Adaptation" the company knows if the product has been a success or a failure. If the product has been marketable the customer base increased the market share of the company.

At this stage the product stability and errors are known. Both determine the required effort for maintaining the software in the sustaining phase.

End of "Sustaining"

At the "End of Sustaining" milestone the product meets current market needs. The product's marketability is limited to the existing customer base. The product has reached its limits in relation to expansion for future market needs. The new market needs are no longer feasible for the existing product.

End of "End of Life"

Usually no formal management review takes place at the end of this phase. At the beginning of this phase the activities are determined and then executed throughout this phase. The product manager, who has been responsible for the product that is about to be taken off of the company's product list, is responsible that these activities take place and reports back when they are done.

Review	Q1. What is the product we are building and why?	Q2. Is this product (technically) feasible as well as achievable and why?	Q3. Is this product marketable and why?	Q4. Is the product functioning at the level of current abstraction and why?	Q5. How are we building this product and why?
End of Innovation	Product idea is known.	Little of technical feasibility is known due to some prototyping	A firm business case has to support the selection of the product option	No information	Some knowledge exists about how to build the product from a technology and methodology perspective.

45

Review	Q1. What is the product we are building and why?	Q2. Is this product (technically) feasible as well as achievable and why?	Q3. Is this product marketable and why?	Q4. Is the product functioning at the level of current abstraction and why?	Q5. How are we building this product and why?
End of Product development	Details of product defined and implemented.	Existence of product is proven.	Solid business case and pre-orders from key customers demonstrate marketability of product	Product has to be running and working to be ready for delivery	Details of technology, methodology and process perspective were defined and used. Processes for maintenance are defined.
End of Product adaptation(I)	Product idea is proven to work	Information about errors, code stability and maintenance exist.	Product is introduced to market and accepted. Marketability is proven to work.	No new information	Concept of building and adapting the product is proven to work. Processes for maintenance are in place.
End of Sustaining	Product becomes obsolete	Not anymore	Limited due to existing functionality.	Not anymore	Not applicable

Table 3.2: Overview of available information at each management review milestone.

In the sub chapters of this chapter we will apply process mapping to demonstrate the information exchange that takes place between the life cycles and the software methodology during the product development phase of the product development life cycle.

3.2 Waterfall Software Development Model

3.2.1 Waterfall Model

The waterfall model was first described and defined for the development of large software systems by W. Royce [Royce, 1987] who designed and built large scale and complex aerospace products. The initial waterfall model (see Figure 3.2) was documentation driven. Berry Boehm recognized that the completion of documentation for each phase can cause problems. He states in [Boehm, 1988] that "*document-driven standards have pushed many projects to write elaborate specifications of poorly understood user interfaces and decision support functions, followed by the design and development of large quantities of unusable code".*

Much focus was given to the testing phase that was identified as the biggest risk of the waterfall model because *"it occurs at the latest point in the schedule when backup alternatives are least available"* [Royce, 1987]. It was also strongly recommended to involve the customer throughout the waterfall process steps. Since then the waterfall model has been adapted throughout the software industry in many ways. For more details about each phase of "Royce's" waterfall model shown in Figure 3.2 refer to [Royce, 1987].

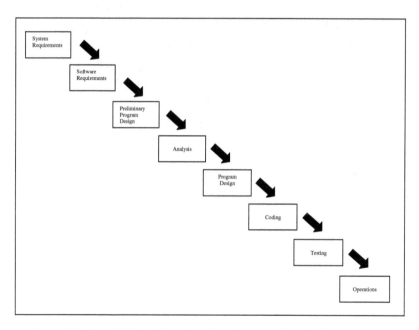

Figure 3.2: Waterfall Model based on Royce's first publication [Royce, 1987].

Although there is more variety of software development methodologies existing these days, a form of the waterfall model is still the most established one in the software industry. The concept is straightforward. A waterfall model consists of several sequential phases. For alternative illustration a version of the waterfall model can be seen in Figure

47

3.3 as applied in the industry. It will be used for further analysis in the next chapters. The phases for this model are principally based on the Royce's waterfall model in Figure 3.2 and the waterfall model with feedback loops as shown in [Boehm, 1988] [Muranko-Drechsler, 2006]. Figure 3.3 aggregates some phases of Royce's waterfall model and introduces an Alpha and Beta phase. Requirements in Figure 3.3 consist of systems and software requirements as shown in Figure 3.2. Design (in Figure 3.3) aggregates preliminary program design, analysis and program design as shown in Figure 3.2. Coding and test are the same as in Figure 3.2. Alpha and Beta phase are added to the original model to point out their increasing importance in software development [Ehrlich-Stampfel, 1990] [Krull, 2000] to increase the likelihood of fulfilling customer acceptance criteria. The production phase represents the same as operations. We use the model of Figure 3.3 for further analysis. The feedback loop as shown in Figure 3.3 demonstrates the opportunity to feedback information from the ongoing phase to the previous one. At the end of each phase the deliverables developed in this phase are reviewed and validated. Changes based on this review get implemented and documented.

Table 3.3 summarizes the main activities for each step of the waterfall model and lists the deliverables. Note that planning activities of the next phase are allocated in the current phase.

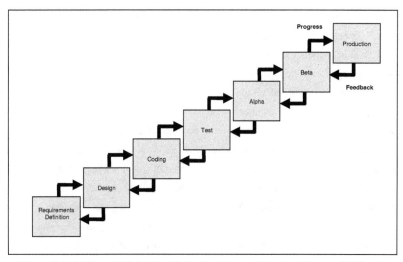

Figure 3.3: A Waterfall Model with feedback loops, based on [Royce, 1987] and [Muranko-Drechsler, 2006].

Process Step	Activity	Deliverables
Requirements Definition	Requirements are gathered, documented, prioritized, specified and decided on.	Requirements document
Design	System architecture is defined. Product features and functionality are designed in detail. Then test plans are written.	Architecture document Preliminary design document Detailed Design document Test Plans
Coding	Implementation of specified and designed features and functionality	Code Review Test cases
Test	Features and Functionality is tested individually, then integrated into the products software base and system tested.	Test Report Alpha test plan
Alpha Test	First internal product validation that executes the Alpha test plans.	Alpha test report Beta test plan
Beta Test	External product validation at key customer sites.	Beta test report
Production	Final product is ready for general customer use.	Technical documentation such as user guide etc.

Table 3.3: Overview of a waterfall model.

Project management usually tracks all development activities of each phase of a waterfall model. The required work load of each phase of a waterfall model would be broken down to a level of granularity that allows assigning time estimates that makes sense to the person that performs the work [PMI, 2004]. The project tracks the deliverables listed in Table 3.3 as milestones within each phase they belong to. At each deliverable milestone the work that is required to meet this deliverable is completed. Project management would monitor the progress of the overall timeline of development. Each phase of a waterfall model finishes with a milestone. In case a phase cannot be completed on time the start of the next phase is delayed. Since a waterfall model is a sequential model time slips of multiple phases add up and move out the overall timeline of the project. When the project cannot be completed on time it might also delay the introduction of the commercial software product to the market. Independent which software development methodology is used product management heavily depends on the status information from project management. It is critical for project management to track the progress of a waterfall development closely. Any changes in the project need to be reflected in the project plan and schedule. Frequent changes to a project can lead to an enormous effort for the project manager to keep all project documents up-to-date and communicate the changes to the project stakeholder. Any change at any phase of the waterfall model can create rework in one or more previous phases and impact the next phases. When changes occur in a project project management is challenged to identify all impacts of this change on the entire project.

The waterfall model has in general the following strengths and weaknesses:

Strengths:

- The waterfall model is straightforward and easy to use. The methodology of the waterfall model does not require intense training of the staff.
- It works well for large scale and stable product developments. Stable developments experience only few requirement changes throughout development.
- As each phase has specified deliverables, progress of development can be easily tracked.

Weaknesses:

- It takes a significant amount of time for going through the stages of the waterfall model before a result can be seen. There are no partial functionality deliveries possible. The development has to go through all the phases before the entire product is available and testable for the customer.
- Once the product is in the testing stage there is no point of return. Due to the sequential nature of the model changes in requirements or design errors that are discovered during the testing phase can require enormous rework.

3.2.2 Product Development Phase of the Waterfall Model

We apply the process mapping to the waterfall model, mapping the product life cycle to the waterfall model via the project life cycle. Figure 3.4 shows the process mapping for the waterfall model. The analysis of Figure 3.4 is described below.

Figure 3.4 shows that the project is initiated with the end of the innovation phase. For details about innovation phase of the product life cycle refer to Chapter 2.2.
The project starts with project initiation.

Project Initiation

When a product is developed by using a waterfall model, the initial product for market introduction gets usually developed within one project life cycle.
During project initiation high-level product requirements would be developed. In order to minimize the risk, Product Marketing works with Engineering on technical feasibility studies for the new product concept. The product development and management association (PDMA) describes a

Definition:	"**Concept**: clearly written and possibly visual description of the new product idea that includes its primary features and consumer benefits, combined with a broad understanding of the technology needed" [PDMA, 2006].

In order to proof it Engineering may create different prototypes.

Once prototyping is completed, management selects one of the prototype options for the project based on Engineering's input and recommendations. A review at the end of project initiation helps management to identify a rough estimate on resources needed to move forward with the project. This is usually the point where management makes their funding decision for the project.

Project Planning

During the Planning phase Engineering breaks down the product requirements into more details. When the requirements have been collected and fully assessed a requirements review takes place that verifies if the requirements are complete and fully understood. The requirements review is a software development specific review milestone.

In the ideal world requirements gathering and assessment should be completed within the initiation phase of the project. In that case the requirements milestone and the initiation milestone would fall together. This would allow having the entire project scope identified before the planning efforts started. When requirements cannot be completed within the project initiation phase, they still may change throughout the project planning phase. Estimates that are created based on changing requirements are less stable than estimates based on completely identified requirements.

In the real world management is often tempted to move the project ahead as soon as possible. As a result frequently management applies resources to the project to start the planning efforts as early as possible when the full scope of the project has not been identified. Under such conditions planning efforts require rework and take up a significant time of the overall project. Estimates have to be revisited each time requirements have changed. An organization needs to be able to monitor closely that the reviews for initiation and requirements occur as close as possible or accept the fact that requirements gathering during the planning phase will require rework and require more time for planning.

Based on the identified requirements Engineering defines the overall architecture of the specific product. The product architecture is the high-level design of the product. The architectural concept is the best product description existing at this point of time. Therefore it builds the baseline for identifying resource needs both in regards of effort and skill set. It requires only a limited number of people to develop the architecture. [DeMarco, 1997] specifies that one of the major challenges of projects is that they get overstaffed at the beginning of the project.

Once the architecture is defined project schedule and project plan can be developed, the project is staffed accordingly for executing and the project documents get approved by the project stakeholder. At this point management should conduct the "End of Planning" project review.

This is likely the most critical review milestone of development. During the planning phase the project team should be able to provide sufficient and satisfying responses to the previously defined six basics review questions. If there are still open points, management needs to verify Engineering understands and feels confident to have enough information to come up with the plan for executing the project.

Definition: "A **project plan** is a formal approved document that defines how the project is executed, monitored and controlled" [PMI, 2004].

If the project team faces problems to identify the overall architecture, management should question the approach taken, and request to build a prototype in order to help with difficult design decisions. Prototypes are especially useful when new technology is used or the staff does not have the required skill set. In both cases the organization needs a cycle of learning before proceeding. Once the team passed the planning review milestone it moves on to project execution. In case a prototype is developed the software methodology can be considered a prototype model [Bahn-Naumann, 1997].

Project Execution

During project execution the project plan is carried out. The team defines the detailed design. Engineering conducts a software development specific review to assess correctness of design and approve the software design. Then the project team implements the code, conducts the unit tests and then the integration tests. A systems test follows the previous test activities if the product needs to be compatible with various platforms or other products. The "End of Implementation" milestone marks when all development has been implemented and integrated.

Alpha Phase

During an Alpha phase the product's features and quality is internally validated and verified. Therefore the developed software product is tested by stakeholders that are part of the organization and the test results are evaluated. Conducting a software development review at the end of the Alpha phase provides the last chance for correcting the directions of the product, and helps identifying if performance values and requirements are met. Based on the results of the Alpha phase outstanding features and discovered software defects can be prioritized. The Alpha phase can also include some time that is dedicated for fixing the problems that were discovered during the test. To address the identified problems helps to increase code stability and identify what functionality will be ready for production.

Beta Phase

A Beta phase follows the Alpha phase. The Beta phase includes testing of the product by key customer and evaluation of the test results.

During the Beta phase key customer are evaluating the new product. The result of this test is their first external validation of the product and helps to identify if they can proceed with the product roll-out. A product roll-out includes all activities that are necessary to introduce a new product to the market.

Some companies have their first external product validation earlier in the development cycle usually at a stage where the product functionality and quality is very limited.

Assessments by customer at such an early stage bear the risk that the customer turn away before they had the chance to understand the full potential of the new product. These early field trials should only occur when the company focuses the product requirements on specific customer needs. After the Beta phase final instabilities of the code get resolved and the product is packaged for market delivery.

After the Beta phase management can already identify how much the product satisfies customer needs. A software development review of the "End of Beta phase" helps to identify priorities for the remaining time left until the product releases to the market. As a result of the review, decisions can be made in regards to setting the date for the product release. If critical functionality is missing, the release date might be moved out and additional development takes place. Also Beta phase results can help to set priorities for the first product adaptation project following product development. If the Beta phase results are satisfying the development will continue as planned.

End of Development

At the end of the product development phase, just before the product release, a software development review takes place to verify that the software fulfils the release criteria. A management review verifies that the software is ready for delivery and that marketing is ready for the product launch. [PDMA, 2006] states that a

Definition: **Launch** is "the process by which a new product is introduced into the market for initial sale."[PDMA, 2006].

Questions

Management makes the decision if the product is ready to leave the company. Based on the milestones we identified in Figure 3.4 and described in this subchapter, we define questions that can be applied to these milestones. Table 3.4 provides a summary of the review questions specific to the milestones for the product development phase. We also relate the six general review questions (see Chapter 2.6) to the specific questions for the product development phase. Note that different basic questions are addressed at different milestones of the product development phase (see column "Related Basic Review Questions" in Table 3.4).

In case one of these questions cannot be answered to full satisfaction of management, management can use process mapping like in Figure 3.4 to identify if the questions are asked at the appropriate time for the underlying software methodology.

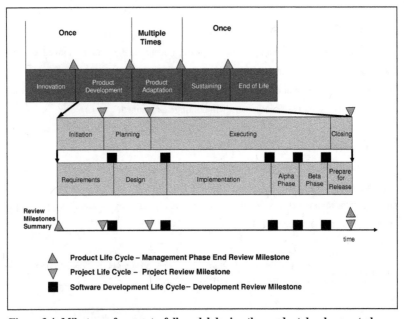

Figure 3.4: Milestones for a waterfall model during the product development phase.

Review Milestone	Focus	Milestone Questions	Related Basic Review Questions (see Table 2.2)
End of Initiation	Project	Can the organization agree on the product? Are first rough estimates for the project identified?	Q1, Q3, Q6
End of Requirements	Software Development	Are the requirements complete? Are the requirements fully understood?	Q1, Q3, Q6
End of Planning	Project	Is the project plan valid? What makes the organization sure that the project is set up for success?	Q1, Q2, Q3, Q5, Q6
End of Design	Software Development	Is the design correct? Is the design approved by the relevant stakeholders?	Q1,Q2,Q5,Q6
End of Implementation	Software Development	Is the implementation of all specified requirements completed? Is the software running?	Q2, Q4, Q6
End of Alpha Phase	Software Development	Can the performance values and the requirements be met? What is the priority of the outstanding work? Is the product working?	Q1, Q2, Q3, Q4, Q5, Q6
End of Beta Phase	Software Development	Does the product meet customer expectations? Can the product rollout proceed as planned? When can the product be released? Is the product working?	Q3, Q4,Q6
Release Readiness	.Software Development	Does the software fulfill the release criteria?	Q3, Q4, Q6
End of product development	Management	Is the software product ready for delivery? Is marketing ready to launch the product?	Q1, Q3, Q4, Q5, Q6

Table 3.4: Review milestone for the product development phase.

In order to understand the level of information and knowledge at each milestone we are applying our six questions that were defined in Chapter 2 to the process described above. Table 3.5 shows an overview about the information at each milestone that is illustrated in Figure 3.4.

Review	Q1. What is the product we are building?	Q2. Is this product feasible as well as achievable and why?	Q3. Is this product marketable and why?
End of Initiation	High-level requirements exist.	Little information for technical feasibility is known.	Existing business case established in innovation is not likely to change
End of Requirements	Details of product requirements defined and understood.	Requirements for technical feasibility positively assessed.	Updates of business case in case key functionality is not technical feasible.
End of Planning	Scope of work is defined based on product's architecture, requirements, and high-level design.	Feasibility of product clarified based on design activities.	Update business case if identified product development costs and / or project schedule change.
End of Design	Know product intend to build.	Feasibility and achievability are known.	Final updates of business case in regard to feasibility of functionality.
End of Implementation	Code of specified requirements exists	Feasibility and achievability are "better" known.	No new information
End of Alpha Phase	Internally that product is Verified and validated what intended to build.	Feasibility and achievability proven during Alpha phase.	Key customer engaged to participate in Beta phase.
End of Beta Phase	Verified and validated externally that product is what we intended to build	Feasibility and achievability proven during Beta phase.	Feedback from key customer that participated in testing activities confirm marketability of product.
Release Readiness	Final product known.	Feasibility proven	No new information
End of product development	Final product known.	Feasibility proven	Solid business case and pre-orders from key customers demonstrate marketability of product

Table 3.5a: Overview of available information at each review milestone (Question 1 to 3).

Review	Q4. Is the product functioning at the level of current abstraction and why?	Q5. How are we building this product?	Q6. Is the plan predictable and realistic and why?
End of Initiation	Not applicable	Consideration of specific technology methodology and processes are done.	First order of magnitude estimate for budget and deadline identified. \
End of Requirements	Identified requirements are proven to be functioning.	Assessment of requirements evaluates if considered technology methodology works.	Plan can build on defined set of requirements.
End of Planning	No new information	Technology, methodology, and processes are selected and defined.	Plan developed based on known product details , methodology and team's input. High predictability.
End of Design	Identified design is proven to be functioning.	Technology, methodology, and processes have been applied.	Meeting deadline for design proves validity of plan.
End of Implementation	Software is running. Not all features might be operational.	Technology methodology and processes have been applied.	Meeting deadline for implementation proves validity of plan.
End of Alpha Phase	Software is running. Not all features might be functioning.	Technology methodology and processes have been applied.	Meeting deadline for Alpha phase proves validity of plan.
End of Beta Phase	Almost all features should be functioning.	Verification and validation that selected methodology and processes have been working.	Meeting deadline for Beta phase proves validity of plan.
Release Readiness	All specified features should be functioning.	Technology methodology and processes have been proven to work	Plan executed.
End of product development	All features should be functional.	Details of technology, methodology and process perspective used.	Lesson's Learned created.

Table 3.5b: Overview of available information at each review milestone (Question 4 to 6).

In Figure 3.5 we show an overview of the information that is exchanged between the software methodology, the project life cycle and the product development life cycle. Looking at the exchange of information we can conclude that some information is created on the methodology level and communicated to product development through the phases of the project life cycle. The granularity of information elaborates into more details from one project review milestone to the next for the waterfall type software development method.

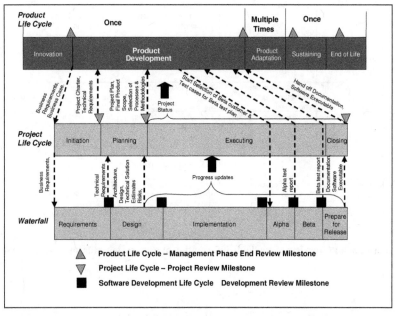

Figure 3.5: Overview of exchanged information during the product development phase.

Figure 3.5 can be used as a checklist to identify what information should be available at any point of time of the project. Figure 3.5 also shows that management requires some information on the product level that originates from the software development level. This illustration provides an opportunity for management to gain an understanding about the source of the requested information.

3.2.3 Product Adaptation Phase

As soon as the product hits the market, plans are made for follow up releases to adopt the product to newly identified customer requirements during its product development life cycle. The product reaches the product adaptation phase. The developments taking place during the product adaptation phase follow the same project life cycle and basically the same waterfall methodology (see Figure 3.4). As the product was validated and verified before it was delivered to the market at the end of the product development phase, Alpha and Beta phase become insignificant for development projects during the product adaptation phase. An Alpha and Beta phase might or might not be needed for a project addressing product adaptations. In reference to Table 3.4 the milestones for "End of Alpha phase" and "End of Beta phase" become optional. At the completion of each "adaptation" project an "End of Product Adaptation" review takes place. As the product is in existence and was delivered when the product adaptation phase is reached there are fewer unknowns for the product and project. As a result the reviews usually take less time than during the initial product development and project execution works with less interruption and fewer changes.

At the beginning of the adaptation phase, frequent releases are occurring. The product is in the early maturity of its market (see Chapter 2.2's Figure 2.1). The more mature the product becomes the less releases are delivered to the market. During the product adaptation stage the development completes the project lifecycle for each release. There are multiple product adaptation projects until the product reaches the sustaining phase. For information about "Sustaining" and "End of life" phases of the product life cycle refer to Chapter 2.3

3.3 Spiral Model Viewpoint

3.3.1 The Classical Spiral Model

The classical spiral model is iterative where planning is mixed with development activities. Each cycle helps to break down the objective into a more granular level of work. If the development is very complex in nature it can take multiple cycles until the product is well enough defined to be approved for implementation. Compared to the waterfall model and agile development methodologies (see Chapter 3.2 and 3.4) the spiral model has been least used in the software industry. The major difference to the other models is that it creates a risk driven approach. Barry Boehm's original model [Boehm, 1988] is initiated by stating the hypothesis that a specific operational mission can be improved by a software effort.

Spiral development itself goes several times through four major phases. Each iteration is called one cycle, see Figure 3.6. During the first phase objectives, alternatives and constraints are identified. Alternative solutions are evaluated using means like prototyping, and then associated risks are identified and solved. The third phase focuses on development and confirmation of the next level (quasi "implementation") of the product. It defines the product in the next level of granularity.

During the fourth phase plans are defined for the next cycle. The first cycle is completed. Before the next cycle starts the stakeholder for this project review all products developed during the previous cycle and plans for the next cycle. Based on the outcome the objectives, alternatives and constraints are developed for the next phase. The classical spiral model goes through multiple cycles until requirements and architectural solutions have been defined. The product implementation follows a waterfall model. The spiral model works on the basis of elaboration where information from the previous phase is applied to work on the details for the next phase.

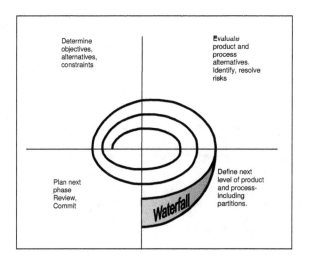

Figure 3.6: Overview of spiral model [Boehm, 1988].

3.3.2 The Next Generation Process Model Extended Win Win Spiral Model

The next generation process model (NGPM) is an extension of the spiral model and is based on Theory W [Boehm-Bose, 1994]. It uses win conditions, like mutual agreements, that are negotiated between the stakeholders of a development. The NGPM model accounts for the fact that constraints can be specific to each stakeholder and therefore can contradict each other which can jeopardize the success of the project. Win conditions are those requirements that have to be determined by negotiating win- win solutions for all involved parties. This guarantees the success of the project. This could lead to waving requirements or modifying requirements to make it work. [Boehm-Ross, 1989]. The spiral model with the NGPM Theory W extension breaks one cycle into seven steps and is referred to WinWin spiral model [Boehm- Egyed, 1998]. Table 3.6 shows how the NGPM relates to the basic model. Berry Boehm and Paul Gruenbacher developed a groupware called EasyWinWin that supports the process to find win-win solutions for the requirements development process during the spiral model [Boehm-Gruenbacher, 2001].

Classical Spiral Model	NGPM extended Win Win Spiral Model
• Determine objectives, alternatives, constraints	• Identify next level stakeholder • Identify stakeholder with conditions • Reconcile win conditions. Establish next level objectives, constraints, alternatives
• Evaluate product and process alternatives. Identify, resolve risks	• Evaluate product and process alternatives. Identify, resolve risks
• Define next level of product and process-including partitions.	• Define next level of product and process-including partitions.
• Plan next phase • Review, Commit	• Validate product and process definitions • Review, commit

Table 3.6: Classical Spiral Model versus Win Win Spiral Model.

Each cycle of the spiral model will create its specific deliverables that need to be reviewed before starting the next cycle. The increase of "spiral" size is not directly related to the duration of the cycle. It is an abstraction of the development process. It is likely that the duration of the project life cycle increases with the number of spiral cycles. The more complex or less known the requirements are at the beginning, the more cycles the project will go through.

The classical spiral model will be used for further assessment.

Table 3.7 provides an overview of the spiral model.

Process Step	Activity	Deliverables
1. Determine objectives, alternatives, constraints	Determine scope of iteration	Scope of iteration
2. Evaluate product and process alternatives. Identify, resolve risks	Identify risks, Prioritize risks, Determine mitigation strategy.	Risk plan.
3. Define next level of product and process-including partitions.	Create models and benchmarks, Identify product concepts, requirements and design,	Concept of iteration, Software requirements, Product design documents.

Process Step	Activity	Deliverables
4. Plan next phase	Validate requirements and design. Planning of product and project specifics for the next iteration. Review and commit to plan.	Requirements plan, Life cycle plan, Development plan Integration and test plan
5. Repeat step 1-4 until ready for product development		
6. Product development using waterfall model	All activities starting with detailed design as listed in Table 3.3	All deliverables starting with detailed design document as listed in Table 3.3.

Table 3.7: Overview of Spiral method activities and deliverables based on [Boehm, 1988].

From a project management perspective the spiral model places a great deal of reliance on the ability of software developers to identify and manage sources of project risks [Boehm, 1988]. Project management practices as described in Chapter 2 can provide guidance for the risk management plan and risk assessment.

From a planning perspective the spiral model behaves similar to the agile development model [see Chapter 3.4]. The total number of iterations might be unknown at the beginning of the project. An initial total number can be anticipated and an estimate for the duration of each iteration could be identified. After each iteration is completed the overall timeline could be updated. Through the initial iterations all the necessary plans and artifacts (see column "deliverables" in Table 3.7) are defined upfront before the waterfall roll-out starts. This can make the execution of a waterfall roll-out more effective. As a result it potentially saves some time as all plans have been developed based on evaluating product and process alternatives and a major risk assessment. For the same reason the product requirements might be more precise and the product might be of better quality.

The spiral model has in general the following strengths and weaknesses:

Strengths:

- Applies to high-risk developments with numerous unknowns. These constraints can typically be found in research projects. The risk driven approach mitigates the risk of uncertainty. The iterative nature helps to progressively elaborate the unknown nature of the development.
- The spiral method addresses the product requirements as well as identifies process alternatives processes (see step 3 of Table 3.7) needed for implementation of the product. Many development approaches take the process question as a given fact rather than a need that has to analyzed and addressed.
- Can respond to changes in requirements as long as it is not in the product development phase.
- Identifying all the product and process details before implementation starts can reduce the rework time.

Weaknesses:

- At the beginning of the project it is unknown how long it will take until a working product is available
- As the iteration can be of different duration the spiral model can be become challenging to track and control the effort.
- Assessing different options can potentially lead to extensive analysis of every possible case. This can become very time intensive and delay the outcome of the project.

3.3.3 Product Development Phase

Section 3.3.1 introduced the spiral methodology. In order to identify the relationship between product life cycle, project like cycle and spiral model, we apply process mapping as used in Figure 3.1. Figure 3.7 shows process mapping for the spiral type model.

As explained in Chapter 3.1 a product idea is selected at the end of the innovation phase of the product life cycle. We assume that with the start of the product development phase the project lifecycle applies. The spiral development starts with the initiation of the project. A project review takes place at the end of the initiation phase. The initiation phase can be shorter than in case of a waterfall type model as details of requirements, design and plans are iteratively refined throughout the cycles of the spiral model. The definition of an overall objective and initial funding for the resources needed for the first spiral cycles are sufficient for the initiation phase.

The spiral process iterates requirements definition, high level design and planning multiple times until the product is ready for implementation. The spiral model defines a review at the end of each cycle (see Figure 3.6), the so called "End of Cycle" review. See development review milestone indicated with "n" in Figure 3.7.

Only when all sufficient product information is identified, the product is implemented following a waterfall type model as introduced in Chapter 3.2. The implementation of the waterfall type model is assigned to the third quadrant of the spiral cycle. As shown in Table 3.7 the third quadrant defines the product and process in more detail. The spiral model does not propose any reviews during the waterfall roll-out. The section of the waterfall model of Chapter 3.2.2 suggests additional reviews in analogy to Figure 3.4. When the "End of Planning" milestone is reached, development reaches the point of starting the waterfall model. At this point requirements and at least high-level design have been completed.
When all design work has been finished an "End of Design" review like described for the waterfall model needs to take place (see Chapter 3.2).

Also reviews at the end of the Alpha phase, Beta phase and project closing apply as described in Chapter 3.2.2.
For the spiral model all questions to be asked at each of the milestones as shown in Figure 3.7 are the same as defined in Table 3.4 with the exception of the "End of Requirements" milestone. Instead the spiral model has an "End of Cycle" review at the end of each spiral cycle. The questions to be asked for the "End of Cycle" review are listed in Table 3.8. We also relate the general defined review question of Chapter 2.6 to

the "End of Cycle" reviews. Note that question 4 (Is the product functioning?) applies to the created prototype of the current cycle.

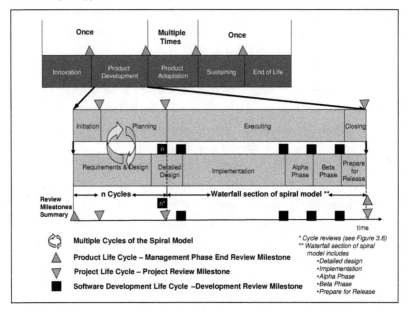

Figure 3.7: Milestones for a spiral model during the product development phase.

Review Milestone	Focus	Milestone Questions	Related Basic Review Questions (see Table 2.2)
End of Innovation	Management	See Table 3.2	See Table 3.2
End of Cycle (n)	Software Development	Are the requirements sufficiently completed at this level of refinement? Are the requirements fully understood at the level of refinement? Is the plan for the next cycle realistic?	Q1, Q2, Q3, Q4, Q5, Q6
Waterfall Milestones of Table 3.4			See Table 3.4
End of product development	Management	See Table 3.2	See Table 3.2

Table 3.8: Questions to be asked at the "End of Cycle" milestone.

In order to understand the level of information at each milestone of the waterfall model (Chapter 3.2) we applied the six defined questions of Chapter 2 to each milestone and summarized the outcome in Table 3.5. Applying the six general questions to the spiral model provides similar results. We apply the basic six questions to the spiral model in order to identify the existing level of information at each milestone (see Table 3.9). Note that the "End of Cycle" milestone replaces the "End of Requirements" milestone in Table 3.4 for the spiral model. The granularity of available information will increase with each cycle. At the point the development is ready for implementing the product by following the waterfall model, the requirements have been defined and assessed in much more detail than in the requirements phase for the waterfall model. Note that at each of the "End of Cycle" reviews some requirements have been proven to work applying prototyping. At the "End of Planning" review the product is much more specified than at the same milestone of the waterfall model. For the rest of available information at each milestone refer to Table 3.5 of the waterfall model.

Review	Q1. What is the product we are building?	Q2. Is this product feasible as well as achievable and why?	Q3. Is this product marketable and why?	Q4. Is the product functioning at the level of current abstraction and why?	Q5. How are we building this product?	Q6. Is the plan predictable and realistic and why?
End of Initiation	See Table 3.5	See Table 3.5	See Table 3.5	See Table 3.5	See Table 3.5	See Table 3.5
End of Cycle $_{(n)}$	Working prototype at level of current level of abstraction exists.	Requirements for technical feasibility positively assessed by using prototyping.	Updates of business case in case key functionality is not technical feasible.	Product proven to work for prototype of current cycle..	Assessment of requirements evaluates if considered technology methodology works for current prototype.	Plan can build on defined set of requirements. Each cycle provides more level of granularity for the plan.
End of Planning	Product requirements and architectural solution are well defined.	Feasibility of product completely clarified for requirements and architectural solution.	Update business case if identified product development costs and / or project schedule change.	Product proven to work on prototype level.	Technology, methodology, and processes are selected and defined.	Plan developed based on known product details, methodology and team's input. Very High predictability.
End of	See Table 3.5	See Table 3.5	See Table 3.5	See Table 3.5	See Table 3.5	See Table 3.5

Review	Q1. What is the product we are building?	Q2. Is this product feasible as well as achievable and why?	Q3. Is this product marketable and why?	Q4. Is the product functioning at the level of current abstraction and why?	Q5. How are we building this product?	Q6. Is the plan predictable and realistic and why?
Design						

Table 3.9: Overview of available information at each review milestone.

Figure 3.8 provides an overview of the information that is exchanged between the software methodology, the project life cycle and the product development life cycle during the product development phase. Like in the waterfall type model described in Chapter 3.2 the granularity of information elaborates into more details from one project review milestone to the next for the waterfall type software development method. In comparison to the previously defined waterfall type model some product related information becomes available at earlier stages. By going through the four sections of the spiral cycles the initial cycles help to define the product in more details before implementing the product. As a result methodologies, processes and technical plans are likely to be in place after the project initiation. Figure 3.8 shows that methodologies, processes and technical plans exist at an earlier stage than in the waterfall type model (Figure 3.5).

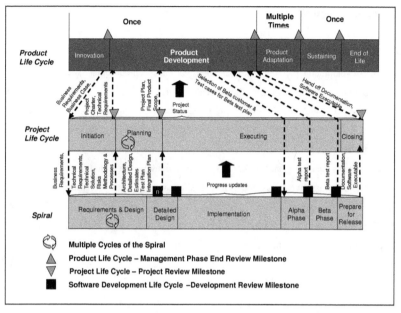

Figure 3.8: Overview of exchanged information during the product development phase.

3.3.4 Product Adaptation Phase

During the product adaptation phase each project could theoretically follow its own spiral methodology. As the product foundation has been developed the spiral model will have a very simplified and short assessment period before entering the waterfall model. Like described in Chapter 3.2.3 the "End of Alpha" and "End of Beta" milestones become of less importance for the product adaptation phase and are optional.

Otherwise the milestones for the adaptation phase are the same as for the product development phase. Please refer to Figure 3.7 and Figure 3.8 for details about milestones and available information.

With respect to "Sustaining" and "End of life" phases there is no difference to the waterfall model (see Chapter 2.3).

3.4 Agile Development

3.4.1 Motivation and Approach

Agile development methodologies include various methodologies such as Extreme Programming, Scrum, Crystal Methods, Feature Driven Development , Dynamic Systems Development Model, Adaptive Software Development or Lean Development [Schwaber-Beedle, 2002] [Beck, 2000], [Abrahamsson, 2002]. Some of them have been around for more than 10 years.

Requirements changes and redirections are common throughout the development lifecycle of a software project. Therefore a more flexible software development methodology is needed.

The agile development methodologies can follow a moving target. Scrum is an important representative amongst the agile development methodologies for project management. Scrum provides the overall management of the development and often applies the development practices of Extreme Programming. See [Beck, 2000] for details on Extreme Programming.

The product is usually developed in increments rather than building the whole system or product at once.

This leaves the necessary room to introduce modifications, additions or changes between the iterations. It also allows applying lessons learned from the previous iteration. In addition the developer can focus on certain features/functionality within the cycle. Priorities will not change within one development cycle. The details are specific to the methodology used. Dependent on what Agile methodology is used for development, one iteration can take between two weeks up to four months. [Koppensteiner-Udo, 2004] [Abrahamsson, 2002]. Figure 3.9 shows the development cycle for Scrum:

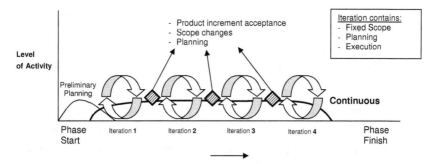

Figure 3.9: Agile Development Cycle [Udo-Koppensteiner, 2003].

In Scrum the duration of one iteration is chosen to be 30 days [Schwaber- Beedle, 2002].

3.4.2 Scrum

Every project using Scrum starts with a preliminary planning phase. This phase begins with a high level project definition, followed by the definition of the architecture. Then a product backlog, an initial list of what the product will consist of, is built and prioritized. Based on this list the first project estimates are provided and releases are planned.

For each iteration (so called Sprint) the team or the customer selects a set of features based on priority. During planning of the Sprint the requested feature set is analyzed and the associated work gets broken down into more details. As a result the schedule is created for this Sprint. The scheduled work is tracked. There are no standard documents defined for a Scrum development. From the first Sprint onwards functioning software is created. By default a Sprint takes 30 days. During the execution of a Sprint the determined software functionality gets designed in detail, developed, unit tested and integrated with previous developed increments. The incremental product must be of shippable quality. This means it is fully tested, documented and available as a software executable. Practices of specific agile methodologies such as Extreme programming might be combined with Scrum and applied within the executing period.

At the end of each Sprint, the product increment is reviewed and has to be accepted by all stakeholders. The customer formally accepts the product functionality developed and at the same time can correct future requirements or priorities for the next Sprint. Sprints are

73

used as control devices to help make it easier to change course during the project, as well as provide some stability. [Udo-Koppensteiner, 2003].

The development Sprints are followed by release iterations that make sure that all product increments of various teams are working together and packaged. Table 3.10 shows an overview of Scrum.

The software projects that follow the Scrum methodology are managed by self-empowered teams. These teams decide for themselves what software development practices they will use, what skill set they need for this development, how to split the work and how to work as a team. Self-empowered teams are co-located to improve the communication between the team members. They are also more likely to seek solutions that keep the administrated effort to manage themselves and their work as low as possible.

Process Step	Activity	Deliverables
Preliminary Planning	Identify product requirements. Define Project. Define Architecture. Prioritize Product requirements and functionality. Estimate product functionality Plan Releases	Product Backlog, Architecture document as far as necessary, Release Plan.
Development **Iterations (Sprints)**	Plan Sprint in detail. Create detailed design, Create test cases Develop code, Perform unit test Perform integrations and system test as appropriate.	Burn-down chart (see Figure 3.10), Detailed Design documented as necessary, Test cases, Product documentation as necessary, Software executable of product increment.
Release **Iterations**	Perform integration and integration testing of various developed product increments. Create software package.	Software release.

Table 3.10: Overview of Scrum activities and deliverables.

Management does not control the team or the project. Instead of a project management role the Scrum master's role is defined. The Scrum master conducts daily meetings called Scrum meetings. These meetings are of very short duration (about 15 minutes). At these meetings each team member provides status of the accomplishments of the previous day, his/her planned tasks for today and any roadblocks he/she might face.

The Scrum master follows up outside the meeting to remove some of these roadblocks. The status of the performed work is tracked by one of the team members and illustrated in a so called burn down chart. See Figure 3.10 for an example of a burn down chart. The burn down chart for a Sprint is based on the effort of all tasks the team needs to accomplish for the current Sprint. It tracks the total time of all remaining tasks efforts over the duration of a Sprint. The total time is determined by adding the estimates of all tasks required for a Sprint together. The work that is completed is subtracted from the total work effort on almost a daily basis. In case one task takes more time than anticipated during planning at the beginning of the Sprint, the additional time is added to the total time of work effort (see point with 810 hours on burn down chart Figure 3.10). A burn down chart is also created for the total time of the project and is updated after each Sprint. The maintenance of the burn down chart is a project management task for tracking progress of the development. Besides the Scrum master role, the burn down chart is the only project management tool defined for Scrum. There are no other project management responsibilities identified in Scrum.

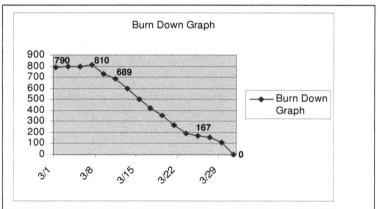

Figure 3.10: Example of a burn down chart.

From a project management perspective Scrum responds to change rather than follows a plan and therefore is prone to scope creep and requirements creep.

Scrum developments can have several advantages for product management. The customer is often considered part of the development team. Each Sprint creates a product increment that is reviewed by all stakeholders. This also includes product management who can then decide when the product is ready for market introduction.

Scrum has in general the following strengths and weaknesses as sated below. Other Agile methodologies have similar strength and weaknesses:

Strengths:

- Delivering working software after each Sprint
- Requirements changes can be introduced between Sprints without slowing down the progress of ongoing development work.
- Building up trusting relationships with stakeholder by demonstrating a piece of working software at the end of each Sprint.
- Scrum methodology is easy to understand and learn.
- Teams are self-managed and co-located. Therefore team cohesion and communication improves

Weaknesses:

- Requires a different role of management that empowers their teams to make their own decisions, even allowing them to fail.
- The team needs a number of Sprints to learn about their capability as a team. Therefore the team members might over-commit themselves first and then underestimate their progress in later Sprints. Only over time estimates will improve.
- It takes true commitment and management support to remove barriers for the team in order to make this approach work.
- Management takes a risk by implementing this management philosophy into an organization that has been driven from the top down in the past or has had a lot of inexperienced employees.

3.4.3 Product Development Phase

We apply the process mapping (see Figure 3.1) to Scrum. Figure 3.11 illustrates the process mapping for Scrum. It shows the milestones for the product development life cycle, the project life cycle and an agile development methodology based on Scrum as described in [Schwaber- Beedle, 2002] and [Schwaber, 2004].

Scrum works best when the product idea is already in place. Both the product idea as well as the associated business case is identified during the innovation phase as described in Chapter 3.1. The product development phase starts with a product level initiation and planning phase that is then followed by multiple Sprints that run partly through all phases of the project management cycle.

During the product level initiation and planning phase the product backlog, an overall project duration and a release plan are identified for the Scrum development.
Each Sprint that follows this phase concept contains planning, executing and closing activities. At the onset of each Sprint features are chosen from the product backlog that can be completed within the duration of one Sprint. Then these features are analyzed and planned in more detail (Planning Phase). The progress of the Scrum team is tracked in a burn-down chart [Schwaber- Beedle, 2002] (see Chapter 3.4.2).

During executing the product increment including the selected functionality is created. The product increment is completed at the end of the Sprint (milestone). The product increment gets reviewed and accepted by all stakeholders at this milestone. This Sprint review is part of the project closing phase. At the same time future requirements or priorities can be changed for the next iterations [Udo-Koppensteiner, 2003]. As the iterations are the control device it appears logical to link the project review to the results of the review of the product increment.

The review of the incremental product is the only review within the Sprint and project cycle. After the review the next cycle starts with the initiation phase (see Figure 3.11) where product direction can be changed, features can be added or removed from the overall feature list, and priorities get new assigned. Next the overall timeline for the product is updated based on the outcome of the previous Sprint and changes to the feature list. These activities occur during the planning phase.

The next Sprint cycle follows the same way as described above or in more detail in Chapter 3.4.2. After several Sprints the product will be ready for release. This defines the end point of the product development phase. The release readiness review may be combined with one of the product increment reviews that take place at the end of each Sprint. As each product increment is integrated with the existing code base during its Sprint cycle, the product can be released whenever sufficient functionality has been implemented. After the release the Sprint content shifts slowly from feature development to enhancements.

Table 3.11 lists the questions that can be asked at "End of Sprint" milestone. We also relate the general defined review question of Chapter 2.6 to the "End of Sprint" reviews. As working software is reviewed at the end of each Sprint all basic questions apply to this milestone. Note that each "End of Sprint" milestone will provide also incremental answers to these questions.

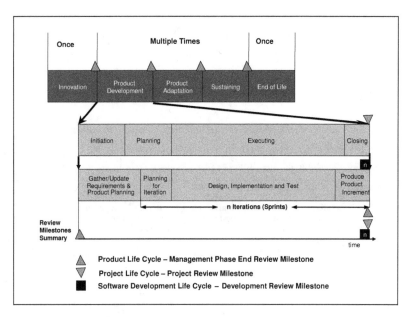

Figure 3.11: Milestones for a Scrum model.

Review Milestone	Focus	Milestone Questions	Related Basic Review Questions (see Table 2.2)
End of Innovation	Management	See Table 3.2	See Table 3.2
End of each Sprint	Software Development, Project Management	Does the product increment meet customer expectations? Has the functionality of the Sprint been fully implemented? Are there any changes to existing requirements and scope (product backlog) required? What is the priority of the outstanding work? Is the product ready for release with this product increment?	Q1, Q2, Q3, Q4, Q5, Q6
End of Product Development	Management	See Table 3.2	See Table 3.2

Table 3.11: Milestones for a Scrum development methodology.

Table 3.12 shows an overview of the existing information at each milestone when applying the six questions we defined in Chapter 2. The management milestones are the same as explained in Chapter 3.1. See Table 3.2 for information existing at each management milestone. By applying process mapping we were able to identify the information available at each "End of Iteration (Sprint)" milestone.

Figure 3.12 provides an overview of the information that is exchanged between the Scrum, the project life cycle and the product development life cycle. More information becomes available with the availability of each product increment.

Review	Q1. What is the product we are building and why?	Q2. Is this product (technically) feasible as well as achievable and why?	Q3. Is this product marketable and why?	Q4. Is the product functioning at the level of current abstraction and why??	Q5. How are we building this product and why?	Q6. Is the plan predictable and realistic and why?
End of Iteration (Sprint)	Product increment of current Sprint available.	Product increment proves feasibility of functionality implemented during Sprint.	Feedback of customer reviewing the product increment confirm marketability.	Product increment is functioning.	Creating one product increment per Sprint.	Each Sprint that delivers the scope identified for the current Sprint improves predictability. Each change as a result of reviewing the current product increment decreases predictability.

Table 3.12: Overview of available information at each review milestone.

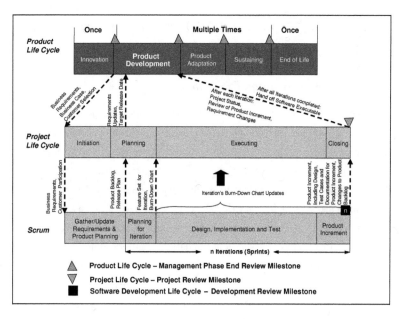

Figure 3.12: Overview of exchanged information during the product development phase.

3.4.4 Product Adaptation Phase

After the release of the product, the product transfers from the product development phase to the product adaptation phase of the product life cycle. The iterative approach applies the same way to the product adaptation as described for the product development phase (see Chapter 3.4.3).

For information about "Sustaining" and "End of life" phases of the product life cycle refer to Chapter 2.3.

Chapter 4: Systems Dynamics Models for Key Software Development Methodologies

4.1 Overview of Systems Dynamics

In the previous chapters we described the correlation between product life cycle, project lifecycle and software methodology. We aligned them to each other and demonstrated that there is a relationship between these processes by applying process mapping (see Figure 3.1) to three software development methodologies: waterfall, spiral and Scrum. Using process mapping we identified the review milestones for each software development methodology. The review milestones were set based on the specifics of each software model. Placing the review milestones at the right point in time enables the information to be exchanged between the product, the project and the methodology and improves the chances for a successful outcome of a project. Further we provided an overview of what information is exchanged between the software development methodology and the product development life cycle through the project life cycle (Figure 3.5, 3.8, 3.12). We established that the project life cycle builds the link between these two processes.

As a next step we evaluate the software models from a timing perspective. We will identify how long each software models will take in specific project scenarios. We use systems dynamics modeling.

In this chapter we identify systems dynamics models for each software model described in Chapter 3. Then we define different scenarios related to all three software development methodologies and let each model run through the same scenarios. Each of these scenarios has an impact on the time the development takes. This will allow us to compare the results for all models with each other and draw conclusions on the behavior of these software methodologies.

4.2 Management of Systems Theory

Traditional management approaches focus on scientific, administrative, process, human relations, and contingency perspectives to management in separation. Therefore it is more action oriented. In contrast systems thinking considers the interaction of all these factors and how they influence each other. Compared to traditional management approaches management that applies a systems thinking focuses on the manager's thought process. It is based on the assumption that a manager's actions cannot be separated from the way he or she thinks.

"Systems Thinking identifies the relationships between the parts of the system" [Cavaleri-Obloj, 1993].

Definition:	**"Systems Thinking** consists of four central dimensions: *Interrelated Thinking*: a thinking in interrelated, systemic structures. *Dynamic Thinking*: a thinking in dynamic processes. *Thinking in Models*: explicitly comprehended models *Steering Systems*: the ability for practical system management and system control" [Ossimitz, 2000].

Applying system thinking helps to gain the insight that changing relationships may affect the structured behavior and performance of a system. Systems thinking is based on ideas originating from engineering, organization theory, natural sciences and philosophy [Bertalanffy, 1976] [Cavaleri-Obloj, 1993] [Senge, 1994].

Definition:	"A **System** is a grouping of component parts that individually establish relationships with each other and interact with their environment both as individuals and as a collective" [Cavaleri-Obloj, 1993].

A system can be defined by its components and the relationship between the components (elements) in a way that

- the elements of a system are connected in an organized way.
- the elements are influenced by its belonging to a system or leaving a system.

83

- the attributes of a system are different from the sum of the attributes of each component.
- the system causes something.
- the system is interesting to someone.

This definition is based on [OpenSystem, 1981] [Thome, 1993] [Chroust, 2002].

Systems are composed of other smaller, less complex systems known as subsystems. Also subsystems can be broken down into smaller interrelated subsystems.

Definition:	"The manner in which a system's elements are organized or interrelated is called the **Structure**" [Sterman, 2000]

By changing the structure of the elements, new forms of relations become possible, and the system will usually generate new patterns of behavior. Therefore structure is the primary determinant of behavior in systems.

Dynamic systems show changing behavior over time. As human beings we have a tendency to assume that each effect in a system is related to one cause [Sterman, 2000]. "*Experiments show people can generally detect linear, positive correlations among variables.......However, we have great difficulty in the presence of random error, non-linearity, and negative correlation, often never discovering the true relationship*" [Brehmer, 1980]. We have also problems to envisioning exponential growth and feedback loops.

Often we ignore feedback, that can result from decisions we made, or non-linearity, or time delays [Sterman, 2000]. The effect of feedback can be demonstrated by using causal loops that are introduced in Chapter 4.4. System Dynamic modeling uses causal loop diagrams to create simulation models that can help the user to understand the system's behavior over time (see Chapter 4.3).

4.3 Dynamic Systems

A system is considered dynamic when it changes over time. Interactions among elements of a system usually establish a pattern over time based on the occurrences of events. There are common behaviors that can be observed in systems over a period of time

(Figure 4.1). Systems can have different behaviors. Essential types of behaviors are listed in Table 4.1.

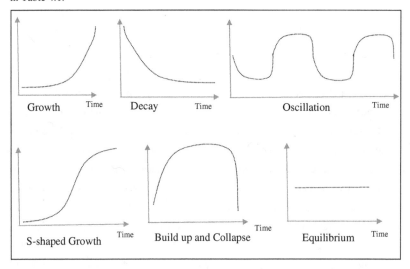

Figure 4.1: Common Models of System Behavior [Cavaleri-Obloj, 1993], [Sterman, 2000].

In many areas of today's world models are used to provide more insight into systems. Systems Dynamics is applied to dynamic systems to learn about their behavior. Virtual worlds are the only way of experiencing the potential outcome without any consequences. They are used for pilot training, aircraft modeling and assessment of how buildings fit into the neighborhood, just to name a few. System Dynamic models are used to assess business problems. They can help management to evaluate problems and identify the impact of their decisions on a system before they take any action.

Behavior of a System	Description
Equilibrium	System has achieved balance
Dynamic equilibrium	The system state shows dynamic fluctuations within a restricted range.
Disequilibrium	State of system shows wide variations,
Entropical behavior	System shows powers of disorganization and disintegration

Table 4.1: Behaviours of a System based on [Cavaleri-Obloj, 1993].

As we will show in our project delay scenario in Chapter 4.4 (Figure 4.1), a causal loop diagrams can help to learn about the behavior of a system.

4.4 Causal Loops

In order to demonstrate how systems theory can be applied to project management we use simple scenario.

A project can be perceived as a system that consists of multiple elements that interact with each other. The elements for a software project include but are not limited to the project team (a subsystem consisting of its team members), the scope of the project (software product which in itself is a system again) and the development that needs to happen to implement the scope. Assuming that a project reports a delay, management might ask the project team for a solution to react to this delay. From this point onwards management decides to track the project delays and tries to identify the underlying cause. Based on the tracked data management identifies that every time requirements change, additional development is added to the scope of the project that adds to the workload of the project team and pushes out the timeline. Every time the timeline of the project increases the project team feels pressured and as a consequence introduces errors. The resolution of these errors adds even more to the existing workload and the project to delay. Whenever we ask "What is causing the situation", we are probing a structure [Anderson-Johnson, 1997]. A causal loop diagram can help to identify how a system works (behavior) and can provide insight into the systems structure. Figure 4.2 shows a causal loop type diagram for our scenario.

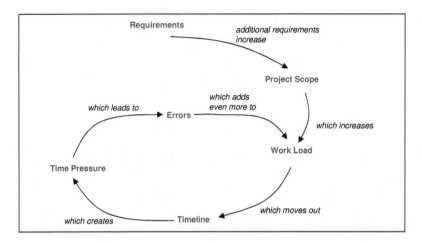

Figure 4.2: Causal loop type diagram for project delays.

The relationship between two parameters can be either reinforcing or balancing. In case one parameter reinforces the behavior of other it is referred to as "positive" or "reinforcing" relationship and marked with a "+" sign at the arrow head. A "balanced" or "negative" relationship is marked with a "-" sign (see Figure 4.3).

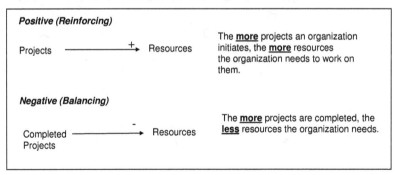

Figure 4.3: Interpretation of positive and negative influence.

Loops in a causal loop diagram indicate feedback. The feedback can either reinforce or balance the behavior [Senge, 1994]. The polarity of a loop can be identified by using the rule of thumb that the product of two negative signs from the links in a loop is equal to a reinforcing behavior of the loop. Therefore negative loop polarity requires an odd number of negative links in the loop [Sterman, 2000]. Figure 4.4 shows an example for a positive and a negative loop. Figure 4.5 shows the complete causal loop diagram for the example we showed in a simplified way in Figure 4.2. It includes the polarity of the links as well as the polarity of the feedback loop.

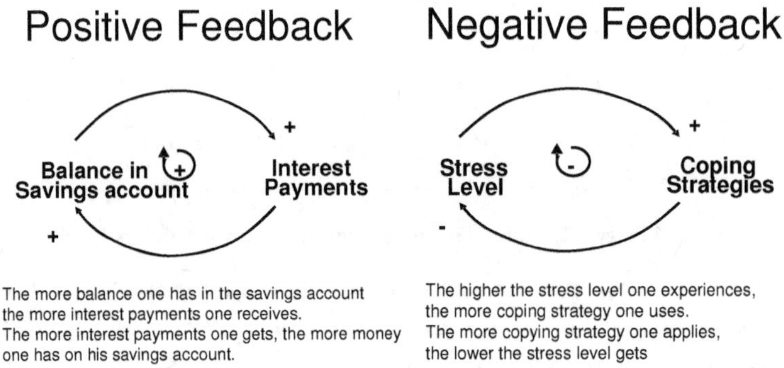

Positive Feedback
Negative Feedback
+
Balance in Savings account
+
Interest Payments
+
Stress Level
-
Coping Strategies
+
-
The more balance one has in the savings account the more interest payments one receives.
The more interest payments one gets, the more money one has on his savings account.
The higher the stress level one experiences, the more coping strategy one uses.
The more copying strategy one applies, the lower the stress level gets

Figure 4.4: Example for positive and negative loop polarity [Sterman, 2000].

Requirements
+
Project Scope
+
Errors
+
+
Work Load
Time Pressure
+
+
Timeline
+

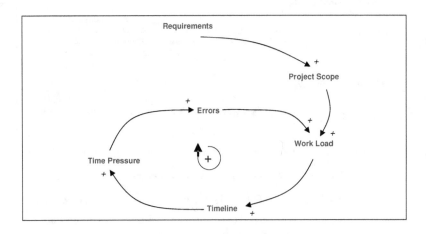

Figure 4.5: Complete causal loop diagram for project delays.

4.5 Modeling by Systems Dynamics

One way to interpret and see effects of systems dynamics models is by using computer application software. In order for systems models to be simulated they need to be translated from a causal loop diagram into a stock and flow diagram.

| Definition: | "**Stocks** are accumulations that build and decline over time" [Sterman, 2000]. |

Therefore stocks are a quantity.

| Definition: | "**Flows** are either the inflows that contribute to the accumulations or outflows that lead to declining stock levels." [Sterman, 2000]. |

Each flow either fills or drains the level of the accumulation with a certain speed, the *rate*. The rate of inflow or outflow determines the level of the accumulation.

| Definition: | "A **Level** is the amount of accumulation at any single point." [Sterman, 2000]. |

Levels are measured in the same unit of the stock at any given time period. Figure 4.6 shows the definition for a flow and stock diagram.

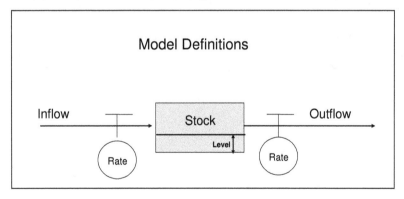

Figure 4.6: Model definitions for a flow and stock diagram [Sterman, 2000].

From the stock and flow diagram we can construct the corresponding differential equation to calculate the value (level) of the Stock variable at every point of time of the simulation:

$d/dt\ (Stock) = Inflow(t) - Outflow(t)$ (4.1)

"*Stocks accumulate or integrate their flows. The net flow into the stock is the rate of change of the stock (inflow less outflow)*" [Sterman, 2000] that corresponds to the integral in (4.1).

The causal loop diagram builds the bases for understanding the structure of a system. In order to translate at a causal loop diagram into a flow and stock diagram stocks can be defined by identifying the parameters that can be counted or measured in the causal loop diagram. Additional auxiliary variables complete the model. The causal loop diagram of the system represents changing (temporal) system's behavior.

Looking at the causal loop diagram of Figure 4.5 we identify project scope, work load, errors and timeline as measurable or stock variables. Time pressure is related to the error rate and therefore represented through the flow variable "error rate". Please see Figure 4.7 for the version of the flow and stock diagram or systems dynamics model used here.

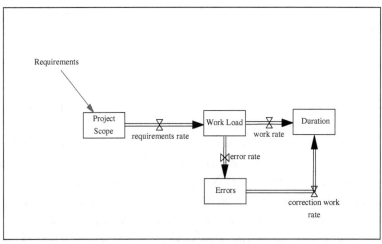

Figure 4.7: Systems dynamics model for project delay example of Figure 4.5 based on [Anderson-Johnson, 1997].

Table 4.2 lists the units for the model's variables. It shows stock variables measured in effort and flow variables measured in time unit per time period.

Variable	Unit
Stock Variables	
Requirements	Effort in Hours
Project Scope	Effort in Hours
Work Load	Effort in Hours
Errors	Effort in Hours
Duration	Effort in Hours
Flow Variables	
Requirements Rate	Hours per Time Period
Work Rate	Hours per Time Period
Correction Work Rate	Hours per Time Period
Error Rate	Hours per Time Period

Table 4.2: Units of each variable of the systems dynamics model.

The translation of the causal loop diagram into flow and stock diagram or systems dynamic model is based on the perspective, subject knowledge and experience of the modelers.

In order to create the systems dynamics models for the software development methods described in Chapter 3, we will apply a generic modeling process to help us defining the systems dynamics models. The modeling process we will use is iterative and follows a six step approach. Figure 4.8 shows the modeling process. It starts with the formulation of the problem. Then a feedback loop structure is defined that is believed to underlie the behavior of the system (Step 2 Dynamic Hypothesis). Next the assumptions and variables for the systems dynamics models are identified (Step 3: Assumptions and Variables). Then a simulation model is formulated (Step 4: Simulation Model) and simulated (Step 5: Simulation). During simulation the results are compared to system that is being studied. Based on the outcome of the previous step the model is analyzed and potentially new policies can be formulated (Step 6: Analysis and Policy Design).

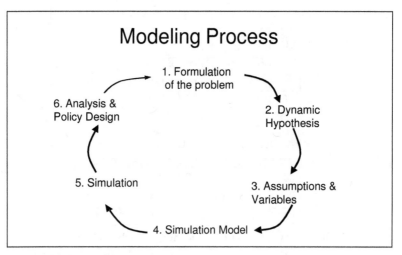

Figure 4.8: The modeling process in systems dynamics based on [Sterman, 2000].

4.6 Systems Dynamic Models for Software Methodologies

Chapter 4 explained the basics of systems and systems dynamics up to this chapter. We also described a generic six step approach for systems modeling that we will follow throughout Chapter 5, 6 and 7 to create and evaluate systems models. We start with defining the problem (step 1: Formulation of the Problem) that is applicable to all software methodologies we will simulate in Chapter 5, 6 and 7. The formulation of the problem builds the foundation for building all the systems dynamics models. We will execute step 2 to step 6 of the modeling process for systems dynamics models (see Figure 4.8) for each software development method. At the end of this chapter we will compare the results of all systems dynamics models with each other. Figure 4.9 shows an overview of the structure for Chapter 5, 6 and 7.

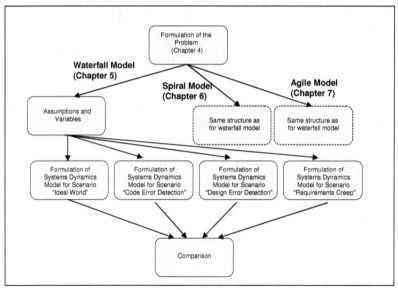

Figure 4.9: Overview of the structure of Chapters 5, 6, and 7.

4.6.1 Formulation of the Problem

Software projects might appear very similar in nature. There are basic software practices in place that help organize the development and guarantee the creation of a high quality software product. These practices and tools relate to configuration management, testing, product validation, verification, setting up and monitoring software metrics, as well as solid project management practices. Several standards [ISO 15288, 2002] [ISO 15504, 1998] [CMMI Product Team, 2001] address these topics. None of these concentrate on the timeliness of the software development method in a project.

Up to this point we cannot tell if choosing a specific software development methodology has an impact on the duration of a project. Simulating each software methodology under similar conditions will enable us to compare the results and provide a qualitative statement of the project durations. Therefore we assume the same environment and circumstances for a project and simulate each previously introduced and assessed software model. We assess the development models without considering any disruptions caused by the operations of the organization or management. This mean we are taking a view of the software methodology and will discuss the implications of the results on the software project later in this chapter and in the result section of this thesis. For the time horizon of the simulations we assume to start with the beginning of the development und to end when all code is produced.

We will use the systems dynamics tool Vensim for the simulations of the systems dynamic models. Vensim stands for Ventana Simulation Environment. It is an integrated framework for conceptualizing, building, simulating, analyzing, optimizing and deploying models of complex dynamic systems [Vensim, 2004]. Vensim uses a workbench-toolbox approach. The user develops first the causal loop diagram for his problem without the tool. Then he translates the causal loop into a systems dynamics model consisting of stocks, flows and variables. The systems model can be designed and simulated with Vensim. The tool provides graphic diagrams and source code listing of the systems model.

We are assuming a number of general rules for building our systems dynamic models:

- We define one systems dynamics model for each software development methodology (waterfall model, spiral model, agile model) as defined in Chapter 3.

- Each systems dynamics model is based on four defined scenarios ("Ideal World", "Code Error Detection", "Design Error Detection", "Requirements Creep", see Table 4.3) of growing complexity. We create our systems model in the simplest way possible by focusing on the overall process characteristics of the selected methodologies. Our systems dynamics models will represent the process steps from requirements to the availability of final production code.

- We are excluding the build versus buy decision process for software products.

- Further we are not including any architectural or design considerations related to how the product will be created. Therefore we are not differentiating component based development from development from scratch.

- The final version of each systems dynamics model of each methodology addresses all four scenarios (Table 4.3).

- The systems dynamics models represent the development process not the development practices.

We are building one systems dynamics model for each software methodology based on four defined scenarios. Table 4.3 lists a summary of all four scenarios:

Scenario *"Ideal World"* takes an idealized view to help us build the baseline systems dynamics model for each software methodology. It represents the basic elements of the software methodology assuming that there are no problems and no errors made during the development process. The development works flawless and creates the perfect product.

95

Although at first sight it might seem absurd to take this view in a theoretical simulation world, it is found sometimes in the real world. This view of the perfect world is often taken in organizations that plan their projects without considering any possibilities for rework during the project. Scenario "Ideal World" also helps us to come up with the baseline model for each methodology from which we can build up the model for scenario "Code Error Detection", "Design Error Detection" and "Requirements Creep".

Scenario *"Code Errors Detection"* assumes that errors are made during development that occur with a certain error rate (bug rate). These errors need to be resolved as part of the project. We assume that these errors can be addressed by fixing the code. No other area of the software development process is impacted by these errors. The overall scope stays the same for the project.

Scenario *"Design Error Detection"* assumes that the discovered errors require not only code changes but also design changes. The design changes result in additional code creation. We assume that the scope will slightly increase of the project due to the design changes.

Scenario *"Requirements Creep"* represents the most realistic case of all scenarios. It assumes that new requirements are identified during the development and errors are found that require code and design changes. Requirements can change due to competitive pressure, change of regulations and many other reasons as described in [Jones, 1996].
These newly identified requirements are implemented in addition to the originally specified ones. With scenario "Requirements Creep" we are simulating scope creep that is one of the major reasons why projects exceed their timeline and/or budget.

Scenario	Description of Scenario
"Ideal World"	Simulation of basic software development model. No errors are discovered or addressed during development
"Code Error Detection"	Fixed error rate is discovered and addressed during the development. These errors (bugs) require only code changes.
"Design Error Detection"	Discovered errors require design changes and code changes.

Scenario	Description of Scenario
"Requirements Creep"	Additional work due to additional requirements to be discovered during the software development.

Table 4.3: Summary of scenarios for systems dynamics models.

Based on the definition of these four scenarios we can see that they build upon each other. From that perspective we can expect that there will be a lesson's learned for managers and project teams from the results of our systems dynamic models.

By defining the assumptions and scenarios for our systems dynamics model we completed the first step (Formulation of the problem) of the generic modeling process (see Figure 4.8). We will apply step 2 to step 6 for each methodology. As part of building a systems dynamics model we will also define the management parameters that can influence these models.

The data used for simulating the selected software methodologies are based on personal experience working in the field of software development, collected from industry data [Jones, 1998] and input from Gerhard Eschelbeck [Eschelbeck, 2006].

4.6.2 Common Assumptions for all Systems Dynamics Models.

All systems dynamics models will be based on the following assumptions:

Basic Project Data

We presume that one requirement translates into 1000 Lines of Code (LoC) [Eschelbeck, 2006]. For our simulations we implement 100 requirements which result into a software product of 100,000 LoC for the initial scenario "Ideal World".

Staffing

We assume that we have a team of five software Engineers available to work on a software development project. The number of Engineers is derived from the effort stated in [Jones, 1998] for this size of a project. We assume that these five Engineers of our project team are evenly assigned across the development activities throughout the entire duration of the project. Realistically not all Engineers will be working on the project until the product is completely finalized.

For the scenarios "Code Error Detection", "Design Error Detection" and "Requirements Creep" we assume that all Engineers will be assigned to the project until the product reaches a "good enough" quality to be released to the market (see Figure 4.10). At this point "most" of the product has been completed and some errors will be left for correction after the release. After the release the project team would likely be reassigned to either expand the product functionality or another product development.

We assume that after the "Most" completion date, only two Engineers out of the five original assigned team members stay on the project to fix and test the remaining bugs. Figure 4.10 shows this staffing assumption.

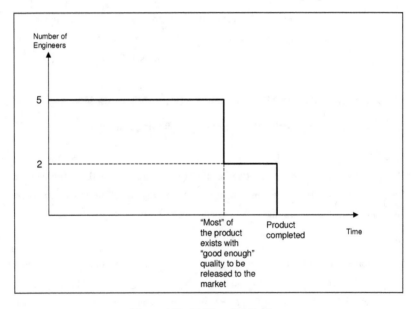

Figure 4.10: Staffing distribution.

Staffing Rates

The simulations of the systems dynamic models of Chapter 5, Chapter 6, and Chapter 7 will provide us with the project durations for each scenarios of each considered software methodology. To calculate the effort and cost we assume that that one person month consists of 160 hours effort and one Engineering hour costs $60 based on the average work hour presented in [Jones, 1998].

Percentage of Errors

The percentage of code defects detected during development depends on the language used for development and other factors. [Jones, 1998] states a code error rate of 9 to 29 bugs per 1000 LoC dependent on specific coding language. For scenario "Requirements Creep" we assume a total defect rate of 30 percent of tested code per time step accounting for code and design errors as well as requirements changes. The higher the percentage of errors (bugs) the longer the overall development takes. More errors are a sign of lower quality of work. The underlying cause can be lack of quality standards or also time pressure.

Chapter 5 Building a Simulation Model for a Waterfall Type Model

5.1 Dynamic Hypothesis

In order to analyze the behavior of a waterfall type methodology over time (see 4.6.1), we apply step 2 (Dynamic Hypothesis) of the generic modeling process (Figure 4.8).

Figure 5.1 shows the causal loop diagram for all four scenarios as described in Table 4.3.

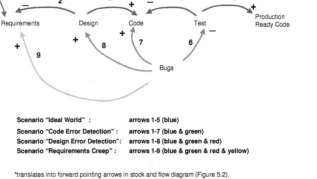

Figure 5.1: Causal Loop Diagram for a waterfall model.

Scenario "Ideal World" (arrows 1-5) takes a very simple and idealistic view, assuming that everything works right the first time and no rework is required. We assume that the requirements exist. They were gathered beforehand. Requirements are the starting point. They are turned into design and code. The amount of code to be generated is proportional to the number of requirements. Design work reduces the number of requirements that are

100

queued up for software development activities. Design work leads to code development. The more design progresses the more features and functionality will be implemented. The Software code is released to testing reducing the amount of outstanding code. As the software is tested it becomes production ready and adds to the final product. This basic scenario is modified to correspond to reality later.

Scenario "Code Error Detection" (arrows 1-7) shows that during the testing stage errors (software bugs) are identified that require some rework. For this scenario it is assumed that rework requires only code changes. This scenario is described by the blue (arrows 1 to 5) and green arrows (arrows 6 and 7). The green arrows are in addition to the blue arrows of Scenario "Ideal World". For each error (bug) that is identified code needs to be fixed.

Scenario "Design Error Detection" (arrows 1-8) builds on the situation defined for scenario "Code Error Detection". In addition to the situation in scenario "Code Error Detection" where errors only cause code fixes now errors can also require design fixes (red arrow 8 in Figure 5.1). We assume that rework in design and coding affects the amount of developed software as well as increases the effort spent on software development activities. We presume that the smaller portion of the tested code requires bug fixing activities. This adds to the amount of development activities. Revised design and code require a second round of testing of the affected code. The bigger portion of the written code qualifies as production code after testing.

For scenario *"Requirements Creep"* (arrows 1-9) new requirements (new scope) are discovered during the testing activities. Hence, the more new scope is identified the more requirements are added to the initial defined requirements. We add the yellow arrow (arrow 9) in addition to the already discussed remainder of Figure 5.1 (arrows 1-8).

We translate the causal loop diagram into a stock and flow diagram that we also refer to as the so called systems dynamics model.

5.2 Assumptions and Variables for the Systems Dynamics Models of the Waterfall Model

All models for the four scenarios (Figure 5.1) of the waterfall model will be based on the assumptions of Chapter 4.6.2.

Staffing

Further we presume that the different sequential phases of a waterfall model overlap. This means as soon as one phase has created tangible output the next phase starts. For example in case a sufficient number of requirements documents have been accomplished the work on design documents can start. Theoretically all phases of the waterfall model could be executed without creating any backlog. This is rarely the case. Often there are not enough resources at any given point of time available and the existing resources need to be spread across all development activities. We assume that all five Engineers will be working on the project from the beginning until the product ships when it reaches a so called "good enough" quality for the market (see Figure 4.10). Then only two Engineers continue to work on the project until the product is completed. For scenario "Code Error Detection", "Design Error Detection" and "Requirements Creep" we assume that no additional manpower can be spend on fixing the identified errors. These errors are fixed as part of the main activities until the product ships. Then two Engineers stay on the project to finish the work.

Processing Speed

[Jones, 1998] shows an example of an application in the same size of our project where design is documented in approximately two times the number of pages as the number of pages for requirements. We assume the same number of design documents as for requirements and account for the amount of design work by having the design work progresses at half of the speed (2 documents per time unit) as compared to requirements (4 documents per time unit). These values as well as the values for code generation speed (1500) and test generation speed (1000) are based on experience data from [Eschelbeck, 2006]. We set the test generation speed by a third lower than the code generation speed to reflect that resources for testing are not always available to keep up the speed with coding.

Error Rates

[Jones, 1998] states that the effort spent for error removal is between 15 and 35 % dependent on the size of the project. We assume that 20 % of the coding activities (200 LoC per time unit) are related to fixing bugs.

For scenario "Design Error Detection" we assume that 5 percent of the errors detected during testing are design changes based on [Jones,1998].

[Jones, 1998] states that the average requirements creep is about 2% but can go up to 15% per month when changes due to market needs or competitive pressure occur. For scenario "Requirements Creep" we assume a change rate of 5% to account for some market needs that might change throughout the duration of development.
Note that the error rate of 30 percent of tested code contains the defect rate for design and requirements changes for scenario "Requirements Creep".

Design translation and requirements translation help to transform LoC into documents.
We can adjust this value to reflect the impact of the change on the scope of the project. We assign a value to these variables that help to generate 5 percent of requirements and design changes. As a result of this design and requirements changes 25 new lines of codes need to be written for each design and each requirements change. This introduces scope creep to the software development project. Refer to Appendix A to see results of simulations that use design and requirements translation values that reflect higher impacts on the project scope.

Summary of assumptions for a waterfall model:
- Project with 100 requirements.
- Staff of five Engineers assigned as shown in Figure 4.10.

- Delays occur between the requirements, design, code and test activities and create a backlog.
- Design documents progress at half the speed of requirements document.
- Total error rate is thirty percent of tested code at each time step.
- Design rework rate is five percent of the errors detected during testing.
- Requirements Creep is five percent of the errors detected during testing.
- Twenty percent of coding activities is spent for bug fixing per time step.
- Bug fixing rate of speed stays constant throughout the entire product development.
- The result of the simulation will provide the duration of the project. Effort and cost can be derived from these values (see Chapter 4.6.2).

Variables

We define the following flow and stock variables for the systems dynamics models for the waterfall model in Table 5.1.

Stock and Flow Parameters	Description	Value	Unit
Assumed Values			
Initial number of Requirements ("Initial number of reqs")[1]	Assigned number of requirements defined at the beginning of development.	100	Documents
Requirements Generation Speed ("reqmtsconstant")[1]	Maximum value for requirements documents that become available at each time step.	4	Documents
Design Generation Speed ("design constant")[1]	Maximum value for design documents that become available at each time step.	2	Documents
Code Translation	Translation factor from document to LoC.	1000	LoC
Code Generation Speed ("code constant")[1]	Maximum value for available Code that becomes available at each time step.	1,500	LoC
Test Generation Speed ("test constant")[1]	Maximum value of code that reaches production quality at each time step.	1000	LoC
Bug Rate Portion ("bug rate constant")[1]	Maximum value for bug rate detected during testing activity	30	Percent
Bug Rework Portion ("bug rework constant")[1]	Maximum value of code that can be fixed at each given time step.	200	LoC
Redesign Portion ("redesign constant")[1]	Percentage of design bugs	5	Percent

---

[1] Name used in actual simulation model as shown in Appendix A.

Stock and Flow Parameters	Description	Value	Unit
Design Translation	Translation of design bug to design document	2.5	LoC/docu ment
Scope Creep Portion ("scope constant") [1]	Percentage of new requirements derived from bugs	5	Percent
Requirements Translation	Translation of bugs to requirements document	2.5	LoC/ Document
Derived Values			
Requirements	Accumulation of requirements.	computed	Documents
Requirements Speed Rate ("spec rate") [1]	Max [Requirements Generation Speed, Requirements]	computed	Documents /week
Design	Accumulation of design documents	computed	Documents
Design Speed Rate ("design spec rate") [1]	Max [Design Generation Speed, Design]	computed	Documents /week
Code	Accumulation of Code	computed	LoC
Code Speed Rate ("code completion rate") [1]	Max [Code Generation Speed, Code].	computed	LoC/week
Test	Accumulation of tested code	computed	LoC
Test Speed Rate ("release ready code rate") [1]	Max [Test Generation Speed, Test].	computed	LoC/week
Production	Accumulation of production ready code	computed	LoC
Bugs	Accumulations of errors.	computed	LoC
Bug Rate	Max [Bug Rate Portion, Test].	computed	LoC/week
Bug Rework Rate	Max [Bug Rework Portion, Bugs].	computed	LoC/week
Redesign Bug Rate	Max [Redesign Portion, Bugs]	computed	Document/ week
New Scope Rate	Max [Scope Creep Portion, Bugs]	computed	Document/ week

Table 5.1: Stock, Flow and auxiliary variables of a waterfall type model.

5.3 Systems Dynamics Model for Waterfall Model with Scenario "Ideal World"

5.3.1 Simulation Model for Scenario "Ideal World"

The initial set up for this systems dynamics model (stock and flow diagram) defines the main phases of a waterfall type model (see Figure 5.2).

Figure 5.2 shows the systems dynamics model of scenario "Ideal World" that simulates the nature of the software methodology's behavior.

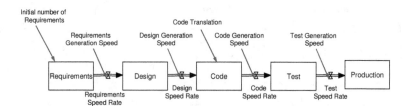

Figure 5.2: Initial system dynamics model for a basic waterfall model of scenario "Ideal World".

At the beginning of the waterfall model the requirements are defined. The total number of the requirements is assumed at the beginning of the simulation. With each time step a certain number of requirements become available for design work ("Requirements Speed Rate") that is reducing the "Requirements". "Design Generation Speed" defines the number of design documents that become available at each time step for coding. Each design document corresponds to one requirements document. The design documents that are ready for coding are accumulated in the stock variable "Design". Each completed design specification is implemented and the "Code Translation" variable translates design documents into 1000 Lines of Code (LoC). The "Code Speed Rate" variable represents the functionality that is implemented and released to testing. With each time step certain code becomes available for testing. Testing is simplified to one activity that usually includes unit test, system test and customer test. The "Test Speed Rate" defines how much code will be finished and ready to be released per time unit. The stock variable "Production" represents all shippable code. At the end of the simulation the complete product is ready for shipment.

As explained in Figure 4.6 the value of a stock variable is computed by its inflow and outflow (4.1). For the scenario "Ideal World" the stock variables are defined in (5.1) to (5.5):

$Requirements(t) = Requirements\ (t\text{-}1) - \int Requirements\ Speed\ Rate\ (t)\ dt$ *(5.1)*

$(d/dt)(Design) = Requirements\ Speed\ Rate\ (t)\ \text{-}Design\ Speed\ Rate\ (t)$ *(5.2)*

$(d/dt)(Code) = Design\ Speed\ Rate\ (t)\ *\ Code\ translation\ \text{-}\ Code\ Speed\ Rate\ (t)$ *(5.3)* *(d/dt)(Test) = Code Speed Rate (t) – Test Speed Rate(t)*   *(5.4)*

(d/dt)(Production) = Test Speed Rate (t)   *(5.5)*

The value of the "Initial number of Requirements" as well as the values of the flow variables define the duration of the development. The higher the number of requirements the longer it will take to design, implement and test them. The value of the flow variables determine how fast the development takes.

The complete systems dynamics model and its source code can be found in Appendix A. It includes auxiliary variables that keep the model in the range of positive values.

5.3.2 Simulation for Scenario "Ideal World"

We simulated the waterfall model shown in Figure 5.2 with the values listed in Table 5.1 (page 105). We assumed that each time step corresponds to one week.

For a variety of simulations of this model refer to Appendix A. The behavior of this simulation is shown in Figure 5.3 to Figure 5.7 and described in Chapter 5.3.3.

For scenario "Ideal World" "Production" accumulates all shippable code that results into 100,000 Lines of Code (LoC) at the end of the development. The accumulation of production quality code in "Production" illustrates how long it takes until the Figure 5.8 summarizes the completion dates of all stock variables in one timeline.

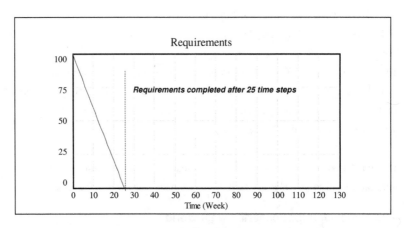

Figure 5.3: Simulation results for "Requirements".

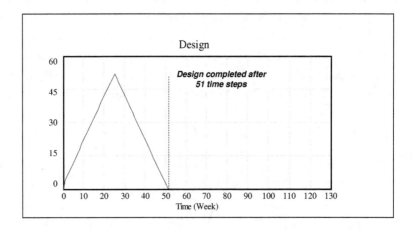

Figure 5.4: Simulation results for "Design".

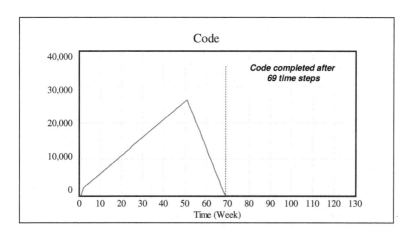

Figure 5.5: Simulation results for "Code".

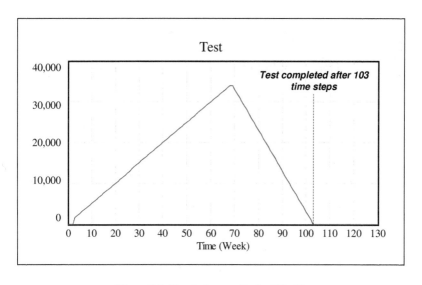

Figure 5.6: Simulation results for "Test".

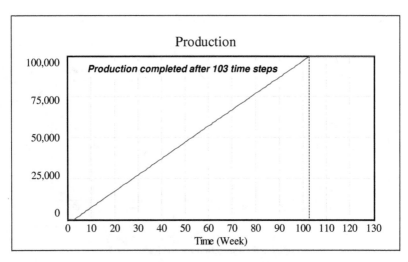

Figure 5.7: Simulation results for "Production".

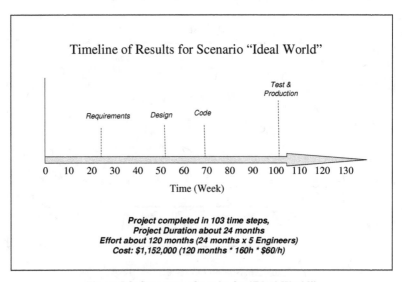

Figure 5.8: Summary of results for "Ideal World".

5.3.3 Analysis and Policy Design for Scenario "Ideal World"

The model in Figure 5.2 shows the following behavior for the values listed in Table 5.1 (page 105):

The phases of the waterfall type model (requirements, design, code, test, production) overlap. As requirements (Figure 5.3) are defined the design work starts, then does coding, testing and production.

Requirements are set to the initial value (100, see Table 5.1, page 105) and passed on to "Design" at a certain rate ("Requirements Speed Rate").

Design (Figure 5.4) issues the design specifications with half the rate as the requirements handed to design. The design specification can only be implemented at a certain rate. "Design" accumulates documents until all Requirements are completed, then the remaining documents are processed until all design work is done. It can be noticed that the design work starts with delay, because the "Requirements" stock variable creates a delay by one time step. We assume that the design speed is faster than the coding speed.

Code development (Figure 5.5) cannot be started unless design documents become available. The stock variable "Code" increases its value until all design work is completed and then processes the documents until all are designed functionality is implemented. As code becomes available software testing starts (see Figure 5.6). Testing creates a backlog as not all functionality can be tested as it becomes available. The restriction on code availability for testing can reflect resource restrictions for development as well as testing.

Both "Test" and "Production" (Figure 5.6 and 5.7) are completed at the same time step. As soon as the last test result becomes available the production code is completed.

The short delay time between the availability of requirements and the first availability of code is rather optimistic and shows a best case scenario. We simulated a project with five Engineers and with an application size of 100,000 LoC that takes 103 weeks to be accomplished (Figure 5.8). This translates in about twenty-four months of project duration with an effort of 120 person months. This agrees with the range stated by [Jones, 1998]. Jones specifies the duration of a project of this size between 17 and 31 months applying approximately five to seven Engineers for development. He further identifies the effort between 91 and 125 person months.

If we assume that one person month consists of 160 hours effort and one Engineering hour costs $60, the project costs for scenario "Ideal World" result into $1,152,000. This does not include any administrative, material or other overhead costs.

In case management would like to influence the duration of the software development project, management could either limit the number of requirements and/or increase the number of the output rate for each phase of a waterfall type model. The output rate of each phase can be improved by e.g. improving the practices used in each phase and/or applying resources with a better skill set or more resources to development activities.

5.4 Systems Dynamics Model for Waterfall Model with Scenario "Code Error Detection"

5.4.1 Simulation Model for Scenario "Code Error Detection"

For the model in scenario "Code Error Detection" (Figure 5.9), we assume that malfunctioning code (Bugs) is detected during testing activities.

Figure 5.9 shows the simulation model for scenario "Code Error Detection". The complete model and its source code can be found in Appendix A.

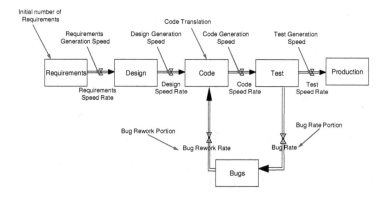

Figure 5.9: Systems dynamics model for scenario "Code Error Detection" of a waterfall type model.

In addition to the variables defined for scenario "Ideal World" of a waterfall type model we add the stock variable "Bugs", the flow variables "Bug Rate" and "Bug Rework Rate" and the constants "Bug Rate Portion" and "Bug Rework Portion". The processing is controlled by "Bug Rate Portion" and "Bug Rework Portion". For a description of these variables see Table 5.1 (page 105).

A certain percentage of the code that is tested at each time step (defined by the "Test Generation Speed") needs to be corrected. This percentage value is specified by the "Bug Rate Portion". The "Bug Rate" demonstrates the out-flowing rate of tested code that requires code rework. The stock variable "Bugs" shows the accumulation of code that requires code fixing. We assume that not all fixes can be done at once concurrently with the coding that takes place at each time step. We suppose that bugs can only be processed at a certain "Bug Rework Rate". The amount of bug fixes that can be completed at each time step is specified by the "Bug Rework Portion". One of the consequences (for "Bug Rate" > "Bug Rework Rate") is that a backlog of bugs will come into existence and may influence the duration of the project.

113

The new stock variable and flow variables are defined by formulas (5.6) to (5.8). See Table 5.1 (page 105) for definitions of variables used in these formulas.

(d/dt)(Bugs) = Bug rate (t) - Bug Rework Rate (t)   *(5.6)*

Bug Rate (t) = Max [Bug Rate Portion, Test(t)]   *(5.7)*

Bug Rework Rate (t) = Max [Bug Rework Portion, Bugs(t)]   *(5.8)*

5.4.2 Simulation for Scenario "Code Error Detection".

We simulate scenario "Code Error Detection" (Figure 5.9) for the values listed in Table 5.1 (page 105). For a variety of simulations of this model refer to Appendix A. The analysis of this simulation is described in Chapter 5.4.3.

For scenario "Code Error Detection" we are using the same values as defined for scenario "Ideal World" and in addition values for the specified key parameters of scenario "Code Error Detection". Jones identifies that 30 percent of the effort for a software development of 100,000 LoC will be dedicated to bug fixing. Our focus is to measure the project duration and not the effort. We specified that thirty percent ("Bug Rate Portion") of the code that is tested needs to be fixed.

Not all fixes can be done concurrently with the coding that takes place at each time step. We assume that only a certain number of LoC ("Bug Rework Rate") worth of bugs can be fixed at each time step. As bugs are fixed new errors are introduced that need to be fixed. The 30 percent of bug fixes also include the so called "bugs of bugs" [Jones, 1998].

The simulation results for the stock variables of Figure 5.9 are shown in the Figures 5.10 to 5.13. Figure 5.14 summarizes the completion dates of all stock variables in one timeline.

The next step (Analysis and Policy Design) discusses the results.

114

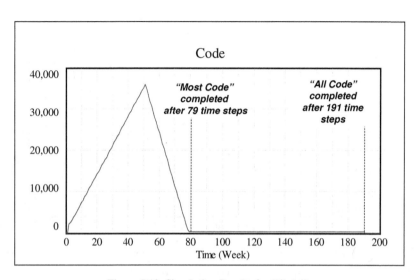

Figure 5.10: Simulation Results for "Code".

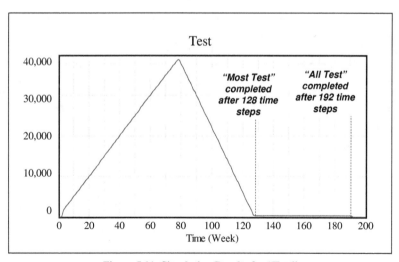

Figure 5.11: Simulation Results for "Test".

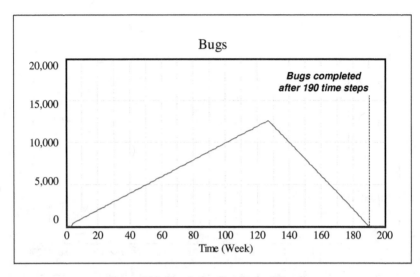

Figure 5.12: Simulation Results for "Bugs".

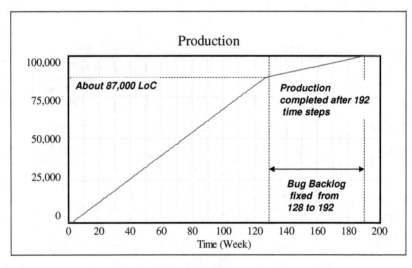

Figure 5.13: Simulation Results for "Production".

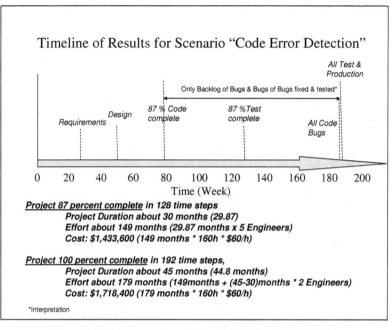

Figure 5.14: Summary of results for "Code Error Detection".

5.4.3 Analysis and Policy Design for Scenario "Code Error Detection"

There are no changes to the completion dates for requirements and design for scenario "Code Error Detection", because there are no additional activities for them compared to scenario "Ideal World". The simulation results for "Requirements" and "Design" are shown in Figure 5.3 and Figure 5.4.

Due to the code rework the most (about 87 percent) of code development can be completed within 79 weeks at the "Most Code" completion date (see Figure 5.10).

The "Most" point is reached when the backlog of a stock variable has been completely processed and from that point onwards the stock variable continues to process only the value that corresponds to the specified error rate.

117

Most of testing can be completed by week 128 at the "Most Test" completion date (Figure 5.11). After that coding and testing are purely related to bug fixing activities that cause enormous delays in project completion. After the "Most Code" completion date only the amount of code specified in "Bug Rework Portion" can be considered. The amount of code that is ready for testing increases until then and then testing works through its backlog. From the "Most Test" completion date onwards only the reworked Code is tested until project completion. This result is based on the model's behavior to continue to address bug fixing at the same rate of speed ("Bug Rework Portion") as during development.

In the "real" world the desire is to ship the product as early as possible. The product would be shipped when it has reached a "good enough" quality. The earliest time for shipping has probably been reached when the main functionality has been implemented and fixed (around the "Most Test" completion date in Figure 5.11). It is likely that this leaves behind an enormous bug count to be addressed after the release. As a result about 13 percent of the code needs to be fixed after the "main" development activities representing the difference between week "Most Test" completion date and "Production" completed. The project duration up to this point is about 30 months and the effort about 149 person months (see Figure 5.14). After the "Most Test" completion date, only two Engineers out of the five original assigned team members stay on the project to fix and test the remaining bugs (see Figure 4.10). The total duration of the project takes about 45 months, 179 person months in effort and creates costs in the amount of $1,718,000 (see Figure 5.14)

The project could be completed earlier when all Engineers stayed on the project to fix the remaining bugs.
Another option could be that management implements additional or/and better quality practices such as code reviews and inspection. Also creating realistic schedules and applying the management of the triple constraints (see Figure 2.5) can influence the error rate.

5.5 Systems Dynamics Model for Waterfall Model with Scenario "Design Error Detection"

5.5.1 Simulation Model for Scenario "Design Error Detection"

For scenario "Design Error Detection" we assume that malfunctioning code (Bugs) result not only into code rework but also in design rework. The total "Bug Rate Portion"-value for scenario "Code Error Detection" stays the same as for scenario "Design Error Detection". This means that the same percentage of tested code is detected as malfunctioning during testing as in scenario "Code Error Detection".

We also assume that the majority of bugs require code fixing (X percent). Only a small percentage (Y percent) of the bugs involves design changes. See Figure 5.15.

Figure 5.16 shows the model of the systems diagram for scenario "Design Error Detection" of a waterfall type model. The complete simulation model and its source code can be found in Appendix A.

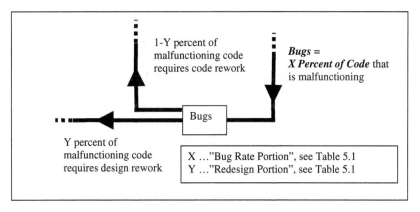

Figure 5.15: Distribution of malfunctioning code (bugs) that require code or design rework.

The constant "Bug Rate Portion"(X) sets the value for the "bug rate" that is detected during testing. "Redesign Portion"(Y) defines the values of Code that can be fixed at each time step.

In addition to the variables defined for scenario "Code Error Detection" of a waterfall type model we add the flow variable "Redesign Bug Rate" and the parameters "Redesign Portion" and "Design Translation" for scenario "Design Error Detection" (see Table 4.3): For a description of these variables see Table 5.1 (page 105).

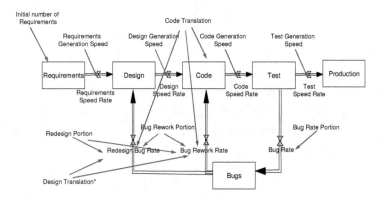

*variable that helps to transform LoC to design documents

Figure 5.16: Systems dynamics model for scenario "Design Error Detection" of a waterfall type model.

The "Redesign Bug Rate" is defined as a percentage of the total amount of rework per time step (value of "Bug Rework Portion") and translated to design documents per week with the help of the variables "Design Translation" and "Code Translation".

As the total amount of rework remains constant, the rework rates for code rework ("Bug Rework Rate") added to design rework ("Redesign Bug Rate") stays also constant. This means that the rework amount as defined in scenario "Code Error Detection stays constant for the total amount of rework:

As we added "Redesign Bug Rate" the stock variables "Design" and "Bugs" are changing from Formula (5.2) and (5.6) to:

120

(d/dt)(Design) = Requirements Speed Rate (t) -Design Speed Rate (t) + Redesign Bug Rate (t)   *(5.9)*

(d/dt)(Bugs) = Bug Rate (t) - Bug Rework Rate (t) - Redesign Bug Rate (t)   *(5.10)*

The new flow variable "Redesign Bug Rate" is defined as in (5.11) and "Bug Rework Rate" evolves from (5.8) to (5.12):

Redesign Bug Rate (t) = Redesign Portion * Bug Rework Portion * Design Translation / Code Translation   *(5.11)*

Bug Rework Rate (t) = Bug Rework Portion - (Redesign Bug Rate (t)* Bug Rework Portion * Code Translation / Design Translation)   *(5.12)*

5.5.2 Simulation for Scenario "Design Error Detection"

We simulated scenario "Design Error Detection" (Figure 5.16) for a waterfall type model for the values listed in Table 5.1 (page 105).

For scenario "Design Error Detection" we are using the same values as defined for scenario "Ideal World" plus the values for the key parameters specified for scenario "Code Error Detection" and "Design Error Detection". We are keeping the total amount of errors as well as the amount of errors that are reworked with each time step at the same percentage as in scenario "Design Error Detection". Out of the amount of code defined by "Bug Rework Portion" that are reworked at each time step 95 percent are code changes and five percent are design changes (set by the variable "Redesign Portion").

The durations of each stock variable are shown in the Figures below. The next step (Analysis and Policy Design) discusses these results.

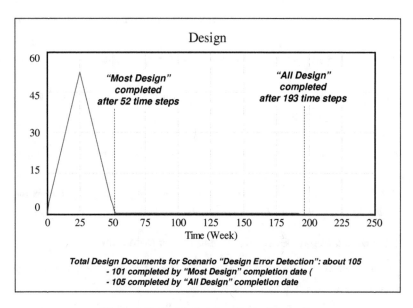

Figure 5.17: Simulation Results for "Design".

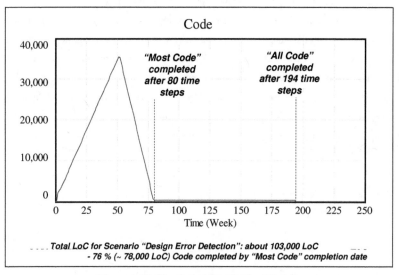

Figure 5.18: Simulation Results for "Code".

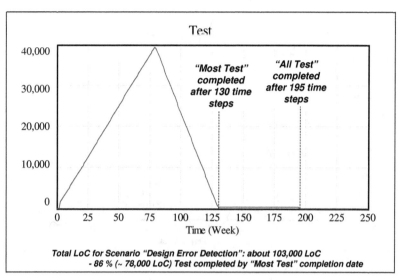

Figure 5.19: Simulation Results for "Test".

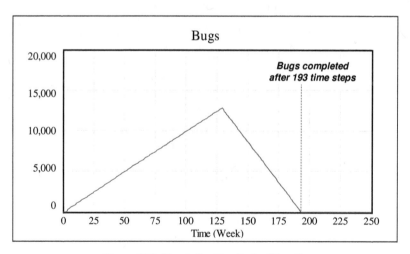

Figure 5.20: Simulation Results for "Bugs".

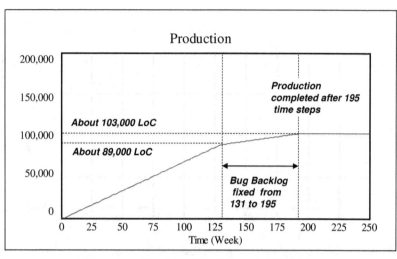

Figure 5.21: Simulation Results for "Production".

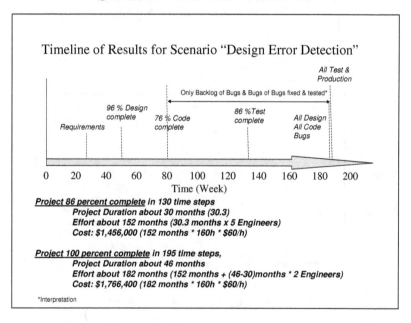

Figure 5.22: Summary of results for "Design Error Detection".

5.5.3 Analysis and Policy Design for Scenario "Design Error Detection"

There are no changes to the completion date for requirements for scenario "Ideal World", because there are no changes made to them (see Figure 5.3).

Most of design work is finished by the "Most Design" completion date (Figure 5.17). Design changes require additional software development. Therefore some code development moves out as compared to scenario "Code Error Detection" and is completed at the "Most Code" completion date. These results show a few weeks increase in duration compared to scenario "Code Error Detection. Also the design rework introduces additional scope and results in development of additional 3 % of LoC.

After the main coding and testing activities are completed only bug fixing activities are executed that cause some delays in project completion (see Figure 5.22). The explanation for this behavior is very similar to the one described in scenario "Code Error Detection": From the "Most Design" completion date onwards design activities focus on design changes only until all design is completed (see Figure 5.17). Until the "Most" code development is completed testing builds up a backlog, then works through it and finishes with time step 195 (Figure 5.19).. The amount of code that is responsible for scope creep (about 3,000 LoC) pushes out the product completion (Figure 5.21). Analog to the description in scenario "Code Error Detection" most development would ship after the majority of functionality has been developed at the "Most Test" completion date when 86% of the code has been developed. At this point the project duration is about 30 months with an effort of 152 person months and costs are at $1,456,000 (see Figure 5.22).

Between the "Most Code" completion date and the final availability of all production code (Figure 5.22) only bug fixing activities take place. Like in the scenario " Code Error Detection" we assume that only 2 Engineers stay on the project. The total project duration is 46 months, with an effort of about 182 person months and associated costs of about $1,766,400.

Design rework can be kept under control when management implements design reviews.

5.6 Systems Dynamics Model for Waterfall Model with Scenario "Requirements Creep"

5.6.1 Simulation Model for Scenario "Requirements Creep"

For scenario "Requirements Creep" we assume that malfunctioning code (Bugs) results not only into code rework but also design rework and new requirements (Figure 5.24). The total "Bug Rate Portion"-value stays the same like in scenario "Code Error Detection" and "Design Error Detection". We still assume that the majority of bugs require code fixing and small percentages require design changes (Y percent) as well as new requirements (Z percent). Figure 5.15 of scenario "Design Error Detection" evolves to Figure 5.23. Figure 5.24 shows systems dynamics model for scenario "Requirements Creep" of a waterfall type model. The complete simulation model and its source code can be found in Appendix A.

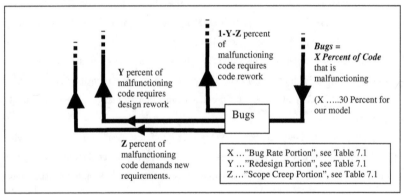

Figure 5.23: Distribution of malfunctioning code (bugs) that require code or design rework or demand new requirements.

In addition to the variables defined for scenario "Design Error Detection" of a waterfall type model we add the flow variable "New Scope Rate" and the variables "Scope Creep

Portion" and "Requirements Translation" for scenario "Requirements Creep (see Table 4.3):

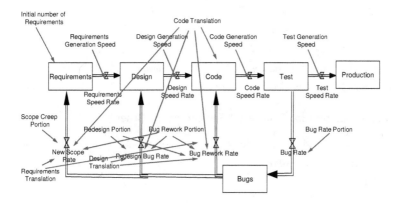

Figure 5.24: Systems dynamics model for scenario "Requirements Creep" of a waterfall type model.

The constant "Scope Creep Portion" defines the amount of requirements that are added to the initial number of requirements. It sets the value for the "New Scope Rate", the amount of requirements that are added to the stock variable "Requirements" at each time step. "Requirements Translation" and "Code translation" help to translate LoC into requirements documents.

The total amount of rework ("Bug Rework Portion") stays constant. Therefore the sum of the rework rates for code rework ("Bug Rework Rate"), design rework ("Redesign Bug Rate") and new requirements ("New Scope Rate") stays constant.

For the model of scenario "Requirements Creep" the stock variables "Requirements", "Bugs" as well as the flow variables "New Scope Rate" and "Bug Rework Rate" are defined as following:

Requirements(t) = Requirements (t-1) - ∫(Requirements Speed Rate (t) + New Scope Rate (t)) dt   *(5.13)*

(d/dt)(Bugs) = Bug Rate(t) - Bug Rework Rate (t) - Redesign Bug Rate (t) – New Scope Rate (t)   *(5.14)*

New Scope Rate (t) = Scope Creep Portion * Bug Rework Portion * Requirements Translation / Code Translation   *(5.15)*

Bug Rework Rate (t) = Bug Rework Constant - (Redesign Bug Rate (t) * Code Translation /Design Translation) - (Scope Creep Portion * Bug Rework Constant * Requirements Translation / Code Translation)   *(5.16)*

5.6.2 Simulation for Scenario "Requirements Creep"

We simulated scenario "Requirements Creep" for a waterfall type model for the values listed in Table 5.1 (page 105).

The durations of each stock variable are shown in the Figures below.

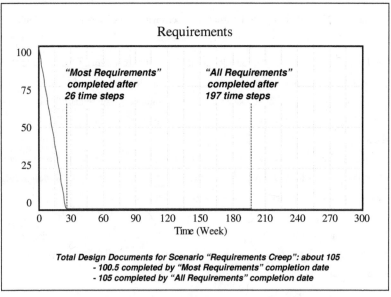

Figure 5.25: Simulation Results for "Requirements".

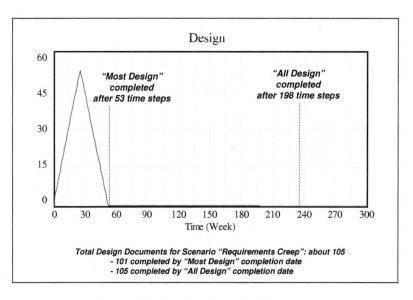

Figure 5.26: Simulation Results for "Design".

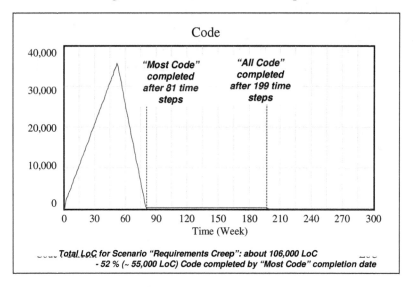

Figure 5.27: Simulation Results for "Code".

129

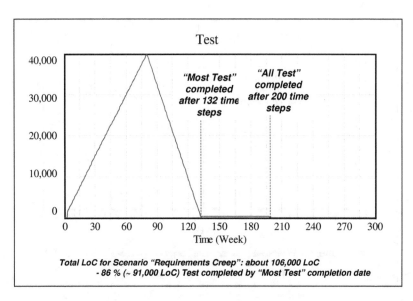

Figure 5.28: Simulation Results for "Test".

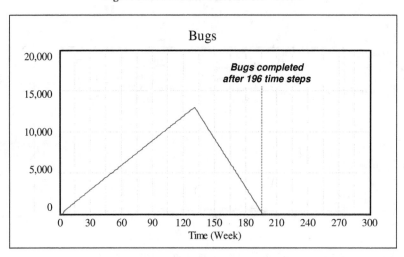

Figure 5.29: Simulation Results for "Bugs".

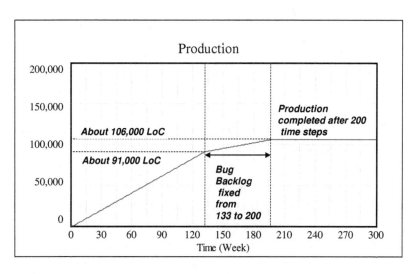

Figure 5.30: Simulation Results for "Production".

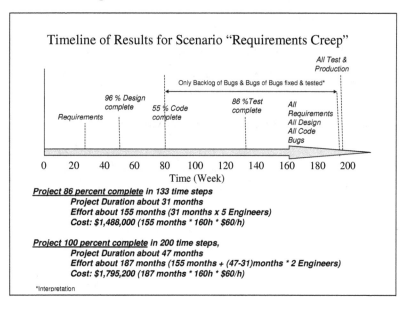

Figure 5.31: Summary of results for "Requirements Creep".

5.6.3 Analysis and Policy Design for Scenario "Requirements Creep"

For scenario "Requirements Creep" we also added new requirements to the development system. These requirements were derived from malfunctioning code (bugs). For this model we assumed that 5 percent of the discovered bugs require requirement changes (see Table 5.1, page 105). "Most" requirements are completed by time step 26 (Figure 5.25). Then only an ongoing low number of changes in requirements (2.5 percent of a requirements document per time step) need to be addressed until all rework can be completed by time 200 (Figure 5.30). At this time step the bug backlog has been processed. We can see by the results that adding minimal new requirements to development moves out the product completion somewhat. New requirements introduce also additional software development activities to the software product. As a result the final product includes 106,000 LoC. This is an increase in code size by 6 percent compared to the application size of scenario "Ideal World" and " Code Error Detection".

Like scenario "Code Error Detection" and "Design Error Detection" the majority of code is completed at the "Most Code" completion date (see Figure 5.27) for scenario "Requirements Creep". Then a rather long time span is spent on rework and new developments until the product is finished "(see Figure 5.31).

The project duration for scenario "Requirements Creep" takes about 47 months, with an effort of 187 person months and associated costs of $1,795,200 (see Figure 5.31)

5.7 Comparison of Results for Waterfall Model

We developed a systems dynamics model for a waterfall type methodology using Vensim, a software simulation tool. We built the model based on four scenarios that we defined in Table 4.3. We created four increasingly complex models in sequential steps starting with scenario "Ideal World". Then we made the necessary additions to scenario "Ideal World" to develop the model for scenario "Code Error Detection". We followed this approach until we reached the stage of the model that satisfies scenario "Requirements Creep". We used the parameter as defined in Table 5.1 (page 105) to run the simulations for each scenario. The results of all scenarios are shown in Table 5.2.

	Ideal World	**Code Error Detection**	**Design Error Detection**	**Requirements Creep**
"Most" Product Completed	Same as total product completed			
Duration [months]	24	30	30	31
Effort [person months]	120	149	152	155
Cost [$]	1,152,000	1,433,600	1,456,000	1,488,000
Duration increase related to "Ideal World" [%]	Base Value	25	25	29
Effort increase related to "Ideal World" [%]	Base Value	24	26	29
Cost increase related to "Ideal World" [%]	Base Value	24	26	29
Total Product Completed				
Duration [months]	24	45	46	47
Effort [person months]	120	179	182	187
Cost [$]	1,152,000	1,718,400	1,766,400	1,795,200
Duration increase related to "Ideal World" [%]	Base Value	87.5	92	96
Effort increase related to "Ideal World" [%]	Base Value	49	52	56
Cost increase related to "Ideal World" [%]	Base Value	49	53	56

Table 5.2: Comparison of scenarios as defined in Table 4.3.

The increase of duration, effort and costs from the state of no error (scenario "Ideal World") to the introduction of code errors (scenario " Code Error Detection") is very significant. The introductions of 5 percent design and requirements changes have visible effect on duration, effort and cost of a project. We assumed a low number of changes to the requirements and design documents. See Appendix A for simulations with variations of changes to these assumed values.

We assumed the product ships with a so called "good enough" quality when "most" of the product is completed (see "Most" product completed in Table 5.2). The difference between the duration for the "Most" product completion data and the "Total" product completion is significant. Fixing the errors takes one third of the project duration. The speed of fixing the bugs can be increased by increasing the manpower to work on this activity. Due to the nature of this systems dynamics model the error fix rate stays the same for each time step throughout the duration of the project.

Figure 5.32 compares the results for "Production" in graphical format for all four scenarios.

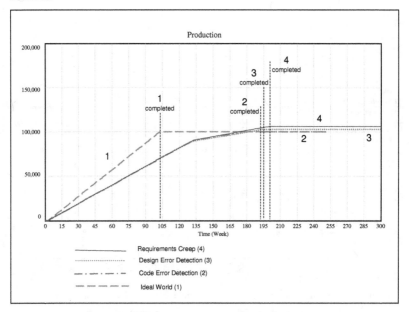

Figure 5.32: Comparison of results for "Production".

Scenario "Ideal World" shows the results for a development that would not require any changes and therefore takes the shortest time to finish development. Scenario "Code Error Detection", "Design Error Detection" and "Requirements Creep" include a 30 percent defect rate. In case of the scenario "Code Error Detection"(see 2 in Figure 5.32) the timeline moves out significantly but does not introduce any new scope.

134

Changes in design (Design Error Detection) and introduction of new requirements (Requirements Creep) create more development work and push out the timeline. This additional amount of created work is generally referred to as scope creep.

Based on the graphs in Figure 5.32 we can see that scenario "Ideal World"(1) takes the least time. With introducing more rework in each scenario the time to accomplish each activity takes longer.

Simulations to Shorten the Project Duration

Once a timeline for a project is defined, management is interested in how it can be reduced. There are obvious ways of achieving it such as reducing the scope of the project or avoiding any changes by implementing rigid change management processes.

The created model allows us to evaluate its behavior under different conditions by changing the parameters listed in Table 5.1 (page 105). We are using the model developed for scenario "Requirements Creep" as the most realistic one and apply different values. The focus of our assessment is to find out what parameters we need to change to reduce the development time. Therefore we double the rate at which requirements (R), design (D) and code (C) work is executed but leave the test rate the same (see "Expedite RDC" in Table 5.3) Then we keep the requirements, design and code at the same pace as for scenario "Requirements Creep" and set the test rate to the same rate as code becomes available for testing (see "Expedite Test" in Table 5.3).

Next we are evaluating how the change in defects can influence the duration of the project. Therefore we reduce the bug rate from 30 to 25 percent (see "Reduce Errors" in Table 5.3).

Then we combine the new three test scenarios by:

- Increasing the speed of execution for each development phase (requirements, design, code)
- Testing code at the rate it becomes available
- Decreasing the defect rate.

135

The parameters for this test case can be found under the column "Shorten Combined" in Table 5.3.

Stock and Flow Parameters	Requirements Creep	Expedite RDC	Expedite Test	Reduce Errors	Shorten Combined	Unit
100	100	100	100		100	documents
Requirements Generation Speed ("reqmtsconstant") ^{2}	4	8	4	4	8	documents
Design Generation Speed ("design constant")^2	2	4	2	2	4	Documents
Code Translation	1000	1000	1000	1000	1000	LoC
Code Generation Speed ("code constant") ^{2}	1500	3000	1500	1500	3000	LoC
Test Generation Speed ("test constant") ^{2}	1000	1000	1500	1000	3000	LoC
Bug Rate Portion ("bug rate constant") ^{2}	30	30	30	25	25	Percent
Bug Rework Portion ("bug rework constant") ^{2}	200	200	200	200	200	LoC
Redesign Portion ("redesign constant") ^{2}	5	5	5	5	5	Percent
Design Translation	2.5	2.5	2.5	2.5	2.5	LoC/Document
Scope Creep Portion ("scope constant") ^{2}	5	5	5	5	5	Percent
Requirements Translation	2.5	2.5	2.5	2.5	2.5	LoC/Document

Table 5.3: Parameters for different test to reduce the duration of the project.

Figure 5.33 and Table 5.4 show the results for these scenarios.

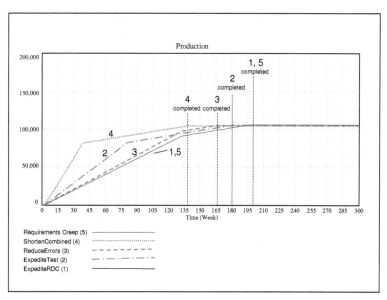

Figure 5.33: Results for different test runs to reduce the project duration.

The duration of the development for the test run "Expedite RDC" is exactly the same as for scenario "Requirements Creep" (see Table 5.4). Figure 5.33 shows the graph for "Production". For scenario "Expedite Test" the corresponding graph in Figure 5.33 shows that development is completed earlier when the code is tested at the rate code becomes available for testing. We can conclude that putting more resources in the testing efforts to test code at the rate it becomes available can help to reduce the duration of the project.

The graph (Figure 5.33) as well as the results in Table 5.4 show a significant decrease in project duration for scenario "Reduce Errors".

When we combine all approaches for scenario " Shorten Combined" we shorten the timeline of scenario "Requirements Creep" significantly (see Table 5.4).

137

	Requirements Creep	Expedite RDC	Expedite Test	Reduce Errors	Shorten Combined
Duration [months]	47	47	43	39	32
Effort [person months]	187	187	142	172	93
Cost [$]	1,795,200	1,795,200	1,363,200	1,651,200	$892,800
Duration decrease related to "Requirements Creep" [%]	Base Value	0	- 8.5	- 17	-32
Effort decrease related to "Requirements Creep" [%]	Base Value	0	- 24	- 8	-50
Cost decrease related to "Requirements Creep" [%]	Base Value	0	- 24	- 8	-50

Table 5.4: Results of scenarios to reduce the project duration.

Note that combining multiple measures has the most effect on the duration of the project. Increasing the speed of executing the development only makes sense when testing is done at the same rate as the code becomes available. Table 5.5 summarizes the measures that help reducing the timeline of a waterfall type model.

Measures	*Example*
Reducing Scope	Reducing features, specifically the ones that are on the wish list and are not mandatory.
Avoiding changes	Implementing change management processes
Implementing quality best practices to reduce defect rate.	Implementing code reviews.
Improving the process time of development	Increase process time of each development. Make sure to assign enough resources to test code in the speed it becomes available.

Table 5.5: Summary of measures that help reducing the project timeline.

Chapter 6: Building a Simulation Model for a Spiral Type Model

In this chapter we create a simulation model for a spiral type model following the generic modeling process as defined in Figure 4.8. The problem articulation in Chapter 4.6.1 builds the baseline for this model. We apply step 2 to step 6 of the generic modeling process for each scenario (see Table 4.3) to build the systems dynamics model for a spiral type model.

6.1 Dynamic Hypothesis

For step 2 (Dynamic Hypothesis) of the generic modeling process we build a causal loop diagram for a spiral type model (see Figure 6.1). One way to interpret a spiral type model is to see it as a combination of iterations and a waterfall model. Figure 6.1 shows the causal loop diagram for a spiral type model that consists of two parts. The initial part demonstrates the iterations and is followed by a waterfall model as shown in Figure 5.1.

The spiral model starts with an iterative part (arrows 1-6 in Figure 6.1). The exact number of iterations is unknown at the start of the spiral. For our simulation model we set an initial value of "Objectives" that will be reduced with each accomplished cycle. Each cycle adds to the clarification of requirements. Each cycle increases the number of requirements. When the number of spiral cycles reaches the value of the pre-defined initial value of "Objectives" the iterative part of our model is completed and the waterfall model starts.

Each cycle (iteration) of a spiral type model consists of four phases that are executed in sequence (see steps 1 to 4 in Table 3.7). Each phase is completed before the next starts. During the first phase the objective is defined for the current iteration. Second risks are identified and alternative solutions are evaluated. Risk assessment reduces the scope that is left to be defined for the next cycles ("Objectives"). The more details are assessed during the "Risk Evaluation", the more information is collected and the product requirements can be broken down into more details during the "Breakdown" phase.

Throughout the fourth phase ("Plan") of the spiral cycle a plan for the next cycle is identified based on the findings and results of the current cycle. The more details the plan includes the more requirements can be clarified in the next cycle (Initial value of requirements). Every completed cycle reduces the amount of spiral cycles that still need to be processed. At the end of the iterative part of the spiral model requirements, product designs and plans have been identified and documented. Finally the development follows a waterfall model to implement and test the software product.

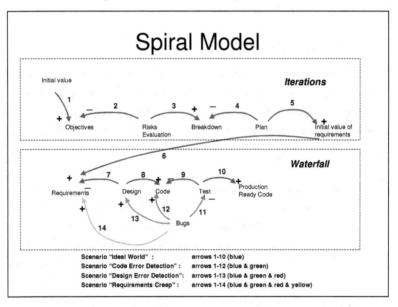

Figure 6.1: Causal Loop Diagram for a Spiral based agile model.

For the waterfall roll-out of the Spiral Model (arrows 7 to 14 in bottom frame of Figure 6.1) we are using the same systems dynamics model as we defined in Chapter 5 for the waterfall type model (see Figure 5.1).

All four scenarios (see Table 4.3), "Ideal World"(arrow 1-10), "Code Error Detection"(arrow 1-12), Design Error" Detection" (arrow 1-13) and "Requirements Creep" (arrow 1-14), start with the same iterative part of a spiral type model.

Note that the differentiation of the four scenarios applies only to the waterfall part of the spiral. Refer to Chapter 5.1 for details about the causal loop diagram of a waterfall type model. We do not assume that testing reveals problems which would re-enter the objective evaluation cycle. This would be considered a major project disaster which probably would make all future predictions impossible.

Practically concurrent development could be executed by spinning off multiple spirals in parallel. For this thesis we assume that the development is executed following a single spiral.

6.2 Assumptions and Variables for the Systems Dynamics Models of the Spiral Model

In order to assess the behavior of a spiral type model over time we apply the systems dynamics model. For the systems dynamics model of a spiral model the general assumptions of Chapter 4.6.2 as well as the assumptions of the waterfall model (Chapter 5.1) apply.

Staffing

We assume two cases for staffing the project applying a spiral model:

First we assume a staffing as shown Figure 4.10 where five Engineers are assigned to the project until the product ships to the market.

For the second option ("Spiral Model Staffing") we assume that only three Engineers are needed for the duration of the iterative part of the spiral process. Then during the implementation of the product that follows a waterfall model five Engineers are assigned to the project until it ships. After shipping only two Engineers continue to work on fixing problems. Figure 6.2 shows the staffing distribution for this case.

141

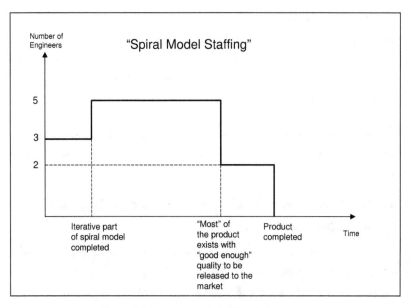

Figure 6.2: Spiral model staffing distribution.

Specific assumptions for the iterative part of the spiral model

For the iterative part of the spiral model we assume that all cycles of the spiral model take the same duration. Table 3.7 lists four phases (step 1-4) of the iteration. We name these phases: "Objective", "Evaluation", "Breakdown" and "Plan". Each of these phases has a defined duration ("Objectives Duration", "Evaluation Duration", "Breakdown Duration", "Plan Duration"). After one phase is completed the next phase starts. Adding the durations of all four phases results in the total duration of one iterative cycle.

Processing Speed

Theoretically the number of required iterations is unknown at the beginning of the spiral process (see Chapter 3.3). Note that for our systems dynamics model we define the number of required iterations upfront (see "Number of Iterations" in Table 6.1,page 145). Each cycle generates and/or clarifies a number of requirements. We assume that the same number of requirements is identified as a result of each cycle (see "Requirements Rate" in Table 6.1, page 145). The value of "Requirements Rate" and the value of "Number of

142

Iterations" are set to create 100 requirements in total. The values listed in Table 6.1 (page 145) for the iterative part of the spiral model are assumptions based on discussions with [Eschelbeck, 2006].

The iterative part reaches the waterfall model (see step 6 in Table 3.7) and the product is implemented. For the spiral model we assume that requirements and design have been defined in more details than in comparison to the waterfall model of Chapter 5 before the implementation of the product starts. The spiral type model defines requirements in more detail as risks and different options are identified and evaluated during the iterative cycles. We account for this assumption by increasing the "Requirements Generation Speed" (from 4 documents per time unit in Table 5.1, page 105, to 6 documents per time unit in Table 6.1, page 145) and the "Design Generation Speed" (from 2 documents per time unit in Table 5.1, page 105, to 4 documents per time unit in Table 6.1, page 145).

Error Rates

We assume that less requirements and design errors are created during implementation than during the implementation process of the waterfall type model of Chapter 5. We reduce the percentage of design bugs from 5 percent in the waterfall model of Chapter 5 to 3 percent (see "Redesign Portion" in Table 6.1, page 145) as well as the percentage of requirements from 5 to 1 percent (see "Scope Creep Portion" in Table 6.1, page 145). Refer to Appendix B to see results for a variety of simulations.

Summary of assumptions for a spiral model

- Project with 100 requirements.
- Staff assigned as shown in Figure 4.10 and Figure 6.2.
- Each spiral cycle has the same duration.
- Each spiral cycle clarifies the same number of requirements
- Design documents progress at two third the speed of requirements document.
- Total error rate is thirty percent of tested code.
- Design rework rate is three percent of the errors detected during testing.
- Requirements Creep is one percent of the errors detected during testing.
- Twenty percent of coding activities is spent for bug fixing per time step.

143

- Bug fixing rate of speed stays constant throughout the entire product development.
- The result of the simulation will provide the duration of the project. Effort and Cost can be derived from these values (see Chapter 4.6.2).

We define the following flow and stock variables for the systems dynamics models for a spiral model in Table 6.1, (page 145). With the exception of the values for "Requirements Generation Speed", "Design Generation Speed", "Redesign Portion", and "Scope Creep Portion" all other assumptions and values for the waterfall model (Table 5.1, page 105) apply to the waterfall part of the spiral model.

Stock and Flow Parameters	Description	Value	Unit
Iterative Part- Assumed Values			
Anticipated Number of Iterations	Defined number of cycles for spiral model	5	iterations
Objectives Duration	Duration of objectives phase	2	weeks
Evaluation Duration	Duration of risk evaluation phase	1	weeks
Breakdown Duration	Duration of breakdown phase	1	weeks
Plan Duration	Duration of plan phase	1	weeks
Number of Iterations	Set number of iterations for spiral	5	weeks
Requirements Rate	Number of requirements that are clarified by each spiral cycle	4	Documents
Iterative Part- Derived Values			
Iteration Start	Calculates start time of next cycle	computed	
Time Rate	Starts each cycle of the spiral process	computed	
Objectives	Accumulation of Objectives per cycle	computed	
Objective Completion Rate	Marks completion of objectives phase and starts next phase	computed	
Risk Evaluation	Accumulation of Risk Evaluation per cycle	computed	
Evaluation Completion Rate	Marks completion of risk evaluation phase and starts next phase	computed	
Breakdown	Accumulations of product breakdowns per cycle	computed	
Breakdown Completion Rate	Marks completion of breakdown phase and starts next phase	computed	
Plan	Accumulation of plans per cycle	computed	
Iteration Completion Rate	Marks completion of each cycle	computed	

Stock and Flow Parameters	Description	Value	Unit
Iterations Time	Counts number of spiral cycles and initiates next cycle until anticipated number of cycles is reached.	computed	
Waterfall Part-Assumed Values			
Requirements Generation Speed ("reqmtsconstant") [2]	Maximum value for requirements documents that become available at each time step.	6	Documents
Design Generation Speed ("design constant") [3]	Maximum value for design documents that become available at each time step.	4	Documents
Redesign Portion ("redesign constant") [3]	Percentage of design bugs	3	Percent
Scope Creep Portion ("scope constant") [3]	Percentage of new requirements derived from bugs	1	Percent

Table 6.1: Stock, Flow and auxiliary variables of a waterfall type model.

6.3 A Spiral Systems Dynamics Model for Scenario "Ideal World"

6.3.1 Simulation Model for Scenario "Ideal World"

For scenario "Ideal World" the development executes through the entire spiral model assuming that no rework is required. Figure 6.3 shows the systems dynamics model (stock and flow diagram) for all scenarios. It shows the iterative part and the waterfall part of the spiral model (refer to Figure 5.2 for the waterfall illustration of scenario "Ideal World"). The complete model and its source code can be found in Appendix B.

---

[2] Name used in actual simulation model as shown in Appendix B.

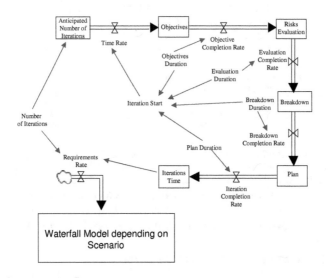

Figure 6.3: Initial system dynamics model for a basic spiral type model.

The following description of the iterative part is applicable for all scenarios of the spiral model: The variable "Anticipated Number of Iterations" is defined by the constant "Number of Iterations". When a spiral starts "Anticipated Number of Iterations" is set to the "Number of Iterations" and the spiral will go through all cycles before implementing the software product using the waterfall model.

The iterative part of the spiral simulation model progresses sequential through all four phases: "Objective", "Risk Evaluation", "Breakdown", and "Plan". Each phase has a defined duration that is set by the corresponding variables: "Objective Duration", "Evaluation Duration", "Breakdown Duration" and "Plan Duration". Every cycle starts with setting up an objective for the cycle. The flow variable "Time Rate" initiates the start of the next cycle by sending a signal (value of 1) to the stock variables "Objectives". Every new cycle reduces the value of "Anticipated Numbers of Iterations". Each phase has a corresponding out-flow value that "informs" the next phase when to start. These are

146

"Objective Completion Rate", "Evaluation Completion Rate", "Breakdown Completion Rate" and "Iteration Completion Rate".

As soon as the last phase of the spiral cycle ("Plan") is completed the "Iteration Completion Rate" increases the "Iterations Time". For a spiral model each phase can have a different duration dependent on how long it takes to satisfy its purpose.
The sum of the durations for each phase results in the duration of the iteration. For this simulation model we assume that all iterations of the model have the same duration.
Figure 6.4 illustrates the timing between the individual four phases.

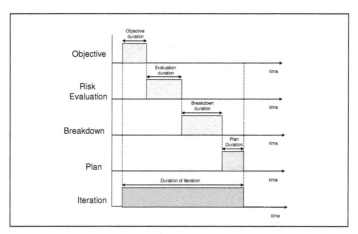

Figure 6.4: Timing interaction between different spiral phases.

When one spiral cycle is completed the next one starts. The start time for the next iteration is calculated based on the total durations of the four phases of the spiral cycle and the number of iterations that have been completed. The number of completed cycles is counted by the stock variable "Iteration Time". "Iteration Start" calculates the start time of the next iteration. Figure 6.5 shows how the start time of each iteration is determined.

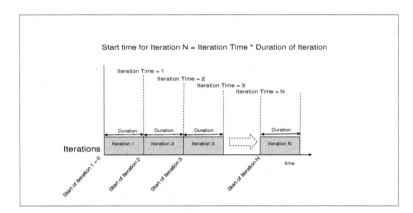

Figure 6.5: Demonstration of how durations of each phase add up to duration of one iteration cycle.

Each completed cycle increments the "Iterations Time". As long as the "Iterations Time" has not received the same value as set in "Number of Iterations" the flow variable "Requirements Rate" increases the number of clarified requirements. As soon as the "Iterations Time" meets the "Number of Iterations", the iterative portion of the spiral model has been completed. No more additional requirements are added to the initial number of requirements for the waterfall type model. The waterfall type model starts with the product implementation as defined for scenario "Ideal World" in Chapter 5.3.

The values for stock variables of the iterative part of a spiral type model described in scenario "Ideal World" (Table 4.3) are defined by the formulas (6.1) to (6.4):

(d/dt)(Objectives) = -objective completion rate(t) + time rate(t)   *(6.1)*

(d/dt)(Risk Evaluation) = +objective completion rate(t) -evaluation completion rate(t)

(6.2)

(d/dt)(Breakdown) = +evaluation completion rate(t) - breakdown completion rate(t) (6.3)

(d/dt)(Plan) = breakdown completion rate(t) -iteration completion rate(t)   *(6.4)*

148

The model of the waterfall model described for "Ideal World" in Chapter 5.3.1 applies to the waterfall part of this spiral model. See Table 5.1 (page 105) and Chapter 5.3.1 for the definitions of the stock and the flow variables of the waterfall model.

6.3.2 Simulation for Scenario "Ideal World"

We simulated the spiral type model of Figure 6.3 for the key parameters and its values listed in Table 6.1 (page 145). We assumed that each time step correlates to one week. Scenario "Ideal World" describes a software development that is based on 100 requirements.

The simulation results for the stock variable "Iterations Time" shows when the iterative part of the spiral model is completed and the waterfall model starts (Figure 6.6). We also show the results for the waterfall part of the spiral model in Figure 6.7 to 6.11. Figure 6.12 summarizes the completion dates of all stock variables in one timeline. The next step (Analysis and Policy Design) discusses the results in detail.

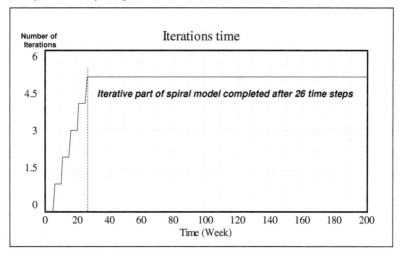

Figure 6.6: Simulation results for "Iterations Time".

149

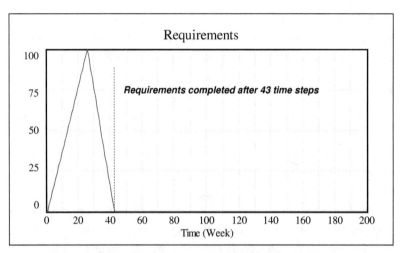

Figure 6.7: Simulation results for "Requirements".

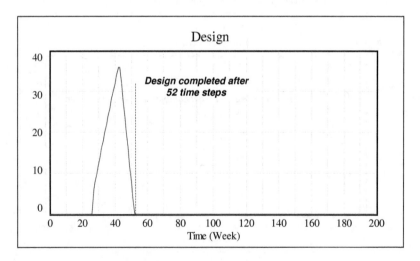

Figure 6.8: Simulation results for "Design".

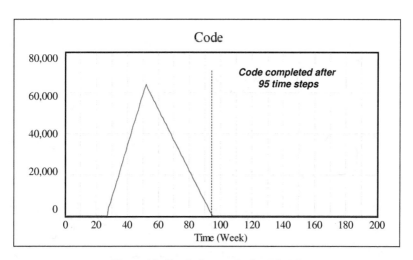

Figure 6.9: Simulation results for "Code".

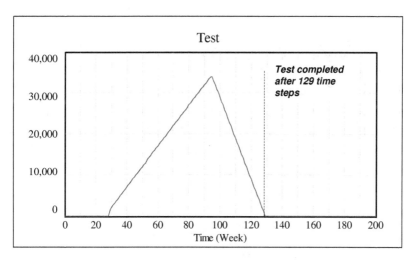

Figure 6.10: Simulation results for "Test".

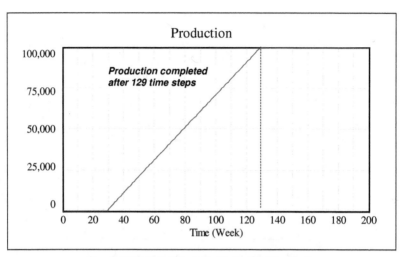

Figure 6.11: Simulation results for "Production".

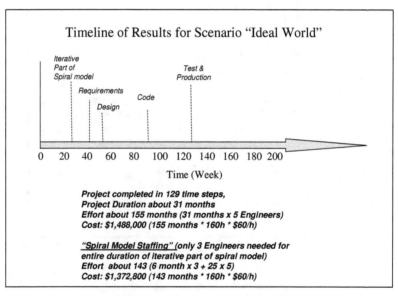

Figure 6.12: Summary of results for "Ideal World".

6.3.3 Analysis and Policy Design for Scenario "Ideal World"

The spiral systems dynamics model shows a similar behavior to a waterfall type model of Chapter 5.2. The main differentiator is the iterative part of the spiral type model.

The stock variables for "Objectives", "Risk Evaluation", "Breakdown" and "Plan" are completed one after the other after the duration specified for each of these phases. They do not accumulate any values. After 26 time steps (see Figure 6.6) all iteration cycles are completed and all requirements are identified and defined. These requirements (Figure 6.7) are then translated into design documents and implemented. Some of the high-level design is already defined during the iterative part of the spiral model. The simulation result for "Design" (Figure 6.8) does not show this activity. In our systems design model we account for existing design at the beginning of the waterfall model by increasing the rate design documents become available for coding. Design activities are completed in 52 weeks. The behavior of the waterfall part of the spiral model follows the same behavior as described in Chapter 5.3.3.

Code becomes available for testing with a rate of 1500 LoC a week. All code is implemented in week 95 (see Figure 6.9). Out of these 1500 Lines of Code 1000 LoC are tested per week. This amount of code has production quality and is added to the stock variable "Production". Production is completed in week 129 (see Figure 6.11). At the end the product entails 100,000 LoC.

It takes about thirty-one months of project duration with an effort of 155 person months to finish this project with a spiral model. This is at the end of the range stated by [Jones, 1998] with a size between 17 and 31 months applying approximately five to seven Engineers for development. The project costs for scenario "Ideal World" result into $1,488,000.

One reason that the results for project duration and effort are rather high can be related to the assumption that the iterations of our spiral model take the same time and that the assumption of 5 weeks is too high. Also there might not be 5 Engineers needed for the entire time of the iterative part of the spiral cycle. In case we assume that in average only

3 Engineers are needed at all time of the iteration the effort goes down to 143 person months and the costs come down to $1,372,800.

In case management would like to influence the duration of the software development project, management could reassign Engineers from Design activities to coding and test activities.

6.4 A Spiral Systems Dynamics Model for Scenario "Code Error Detection"

6.4.1 Simulation Model for Scenario "Code Error Detection"

For the model of scenario "Code Error Detection" we assume that some of the tested code in the waterfall portion of the spiral works incorrectly (Bugs) and only requires code fixing. The conditions of the iterative part of the spiral stay the same as in scenario "Ideal World". The definitions for this scenario are explained in scenario "Code Error Detection" of the waterfall type model in Chapter 5.4.

The systems dynamic model of the spiral type model is the same as shown in Figure 6.3. The waterfall type model for scenario "Code Error Detection" as shown in Figure 5.9 applies to the waterfall part of the spiral type model for this scenario. The complete model and its source code can be found in Attachment B.

6.4.2 Simulation for Scenario "Code Error Detection"

We simulated the spiral type model for scenario "Code Error Detection" applying the values of the key parameters as listed in Table 6.1 (page 145).

The simulation results are shown from Figure 6.13 to Figure 6.17.

The next step (Analysis and Policy Design) discusses the results in detail.

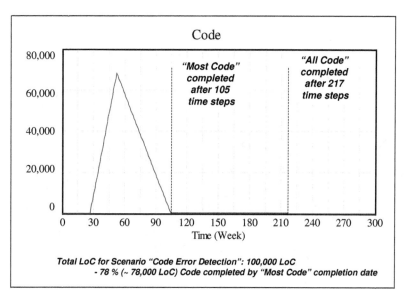

Figure 6.13: Simulation results for "Code".

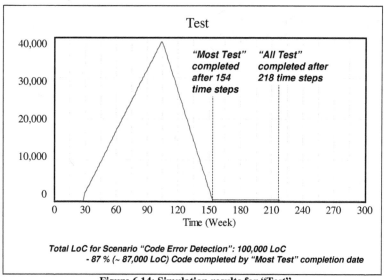

Figure 6.14: Simulation results for "Test".

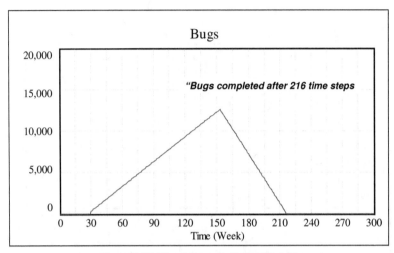

Figure 6.15: Simulation results for "Bugs".

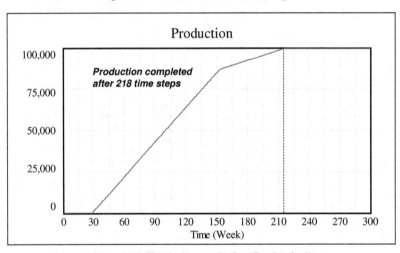

Figure 6.16: Simulation results for "Production".

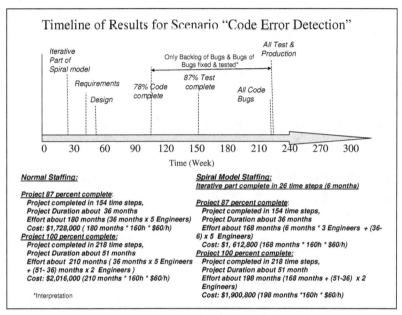

Figure 6.17: Summary of results for "Code Error Detection".

6.4.3 Analysis and Policy Design for Scenario "Code Error Detection"

There are no changes to the iteration part of the spiral. The iteration part remains constant for all scenarios of this model. See Figure 6.6 for the simulation result of "Iterations Time". The waterfall part of the spiral exhibits the same behavior as the waterfall model of scenario "Code Error Detection" in Chapter 5.4. Requirements and design stay exactly the same for scenario "Code Error Detection"(see Figure 6.7 and 6.8). Most code development can be completed within 105 weeks. Most of testing can be completed by week 149. We assume that the product would be shipped at this point of time. Afterwards coding and testing are purely related to bug fixing activities. The product is completed after 218 weeks. Bug fixing results in a major delay of product completion. An increase in the rate of rework would complete the development earlier.

Figure 6.17 lists also the results for project effort and cost for both the general staffing assumption (Figure 4.10) and the spiral model staffing assumption (Figure 6.2).

Notice that the effort and cost for the spiral model assumption is somewhat lower than the for the general staffing assumption due to the fact that less resources are assigned to the iterative part of the spiral model.

6.5 A Spiral Systems Dynamics Model for Scenario "Design Error Detection"

6.5.1 Simulation Model for Scenario "Design Error Detection"

For scenario "Design Error Detection" design changes are detected during development in addition to the incorrect working code in scenario "Code Error Detection". The same definitions for all variables of a waterfall type model apply to the waterfall roll-out of the spiral type model and can be referred to in Chapter 5.5. Please see Figure 6.3 for the systems dynamics model of the spiral type model for scenario "Design Error Detection". The waterfall type model for scenario "Design Error Detection" as shown in Figure 5.16 applies to the waterfall part of the spiral type model for this scenario.

One of the benefits of the spiral model is the upfront clear definition of requirements. Better interpretation of requirements lead also to better design decisions. Therefore the parameter for the design rework ("Redesign Portion") is set to a lower value for the waterfall roll-out of the spiral than for the waterfall type model "(see Table 6.1, page 145).

Figure 6.3 illustrates a simplified model of the spiral model. Please refer to Appendix B for the complete model and its source code.

6.5.2 Simulation for Scenario "Design Error Detection"

We applied the values from Table 6.1, (page 145). "Rework Portion" is lowered from five percent to three percent for the spiral type model to adjust to the fact the requirements and design have been defined in more details before the waterfall type development starts.

158

Figure 6.18 to 6.23 show the results for the simulation of the scenario "Design Error Detection". The results for "Iterations Time" and "Requirements" are shown in Figure 6.6 and Figure 6.7. The next step (Analysis and Policy Design) discusses the results.

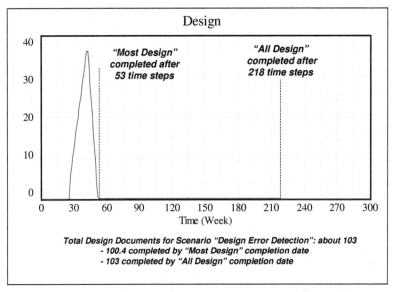

Figure 6.18: Simulation results for "Design".

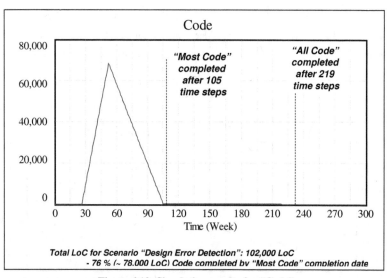

Figure 6.19: Simulation results for "Code".

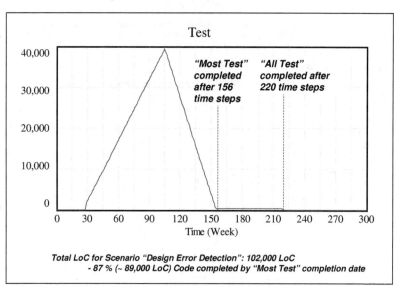

Figure 6.20: Simulation results for "Test".

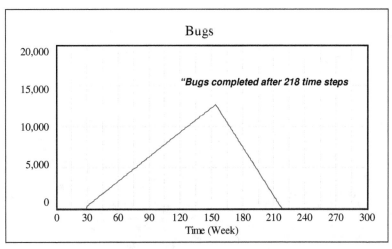

Figure 6.21: Simulation results for "Bugs".

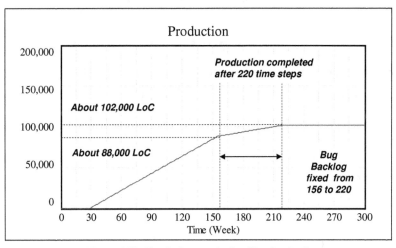

Figure 6.22: Simulation results for "Production".

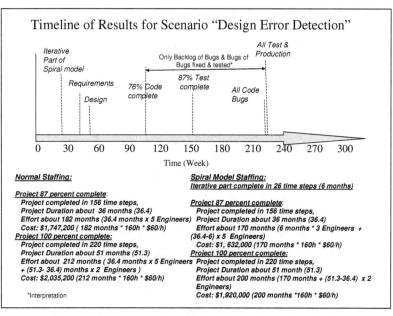

Figure 6.23: Summary of results for "Design Error Detection".

6.5.3 Analysis and Policy Design for Scenario "Design Error Detection"

The iterative part of the spiral model clarifies requirements in detail before they are implemented. Also some design aspects may be evaluated as part of the risk analysis. As a result rework in design is anticipated to be very low for the spiral model. The main number of design documents are completed by week 53. From then onwards only the rework number of design documents is addressed. The duration of the development for this scenario does not take much longer than for scenario "Code Error Detection". The design rework adds minimal additional code development. The end product results in about 102,000 LoC. In week 156 about 89,000 LoC are developed that have production quality. The rest of the code is developed and tested by week 220. Code and design rework also influence the size of the project minimal. The end product consists of two percent more code due to design rework only. The effort, and cost data of the project are calculated in Figure 6.25. Both staffing distributions (Figure 4.10 and Figure 6.2) show similar results for the project.

6.6 A Spiral Systems Dynamics Model for Scenario "Requirements Creep"

6.6.1 Simulation Model for Scenario "Requirements Creep"

For scenario "Requirements Creep" we assume that in addition to the design changes and code changes we also face scope changes that result into changes of the requirements. We only focus on requirements changes during the waterfall roll-out of the spiral model.

As the spiral model spends a significant amount of time upfront on identifying the requirements the chances for scope changes can be anticipated to be rather minimal for the spiral type model. The iterative part of the spiral type model that identifies the requirements stay the same as in scenario "Ideal World".

The variables of the waterfall roll-out are defined as for the waterfall type model.

Please refer to section 5.6 for more details.

The systems dynamic model of the spiral type model is the same as shown in Figure 6.3. The waterfall type model for scenario "Requirements Creep" as shown in Figure 5.24 applies to the waterfall part of the spiral type model for this scenario. The complete versions of the systems dynamics model and its source code can be referred to in Appendix B.

6.6.2 Simulation for Scenario "Requirements Creep"

We simulated this model for the values listed in Table 6.1 (page 145).

The spiral model spends a significant amount of time upfront on identifying the requirements. Therefore we set the value for "Scope Constant" to 1 percent.

The results of this simulation are shown from Figure 6.24 to 6.29. Figure 6.30 shows the timeline for the simulation results of scenario "Requirements Creep". The simulation result for "Iterations Time" is shown in Figure 6.6. The next step (Analysis and Policy Design) discusses the results.

163

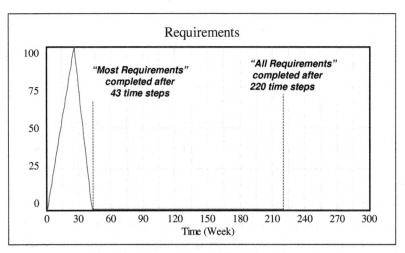

Figure 6.24: Simulation results for "Requirements".

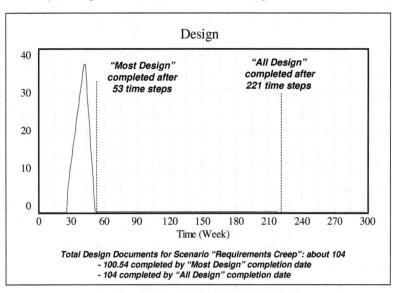

Figure 6.25: Simulation results for "Design".

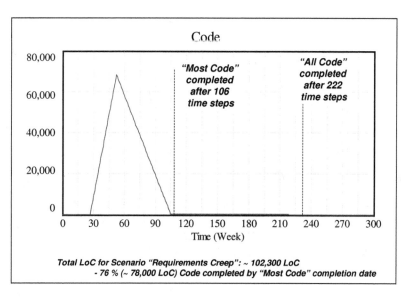

Figure 6.26: Simulation results for "Code".

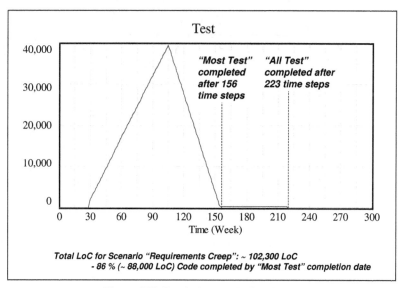

Figure 6.27: Simulation results for "Test".

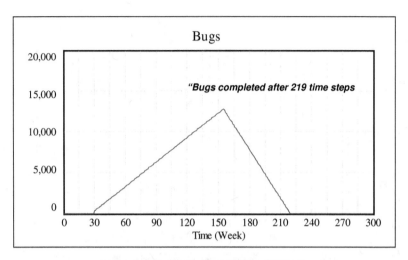

Figure 6.28: Simulation results for "Bugs".

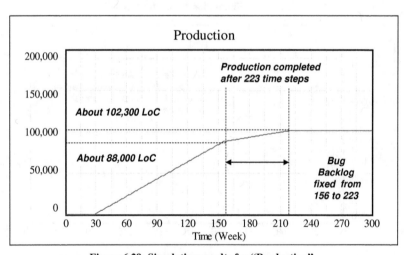

Figure 6.29: Simulation results for "Production".

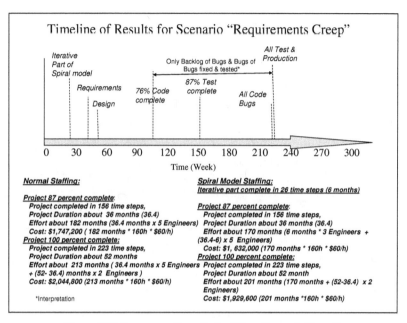

Figure 6.30: Summary of results for "Requirements Creep".

6.6.3 Analysis and Policy Design for Scenario "Requirements Creep"

For scenario "Requirements Creep" we also added new requirements to the development system. These requirements were derived from malfunctioning code (bugs) like in scenario "Requirements Creep" of a waterfall type model. We assume that only 1 percent of the discovered bugs require requirements changes for the spiral model. We only add minimal requirements of 2 percent of a requirements document per time step to the list of requirements. The majority of the requirements are completed by time step 43. Then only an ongoing low number of changes in requirements (1 percent of a requirements document) need to be addressed until all rework can be completed by time step 223. As a result the final product includes about 102,000 LoC.

Figure 6.30 shows the results for effort and cost of the project. As the requirements creep is very low project duration, effort and cost have only increased very little compared to the previous scenarios "Code Error Detection" and "Design Error Detection".

6.7 Comparison of Results for a Spiral Type Model

We developed a systems dynamics model for a spiral type methodology. We simulated four scenarios ("Ideal World", "Code Error Detection", "Design Error Detection", "Requirements Creep") using Vensim (software simulation tool). We used the parameter as listed in Table 6.1 (page 145) to simulate each scenario. We calculated the project effort, and cost for two staffing distributions (Figure 4.10 and Figure 6.2). The results for all scenarios are listed in Table 6.2 for the general staffing distribution and in Table 6.3 for the spiral model staffing distribution.

	Ideal World	Code Error Detection	Design Error Detection	Requirements Creep
"Most" Product Completed	Same as total product completed			
Duration [months]	31	36	36	36
Effort [person months]	155	180	182	182
Cost [$]	1,488,000	1,728,000	1,747,200	1,747,200
Duration increase related to "Ideal World" [%]	Base Value	16	16	16
Effort increase related to "Ideal World" [%]	Base Value	16	17	17
Cost increase related to "Ideal World" [%]	Base Value	16	17	17
Total Product Completed				
Duration [months]	31	51	51	52
Effort [person months]	155	210	212	213
Cost [$]	1,488,000	2,016,000	2,035,200	2,044,800
Duration increase related to "Ideal World" [%]	Base Value	65	65	68
Effort increase related to "Ideal World" [%]	Base Value	35	37	37
Cost increase related to "Ideal World" [%]	Base Value	35	37	37

Table 6.2: Results of all scenarios for general staffing distribution (Figure 4.10).

	Ideal World	Code Error Detection	Design Error Detection	Requirements Creep
"Most" Product Completed	Same as total product completed			
Duration [months]	31	36	36	36
Effort [person months]	143	168	170	170
Cost [$]	1,372,800	1,612,800	1,632,000	1,632,000
Duration increase related to "Ideal World" [%]	Base Value	16	16	16
Effort increase related to "Ideal World" [%]	Base Value	17	19	19
Cost increase related to "Ideal World" [%]	Base Value	17	19	19
Total Product Completed				
Duration [months]	31	51	51	52
Effort [person months]	143	198	200	201
Cost [$]	1,372,800	1,900,800	1,920,000	1,929,600
Duration increase related to "Ideal World" [%]	Base Value	65	65	68
Effort increase related to "Ideal World" [%]	Base Value	38	40	41
Cost increase related to "Ideal World" [%]	Base Value	38	40	41

Table 6.3: Results of all scenarios for a spiral model staffing distribution (Figure 6.2).

The results for both staffing distributions (Table 6.2 and Table 6.3) show a significant increase in duration, effort and cost from scenario "Ideal World" (no errors) to scenario "Code Error Detection" (considering code errors). The consideration of design errors (scenario "Design Error Detection") and requirements creep (scenario "Requirements Creep") show only very little change to the scenario "Code Error Detection".

Notice that there is somewhat difference in results for the general staffing distribution (Figure 4.10) and the spiral model distribution (Figure 6.2). The spiral model distribution assumes that less Engineers (three) work on the iterative part of the spiral process than the general staffing distribution (five). As a result the numbers for effort and cost are lower for the spiral model staffing assignment. The results for the project duration is for both staffing assumptions the same.

We also assumed that the product ships with a so called "good enough" quality when "most" of the product has been completed. Table 6.2 and 6.3 show the results for "most" product completion and total product completion. The difference between the two is significant. There is an increase of 42 percent for the duration and 18 percent for the effort and costs from the "most" product completion to the total product completion.

Between the "most" and total completion time we assume that only the bugs and the bugs of bugs are fixed and tested.

Figure 6.31 compares the results for "Production" in graphical format for all scenarios.

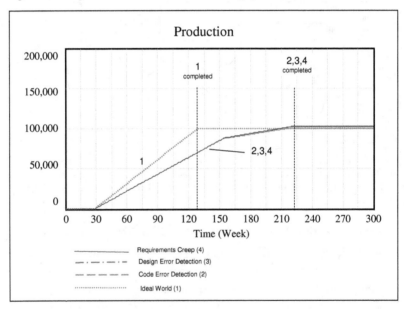

Figure 6.31: Comparison of results for "Production".

Scenario "Ideal World" (see 1 in Figure 6.31) takes the shortest time to complete development. The graph of production is zero until the waterfall part starts and production code becomes available The behavior of the graphs are similar to the waterfall type model as shown in Figure 5.32 and explained in Chapter 5.7. The waterfall type model at the end of the spiral takes the majority of the development time. As we add more rework the development takes longer. One of the biggest advantages of the spiral model is the risk driven approach that allows clarifying the requirements and plans before the implementation. We can assume that the design rework and scope creep is rather low for a spiral type model. This explains why the results for scenario "Code Error Detection", "Design Error Detection" and "Requirements Creep" in Figure 6.31 look very similar. Design rework and scope creep show only a modest impact on the timeline for a spiral model.

Simulation to shorten the Project Duration

The duration of a software project applying a spiral model for development can be reduced by decreasing the number of iterations of the spiral model or improving the execution of the waterfall type model.

The number of iterations might be reduced by assigning resources to the project who are domain experts in their field. Domain experts can help to identify the objectives and provide knowledge about the options for potential alternatives. In addition the help of a project manager who is an expert in risk management and understands the software development life cycle of a spiral type model can reduce the time necessary to go through the methodology process. Reducing the number of spiral cycles would reduce the duration of "Iterations Time". The results of our simulations (Figure show that the majority of development time of a spiral model is spent on product implementation using the waterfall model.

Another way to reduce the timeline is to optimize the development time of the waterfall part of the spiral model. We identified already in Chapter 5.7 that the combination of maximizing the speed of execution for each phase decreases the project duration (scenario "Shorten Combined" in Chapter 5.7) for the waterfall model. This includes testing code as it becomes available, increasing the speed of execution for coding and testing and, decreasing the defect rate. Table 6.4 lists the parameters of the "Shorten Combined" scenario for the simulation run of the spiral model. The execution time of requirements (6 documents per time unit) and design (4 documents per time unit) stay the same as original defined in Table 6.1 (page 145).

Stock and Flow Parameters	Shorten Combined	Unit
Initial number of Requirements ("Initial number of reqs")[3]	100	documents
Requirements Generation Speed ("reqmtsconstant")[4]	6	documents
Design Generation Speed ("design constant")[4]	4	Documents
Code Translation	1000	LoC
Code Generation Speed ("code constant")[4]	3000	LoC
Test Generation Speed ("test constant")[4]	3000	LoC
Bug Rate Portion ("bug rate constant")[4]	25	Percent
Bug Rework Portion ("bug rework constant")[4]	200	LoC
Redesign Portion ("redesign constant")[4]	3	Percent
Design Translation	2.5	LoC/Document
Scope Creep Portion ("scope constant")[4]	1	Percent
Requirements Translation	2.5	LoC/Document

Table 6.4: Parameters for the "Shorten Combined" scenario.

Figure 6.32 shows the graphic results for "Shorten Combined" scenario for "Production" in addition to the four scenarios "Ideal World", "Code Error Detection", "Design Error Detection", and "Requirements Creep".

---

[3] Name used in actual simulation model as shown in Appendix B.

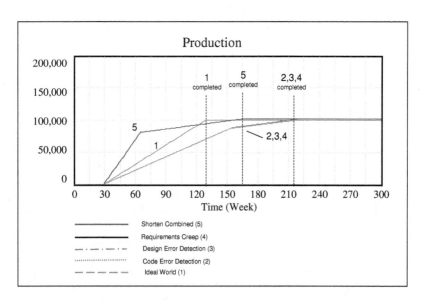

Figure 6.32: Comparison of "Shorten Combined" test case with the four scenarios.

	Requirements Creep, General staffing	Shorten Combined, General staffing	Requirements Creep, Spiral model staffing	Shorten Combined, Spiral model staffing
Duration [months]	52	39	52	39
Effort [person months]	213	123	201	111
Cost [$]	2,044,800	1,180,800	1,929,600	1,065,600
Duration decrease related to "Requirements Creep" [%]	Base Value	-25	Base Value	-25
Effort decrease related to "Requirements Creep" [%]	Base Value	-42	Base Value	-45
Cost decrease related to "Requirements Creep" [%]	Base Value	-42	Base Value	-45

Table 6.5: Results for the "Shorten Combined" scenario.

When comparing the results (Figure 6.32 and Table 6.5) for the "Shorten Combined" scenario with the results for the four scenarios (Table 6.3) it shows that the combination of improvement measurement provides the best results. The timeline for the "Shorten Combined" test case is the shortest with the exception of scenario "Ideal World". This result is strongly influenced by the increase of implementation and testing speed for "Shorten Combined". As requirements and plans have been clarified upfront, a faster implementation of these requirements might be possible. Therefore we can conclude that assigning more resources to implementation and test can decrease the timeline significantly for a spiral type model.

To reduce the timeline of a spiral type software project, management can apply the measures as defined for a waterfall type model in Table 5.5 and the measures specific to the spiral model in Table 6.6.

Measures	Example
Reducing Number of Spiral Cycles	Assign domain experts and project manager with spiral methodology knowledge to the project.
Appropriate Resource assignment	Less time is required for requirements and design work which allows a higher process time in implementation and testing. Allocate appropriate resources to code and test.

Table. 6.6: Summary of measures that help reducing the project timeline.

Appendix B shows the results of a variety of simulations.

Chapter 7: Building a Simulation Model for an Agile Type Model

7.1 Dynamic Hypothesis

We are following the generic modeling process as defined in Figure 4.8 to create a simulation model for an agile type method (Scrum). The problem articulation in Chapter 4.6.1 builds the baseline for this model. We apply step 2 to step 6 of the generic modeling process for each of the four scenarios as described in Table 4.3.

Figure 7.1 shows the causal loop diagram for all scenarios of the agile type methodology. We build our simulation model based on the Scrum method.

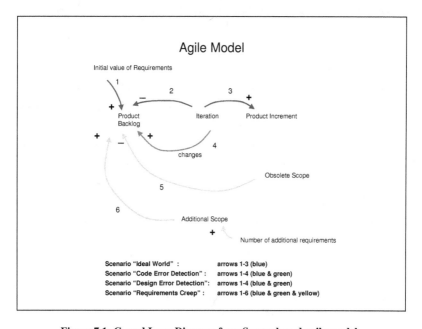

Figure 7.1: Causal Loop Diagram for a Scrum based agile model.

Figure 7.1 shows clearly the difference to the other models (waterfall type model in Chapter 5 and spiral type model in Chapter 6): Requirements are explicitly deleted as a result of each iteration. There is no differentiation made between specifications, design or code on the product backlog list. Additional scope can be a result of the review of the product increment at the end of an iteration or can come from other sources such as a customer. The product is build in increments.

Scenario "Ideal World" (arrow 1-3) assumes that the developed code works right the first time and does not require any rework or changes. An initial value for requirements builds the baseline for the product development. The initial requirements are gathered before the project starts. Then they are consolidated in a product backlog list and prioritized. The more requirements are collected, the longer the product backlog list becomes and the more time it takes to complete the product development. Each completed iteration reduces the number of requirements that remain on the backlog list (see Chapter 3.4).

At the end of each iteration a product increment becomes available that is reviewed by the project stakeholders. In scenario "Ideal World" we assume that each product increment is accepted by all stakeholders as is and is added to the overall end product without any changes. The more iterations are executed the more product increments are developed. The collection of product increments represents the final product.

For *scenario "Code Error Detection"* (arrows 1-4) rework requires code changes and for scenario *"Design Error Detection"* (arrows 1-4) bugs can also require rework in design. Due to the nature of Scrum all development activities for a specific pre-selected subset of requirements are executed within one iteration. Software code and design changes to the scope can be identified as part of the review meeting at the end of the iteration. Changes of code and design are added to the product backlog right after the iteration. At the time the change is identified it might not be clear what might be affected by the change. We show scenarios "Code Error Detection" and "Design Error Detection" in one set of

176

additional arrows (1-4). Both scenarios will be represented by one systems dynamics model (see Chapter 7.4).

For scenario *"Requirements Creep"* (arrow 1-6) new or changed requirements are added to the product backlog list and obsolete functionality is removed from the product backlog. Additional scope as well as obsolete scope can origin from customer requests as well as from discoveries made by the development team. In both cases the product backlog is updated with these changes. The requirements on the product backlog list are prioritized before every iteration (not explicitly modeled). The scope of the iteration that is currently under development is frozen and cannot be changed.

7.2 Assumptions and Variables for the Systems Dynamics Models of an Agile Type Model

All model of the agile model will be based on the assumptions of Chapter 4.6.2.

Staffing

We assume that all Engineers are assigned equally across all development activities. The same number of Engineers is working on the project until the decision is made to ship the product. From then onwards only two Engineers continue to work on the product until it is completed (see Figure 4.10). As errors can be addressed at time during any iteration to a different degree in Scrum, we assume that the product will be shipped at a code completion equivalent to the number of LoC completed at the "Most" product completion point for a waterfall methodology. This point is reached at about 86 percent of total LoC (See Figure 5.14, 5.22 and 5,31).

Processing Speed

Scrum defines the duration of one iteration (Sprint) with 30 days. For our simulation we assume that one time step is equivalent to one Sprint. During one Sprint all development activities are addressed. We presume that during one Sprint all development activities for four requirements can be completed (based on [Eschelbeck, 2006]).

Error Rates

Agile development methodologies are responding well to changes in software development [Udo-Koppensteiner, 2003]. We assume that Scrum would be applied to developments that experience more requirements changes than developments using a waterfall model or a spiral mode. We split the thirty percent change rate into twenty percent change rate for code and design errors and ten percent for requirements changes.

Summary of assumptions for an agile type model:

- Project with 100 requirements.
- Staff of five Engineers assigned as shown in Figure 4.10.
- We assume that the "Most" product completion point for a Scrum development is reached at 86 percent of total LoC.
- Four requirements can be accomplished within a Sprint.
- The product increments are of similar size.
- All development activities are executed as part of a Sprint.
- Total error rate is thirty percent of the developed code.
- Code and design rework rate is twenty percent of developed code.
- Requirements Creep is ten percent of the "Initial number of requirements".
- More additional requirements are identified than become obsolete during the project duration.
- Bug fixing is executed as part of the development activities during a Sprint.
- Bug fixing rate of speed stays constant throughout the entire product development.
- The result of the simulation will provide the duration of the project. Effort and Cost can be derived from these values (see Chapter 4.6.2).

Variables

We define the following flow and stock variables for the systems dynamics models for a Scrum model in Table 7.1 (page 179).

Stock and Flow Parameters	Description	Value	Unit
Assumed Values			
Initial Number of Requirements	Assigned number of requirements defined at the beginning of development.	100	Documents
Requirements Generation Speed ("reqmtsconstant")[4]	Maximum value for requirements documents that become available at each time step.	4	Documents
Code Translation	Translation factor from document to LoC.	1000	LoC
Increment Generation Speed ("increment constant")[5]	Maximum value of Code that becomes available with each time step	4000	LoC
Change Portion ("change constant")[5]	Percentage of code and design bugs	20	Percent
Number of Additional Requirements	Maximum value of requirements that are added to original scope	10	Documents
Additional Scope Portion	Maximum number of requirements that are added per time step.	0.3	Documents
Reduced Scope Portion	Maximum number of requirements that are removed from backlog per time step.	0.1	Documents
Derived Values			
Product Backlog	Accumulation of requirements on product backlog	computed	Documents
Requirements Speed Rate ("Spec Rate")[5]	Max[Requirements Generation Speed, Product Backlog]	computed	Documents / time unit
Iteration	Accumulation of developed code	computed	
Completion Rate	Max[Increment Generation Speed, Iteration]	computes	LoC/time unit
Product increments	Accumulation of product increments	computed	LoC
Change Rate	Max[Change Portion, Iteration]	computed	LoC/time unit
Additional Scope	Accumulation of additional requirements	computed	Documents
Additional Scope Rate	Max[Additional Scope Portion, Additional Scope]	computed	Documents
Obsolete Scope	Accumulation of removed requirements	computed	Documents
Reduced Scope Rate	Max[Reduced Scope Portion, Obsolete Scope]	computed	Documents /time unit

Table 7.1: Stock, Flow and auxiliary variables of an agile type model.

---

[4] Name used in actual simulation as shown in Appendix C

7.3 An Agile Systems Dynamics Model for Scenario "Ideal World"

7.3.1 Simulation Model for Scenario "Ideal World"

For scenario "Ideal World' we assume that all developed code fulfills the requirements and quality criteria right the first time and no errors occur during development.

The initial model for this simulation includes the key parts of the methodology (see Figure 7.2).

Figure 7.2 shows the systems dynamics model for scenario "Ideal World" of a Scrum methodology. For the comprehensive model and its source code please refer to Appendix C.

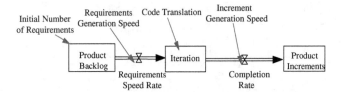

Figure 7.2: Initial system dynamics project model for a basic agile model

At the beginning of a Scrum based methodology the requirements are identified and listed in the product backlog. We assume that the "Initial Number of Requirements" were gathered before the start of development. of the simulation the product backlog is the initial list of requirements for development. At the beginning of the simulation the "Product Backlog" stock variable is set to the value of the "Initial Number of Requirements". For each Sprint a certain number of requirements ("Requirements Generation Speed", see Table 7.1, page 179) is selected for the next iteration ("Requirements Speed Rate") which is subtracted from the product backlog. The development activities take place as part of the iteration. Different software development practices can be applied for the development activities that take place during the iteration. Often Scrum is paired with the core practices of XP [Larman, 2004].

During the iteration the requirements are implemented. The "Code Translation" variable translates them into a number of Line of Code. The "Completion Rate" represents the amount of code that is implemented and approved by stakeholders.

With each completed Sprint a product increment of a size defined by the variable "Increment Generation Speed" becomes available.

Over time "Product Increments" adds up to the complete product.

The stock variables are defined in the formulas (7.1) to (7.3).

(d/dt)(Product Backlog) = Product Backlog (t-1) – Requirements Speed Rate (t)   *(7.1)*

(d/dt)(Iteration) = (Requirements Speed Rate (t)* Code Translation) - Completion Rate(t)

(7.2)

(d/dt)(Product Increments) = Completion Rate(t)   *(7.3)*

7.3.2 Simulation for Scenario "Ideal World'

We simulated the Scrum model for scenario "Ideal World" with the values listed in Table 7.1 (page 179). Each time step correlates to one Sprint (30 days). We assumed 100 requirements that result into a software product of 100,000 Lines of Code. The simulation results for the stock variable of Figure 7.2 are shown in Figure 7.3 to 7.5. Figure 7.6 summarizes these results into one timeline. The next step (Analysis and Policy Design) discusses these results.

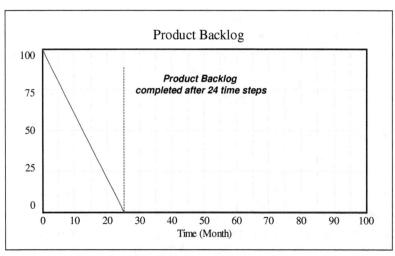

Figure 7.3: Simulation results for "Product Backlog".

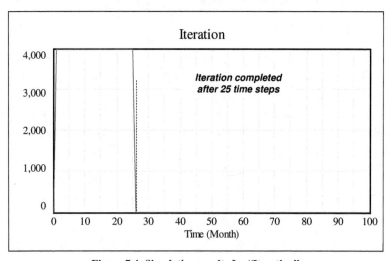

Figure 7.4: Simulation results for "Iteration".

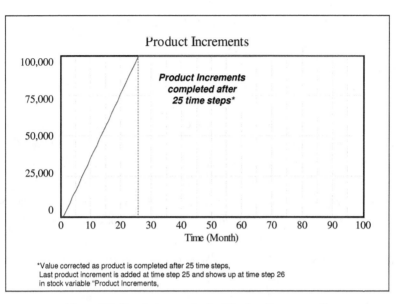

Figure 7.5: Simulation results for "Product Increments".

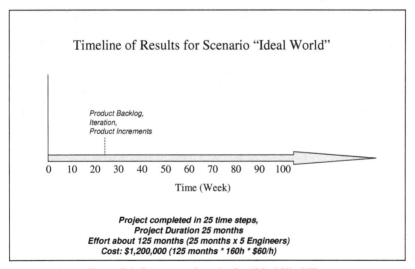

Figure 7.6: Summary of results for "Ideal World".

7.3.3 Analysis and Policy Design for Scenario "Ideal World'

Figures 7.3 to 7.5 show that after 25 iterations (Sprints) all requirements from the product backlog are implemented. All selected requirements for the next iteration are transformed into a working and fully executable portion of a software product. The development of each iteration is completed at the end of each Sprint and the stock variable "Iteration" does not accumulate any outstanding work (Figure 7.4). With the completion of each iteration a product increment becomes available that is added to "Product Increments" (Figure 7.5). The first production ready code is available with the completion of the first iteration The software product of 100,000 LoC is accomplished after 25 months or iterations (Sprints). The effort of this project is 125 person months with costs of $1,200,000. With these numbers the project falls into the examples listed in [Jones, 1998] for this project size.

The simulation model for scenario "Ideal World' demonstrates the iterative nature of Scrum. Scrum creates an operating product increment with each iteration. Every increment is integrated in the existing set of product increments. Compared to a Scrum based methodology the spiral type model clarifies requirements with each cycle and implements the entire product in the waterfall roll-out of the last cycle.

7.4 An Agile Systems Dynamics Model for Scenarios "Code Error Detection" and "Design Error Detection"

7.4.1 Simulation Model for Scenarios "Code Error Detection" and "Design Error Detection"'

The systems dynamics model for scenario "Code Error Detection" and "Design Error Detection" also demonstrates the ability of Scrum to respond to changes during development.

For modeling of these scenarios we assume that code as well as design changes are detected during the iteration. In Scrum the team can decide whether these changes need to be addressed at the expense of the implementation of other requirements for the ongoing iteration. In case these changes are critical to the development they would be addressed right away. In the event that these changes are not of importance to the current progress these changes will be addressed in future iterations. The product backlog is updated with the latest findings after the previous iteration (Sprint) and before the start of the next one.

Figure 7.7 shows the systems dynamics model that addresses the scenarios of "Code Error Detection" and "Design Error Detection" (see Table 4.3) for Scrum, an agile type model. The comprehensive version of the simulation model and its source code can be found in Attachment C.

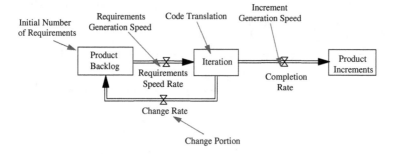

Figure 7.7: System dynamics model for scenarios "Code Error Detection" and "Design Error Detection" of an agile type model.

In Figure 7.7 the "Change Rate" variable demonstrates the out-flowing rate of code rework and design rework from the stock variable "Iteration". The change rate figure derives from the incremental product that is available after each iteration It is a proportion of the product increment that is defined by "Change Portion" (see Table 7.1, page 179).

The stock variable "Change Rate" is defined in formula (7.4). "Iteration" changes from (7.2) to (7.5). "Product Backlog" evolves from (7.3) to (7.6).

Change Rate (t) = Increment Generation Speed * Change Portion / Code Translation

(7.4)

(d/dt)(Iteration) = (Requirements Speed Rate (t)* Code Translation) - Completion Rate (t) – (Change Rate (t)*Code Translation)   *(7.5)*

185

(d/dt)(Product Backlog) = -Requirements Speed Rate (t) + Change Rate (t) (7.6)

7.4.2 Simulation for Scenario "Code Error Detection"' and scenario "Design Error Detection"

We simulated this scenarios with the parameters listed in Table 7.1 (page 179). We used the same values as defined for scenario "Ideal World" and in addition the value for "Change Portion". We assumed a change rate of 20 percent. Changes include design and code changes.

The simulation results are shown in Figure 7.8 to 7.11. The next step (Analysis and Policy Design) discusses these results.

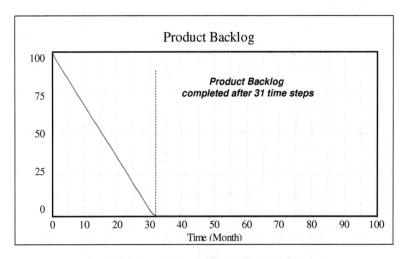

Figure 7.8: Simulation results for "Product Backlog".

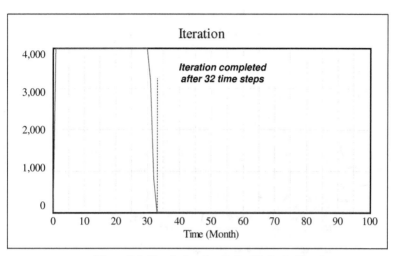

Figure 7.9: Simulation results for "Iteration".

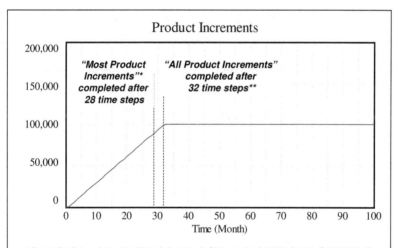

* Assumption that product can be shipped when "most" of it is completed at 86% of total LoC (100,000 LoC)

** Value corrected, Last product increment is added in previous time step and and shows up at time step later in stock variable "Product Increments".

Figure 7.10: Simulation results for "Product Increments".

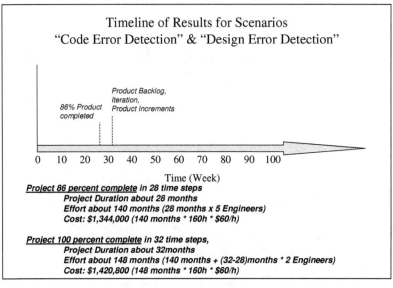

Figure 7.11: Summary of results for "Code Error Detection" and "Design Error Detection".

7.4.3 Analysis and Policy Design for Scenario "Code Error Detection" and scenario "Design Error Detection"

The development takes 32 iterations to be completed. Each iteration produces 4000 LoC where 20 percent of it requires rework. This rework introduces a delay of the completion of development but does not produce any additional code. Therefore the end product still consists of 100,000 LoC at the end of the project.

Usually the product is shipped with a so called "good enough" quality. We assume that this point is reached with 86 percent of product completion. This value is based on the results from a waterfall type model

Figure 7.11 lists the results for project effort (148 person months) and cost ($1,420,800).

7.5 An Agile Systems Dynamics Model for Scenario "Requirements Creep"

7.5.1 Simulation Model for Scenario "Requirements Creep"

Scrum's distinguishing features include the introduction of requirement changes between the iterations that is demonstrated in scenario "Requirements Creep".

For scenario "Requirements Creep" scope changes are detected during the development cycles. Figure 7.12 illustrate the systems dynamics model for this scenario. The complete model and its source code can be found in Appendix C.

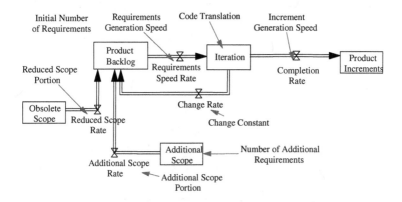

Figure 7.12: System dynamics model for a basic Agile/Scrum model for scenario "Requirements Creep".

Scope changes in scenario "Requirements Creep" entail newly identified requirements as well as requirements that are no longer needed by the customer. The product backlog is updated between the iterations to reflect these changes. Both new and obsolete requirements are defined by stock variables. The stock variable for new requirements is called "Additional Scope". The initial value of the "Additional Scope" variable is set to the "Number of Additional Requirements" that can be expected throughout the duration

189

of the entire development. The flow variable "Additional Scope Rate" adds a percentage of the total number of additional requirements to the product backlog at each iteration. This portion of requirements is defined by the "Additional Scope Portion".

The stock variable for obsolete requirements "Obsolete Scope" has an initial value of zero requirements. The flow variable "Reduced Scope Rate" reduces the product backlog by a predefined number ("Reduce Scope Portion") at each iteration and accumulates this value in "Obsolete Scope".

Both obsolete and additional scope are reflected in the value of the product backlog. "Product Backlog" evolves from (7.6) to (7.7). The new stock variables are specified from (7.8) and (7.9).

$(d/dt)(Product\ Increments) = -Requirements\ Speed\ Rate\ (t) + Change\ Rate(t) - Reduced\ Scope\ Rate\ (t) + Additional\ Scope\ Rate\ (t)$ 　　　　　　(7.7)

$(d/dt)(Additional\ Scope) = -Additional\ Scope\ Rate\ (t)$ 　　　　　　(7.8)

$(d/dt)(Obsolete\ Scope) = Reduce\ Scope\ Rate\ (t)$ 　　　　　　(7.9)

The definition for the stock variable "Iteration" stays as previously defined in (7.5) for the scenarios "Code Error Detection" and "Design Error Detection". "Product Increments" remains as specified in (7.3) in scenario "Ideal World".

7.5.2 Simulation for Scenario "Requirements Creep"

We simulated scenario "Requirements Creep" of the Scrum model using the values listed in Table 7.1 (page 179). Each time step correlates to one Sprint (30 days). At the end of the project the complete product consists of 106,800 Lines of Code. Figure 7.13 to 7.18 show the results for this simulation. The next step (Analysis and Policy Design) discusses the results.

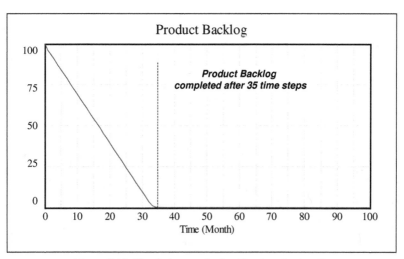

Figure 7.13: Simulation results for "Product Backlog".

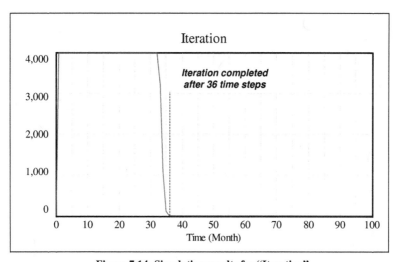

Figure 7.14: Simulation results for "Iteration".

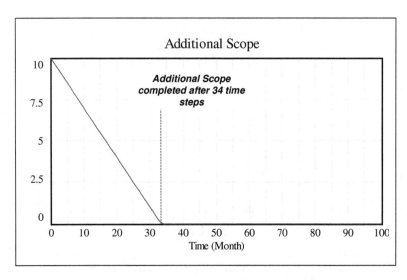

Figure 7.15: Simulation results for "Additional Scope".

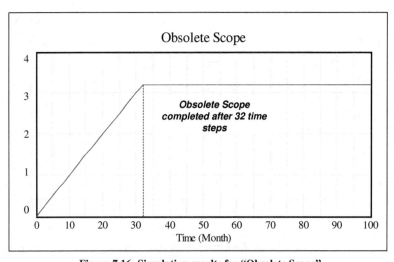

Figure 7.16: Simulation results for "Obsolete Scope".

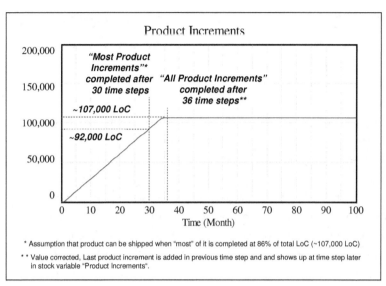

Figure 7.17: Simulation results for "Product Increments".

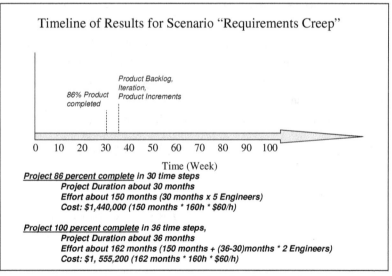

Figure 7.18: Summary of results for "Requirements Creep".

7.5.3 Analysis and Policy Design for Scenario "Requirements Creep"

The product backlog lists 100 requirements at the beginning of the development (see "Initial Number of Requirements" in Table 7.1, page 179). At each iteration (Sprint) additional requirements are added to the product backlog. This number is only partially compensated by the number of requirements that become obsolete. Over the duration of the project more requirements are added to the scope than removed from the scope.
As a result more development takes place that creates an end product with 106,800 LoC. The product is completed after 36 iterations.

As long as the number of requirements on the product backlist is higher than the number of requirements selected for the next iteration, obsolete requirements are removed from the product backlog and changes for rework are identified. Based on the results shown in Figure 7.16 requirements are removed until Iteration 32. Obviously from that point onwards only the predefined number of additional requirements continues to drive additional iterations until all requirements are implemented after 35 time steps. The number of requirements that are addressed between time steps 32 to 35 is smaller than the predefined rate per iteration ("Requirements Generation Speed"). The product increment for time steps 35 and 36 is less than in all other iterations ("Increment Generation Speed"). We can interpret that in these two last time steps the product is finished up. Another way of interpreting is that the project could be completed between 34 and 36 iterations assuming that all product increments have the same size.
Figure 7.18 lists the results for project effort and cost.

7.6 Comparison of Results for an Agile type Model

We developed a systems dynamics model for Scrum, an agile type methodology using Vensim, a software simulation tool. The model is based on four scenarios that we defined in Table 4.3. We simulated the four scenarios for the parameters listed in Table 7.1 (page 179). The scenario "Code Error Detection" and "Design Error Detection" were simulated with the same model (see Chapter 7.4). The results of each scenario are listed in Table 7.2.

	Ideal World	Code Error Detection & Design Error Detection	Requirements Creep
"Most" Product Completed	Same as total product completed		
Duration [months]	25	28	30
Effort [person months]	125	140	150
Cost [$]	1,200,000	1,344,000	1,440,000
Duration increase related to "Ideal World" [%]	Base Value	12	20
Effort increase related to "Ideal World" [%]	Base Value	12	20
Cost increase related to "Ideal World" [%]	Base Value	12	20
Total Product Completed			
Duration [months]	25	32	36
Effort [person months]	125	148	162
Cost [$]	1,200,000	1,420,800	1,555,200
Duration increase related to "Ideal World" [%]	Base Value	28	44
Effort increase related to "Ideal World" [%]	Base Value	18	30
Cost increase related to "Ideal World" [%]	Base Value	18	30

Table 7.2: Results of all four scenarios for an agile type model.

Figure 7.19 compares the results in graphical format for all scenarios.

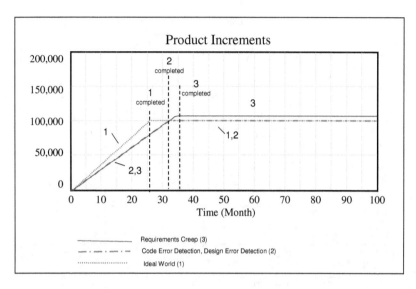

Figure 7.19: Comparison of test results for "Product Increments".

Table 7.2 lists the results for project duration, effort and cost for all scenarios (see Table 4.3) and Figure 7.19 compares the results for "Production. Scenario "Ideal World' shows the shortest duration of the project. No changes during software development are considered for scenario "Ideal World". This is an idealistic case as agile development methodologies in particular are designed to address changes. There is a significant difference between the results for scenario "Ideal World" with no errors and the other scenarios.

Also assuming that only code and design changes occur during the duration of a Scrum project is highly unlikely (scenario "Code Error Detection" and scenario "Design Error Detection"'). Scenario "Requirements Creep" provides the most realistic approach for Scrum. The duration for this scenario takes the longest. As changes can be introduced throughout the duration of the project agile methodologies are assumed to have more scope creep than other methodologies. It appears that adding and removing requirements could be a suitable tool to keep the scope in line with the requirements. We can conclude that increasing the amount of change would increase the project duration to some extend.

196

The complete size of the product for scenario "Requirements Creep" is about 7 percent greater with about 100,000 LoC than for scenario "Ideal World" and scenario "Code Error Detection/Design Error Detection" (106,800 LoC).

We assumed that the product would be shipped at 86 percent of code completion (see "most" product completed in Table 7.2). The results for "total" product completed and "most" product completed are not significantly different. Errors and rework are addressed as part of the development activities during the iterations (Sprints) and can be spread across the duration of the project.

Simulations to Assess Requirements Creep

In order to evaluate the impact of changes on requirements creep for the agile type model we define three additional scenarios. The parameter and values of these scenarios are listed in Table 7.3. We are simulating these scenarios on the most realistic systems dynamics model that we developed for scenario "Requirements Creep" (see Figure 7.12).

Stock and Flow Parameter	Total Requirements Creep	Reducing Requirements Creep	Balancing Requirements Creep	Unit
Initial Number of Requirements	100	100	100	Documents
Requirements Generation Speed ("reqmtsconstant")[6]	4	4	4	Documents
Code Translation	1000	1000	1000	LoC
Increment Generation Speed ("increment constant")[6]	4000	4000	4000	LoC
Change Portion ("change constant")[6]	50	50	50	Percent
Number of Additional Requirements	33	33	33	Documents
Additional Scope Portion	0.5	0.6	0.7	Documents
Reduced Scope Portion	0	0.2	0.5	Documents

Table 7.3: Parameters for scenarios to asses the impact of change on Scrum.

We assume three additional scenarios derived from "Requirements Creep": "Total Requirements Creep", "Reducing Requirements Creep" and "Balancing Requirements

---

[6] Name used in actual simulation model as shown in Appendix C.

Creep" 50 percent changes in code and design, as well as one third of additional requirements. In total 33 additional requirements are added to the initial backlog throughout the duration of the project.

For scenario *"Total Requirements Creep"* we assume that no requirements are removed from the product backlog. This means that only requirements are added.

For scenario *"Reducing Requirements Creep"* we decrease the requirements on the product backlog by 0.2 requirements ("Reduced Scope Portion") per time step.

In scenario *"Balancing Requirements Creep"* we increase the amount of requirements that are removed from the product backlog (see "Reduced Scope Portion" in Table 7.3) Figure 7.20 and Table 7.4 show the results for these scenarios.

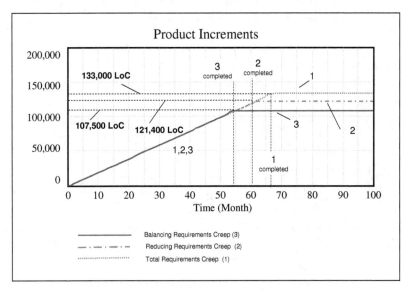

Figure 7.20: Comparison of test results for "Product Increments".

	Total Requirements Creep	Reducing Requirements Creep	Balancing Requirements Creep
Total Product Completed			
Duration [months]	68	61	54
Effort [person months]	310	281	249
Cost [$]	2,976,000	2,697,600	2,390,400
Duration increase related to "Ideal World" [%]	Base Value	-10	-21
Effort increase related to "Ideal World" [%]	Base Value	-9	-20
Cost increase related to "Ideal World" [%]	Base Value	-9	-20

Table 7.4: Results for scenarios to asses the impact of change.

The scenario "Total Requirements Creep" results into a tremendous increase in project duration and size of the end product. The total product size is 33 percent larger compared to scenario "Ideal World' or scenarios "Code Error Detection" and "Design Error Detection"'. This case represents the worst case scenario for an agile type model when changes and requirements are only added to the scope and no scope reduction occurs.

In scenario "Reducing the Requirements Creep" we reduced the product backlog by 0.2 requirements per time step. This accounts in total for 12 requirements that are removed from the product backlog throughout the duration of the project. The project duration and scope creep of this case is reduced compared to the previous case.

In the third case "Balancing Requirements Creep" we increase the "Reduced Scope Rate" to 0.5 requirements per iteration. As a result 27 requirements are removed from the product backlog throughout the duration of the project. As the number of removed requirements balance almost the number of added requirements the scope stays close to the original anticipated 100,000 LoC.

The amount of software code produced for scenario "Requirements Creep" and the "Balancing Requirements Creep" case are in the same range (see Table 7.1, page 179).

The results for the timelines are very different. We can conclude that the increased changes for the "Balancing Requirements Creep" case increase the timeline significantly.

When using an agile methodology for a software project, management may need to pay attention on controlling the requirements creep. The introduction of changes and additional requirements throughout the duration of the project increases the project duration. The Scrum based methodology explicitly includes the process of removing requirements throughout the duration of the project. Management needs to ensure that the project team and the project stakeholder also reduce the project scope at each iteration. This is the only available controlling device for requirements creep and reducing the duration and effort for an agile type software project.

Another way to improve the project performance is to reduce the defect rate. This can be done by assigning experienced software Engineers to the project that are familiar with so called software "best practices".

Table 7.5 summarizes the measures that help reducing the timeline of a Scrum (agile) type model.

Measures	Example
Balancing Scope	Review history of product backlog at each product review at the end of each iteration (Sprint).
Reduce Defect Rate.	Assigning experiences Engineers who apply best practices.

Table 7.5: Summary of measures that help reducing the project timeline.

200

Chapter 8: Comparing Results of Simulation Models.

8.1 Summary of Common Assumptions

In order to assess the temporal behavior of a waterfall, a spiral and an agile type methodology we developed systems dynamics models for each of them by following the modeling process steps: Formulation of the problem, Dynamic Hypothesis, Assumptions and Variables, Simulation Model, Simulation, Analysis and Policy Design (shown in Figure 4.8).

We developed all systems dynamics models based on four scenarios: "Ideal World", "Code Error Detection", "Design Error Detection", and "Requirements Creep" (see Table 4.3): Scenario "Ideal World" is the most idealistic scenario, assuming that development can be done without any errors. With scenario "Code Error Detection" we assumed that errors occur when writing software code. In scenario "Design Error Detection" code and design errors are detection. The most realistic scenario is scenario "Requirements Creep" assuming that in addition to code and design errors also new requirements are identified throughout the duration of the project.

We simulated all three models: waterfall model (Figures 5.2, 5.9, 5.16, 5.24), spiral model (Figures 6.3) and agile model (Figures 7.2, 7.7, 7.12) using Vensim, a software simulation tool, for these four different scenarios. The results are shown in Tables 5.2, 6.2, 7.2.

We assumed similar conditions for these simulations (see Chapter 4.6.2):

- Project with 100 requirements that results in product with 100,000 LoC.

- Five Engineers assigned for most of the project duration (Figure 4.10).

- Thirty percent defect rate of tested code.

The parameters were set to simulate a project with 100 requirements that results into a software product with 100,000 LoC for the most idealistic scenario ("Ideal World"). For "Ideal World" no errors are introduced and no rework is required during the product development. The number of defects was set to 30 percent of tested code for the most realistic scenario "Requirements Creep" (e.g. that new requirements appear during development). This includes the error and rework for code and design errors as well as newly discovered and changed requirements.

Further we assumed that five Engineers were assigned to the project for most time of the development (see Figure 4.10). When the product was considered "good enough" to be shipped to the product most of the product was completed and only two Engineers continued to finish the product. For the spiral model we also introduced a spiral model specific staffing distribution for the project (see Figure 6.2). We assumed that fewer Engineers are required during the iterative part of the spiral.

We compared the results of the simulations for each methodology (see Chapters 5.7, 6.7 and 7.6) and defined different measurements management can take to influence the duration of each methodology (Tables 5.5, 6.6, 7.5).

8.2 Comparison of Results

In the Chapters 5.7, 6.7 and 7.6 we listed the results for each scenario of each methodology. The results of scenario "Ideal World" establishes the baseline. We compared the results for duration, effort and cost off all other scenarios against the results of scenario "Ideal World".

The assumptions of all software methodologies and their systems dynamics model are not completely the same. They are similar enough to compare some of the results with each other. We contrast the results of all software methodologies (waterfall, spiral, agile) for each scenario with each other. For this assessment we take the results that we calculated based on the assumption of the staffing distribution shown in Figure 4.10. The results of the spiral model show the results for the spiral specific staffing distribution (see Figure 6.2) in brackets ( ) next to the results for the general staffing distribution.

Comparing Scenario "Ideal World"

Table 8.1 lists the results for scenario "Ideal World".

	Waterfall Model	Spiral Model	Agile Model
Duration [months]	24	31 (31)	25
Effort [person months]	120	155 (143)	125
Cost [$]	1,152,000	1,488,000 (1,372,800)	1,200,000

Table 8.1: Results for scenario "Ideal World".

For *scenario "Ideal World"* the spiral model shows the longest project duration taking the most effort and cost for both staffing assumptions. The results for the waterfall type model and the agile (Scrum) model are very close with the waterfall type taking the shortest duration, effort and cost for scenario "Ideal World". Effort is calculated based on the duration of the project and the number of staff working on the project during that time. Based on our general staffing assumption that five Engineers are assigned throughout the project until the product has a "good enough" quality to be released, the project with the longest duration takes the most effort.

Comparing Scenario "Code Error Detection"

Table 8.2 compares the results for scenario "Code Error Detection".

	Waterfall Model	**Spiral Model**	**Agile Model**
"Most" Product Completed			
Duration [months]	30	36 (36)	28
Effort [person months]	149	180 (168)	140
Cost [$]	1,433,600	1,728,000 (1,612,800)	1,344,000
Duration increase related to "Ideal World" [%]	25	16 (16)	12
Effort increase related to "Ideal World" [%]	24	16 (17)	12
Cost increase related to "Ideal World" [%]	24	16 (17)	12

	Waterfall Model	**Spiral Model**	**Agile Model**
Total Product Completed			
Duration [months]	45	51 (51)	32
Effort [person months]	179	210 (198)	148
Cost [$]	1,718,400	2,016,000 (1,900,800)	1,420,800
Duration increase related to "Ideal World" [%]	87.5	65 (65)	28
Effort increase related to "Ideal World" [%]	49	35 (38)	18
Cost increase related to "Ideal World" [%]	49	35 (38)	18

Table 8.2: Results for scenario "Code Error Detection".

Also for *scenario "Code Error Detection"* the spiral type model appears to take the longest duration and the most effort and cost. The agile type model (Scrum) takes the least duration efforts and cost.

We assumed a defect rate of 20 percent for code and design changes (see Table 7.1, page 179). Requirements were assumed separately with 10 percent for scenario "Requirements Creep" (see Chapters 7.4 and 7.5). This fact benefits the outcome of the agile type model.

Note that when introducing defects in scenario "Code Error Detection" the increase of duration, effort and cost compared to the scenario "Ideal World" is the highest for the waterfall type model. This might be a result of the sequential nature of the waterfall model. Change in a project using a waterfall type model means often rework in one or more phases or deliverables (see Chapter 3.2).

The waterfall type model and the spiral type model show significant differences in the results for the "most" product completion point and the total product completion point (see Table 8.2). In our simulations we assumed that the code cannot be processed in the same speed as requirements and design documents are created. Consequently errors cannot be addressed in the same rate they are discovered. A backlog of errors accumulates over the duration of the development and is addressed after most of the product has been implemented.

Comparing Scenario "Design Error Detection"

Table 8.3 lists the results for scenario "Design Error Detection".

	Waterfall Model	Spiral Model	Agile Model
"Most" Product Completed			
Duration [months]	30	36 (36)	28
Effort [person months]	152	182 (170)	140
Cost [$]	1,456,000	1,747,200 (1,632,000)	1,344,000
Duration increase related to "Ideal World" [%]	25	16 (16)	12
Effort increase related to "Ideal World" [%]	26	17 (19)	12
Cost increase related to "Ideal World" [%]	26	17 (19)	12
Total Product Completed			
Duration [months]	46	51 (51)	32
Effort [person months]	182	212 (200)	148
Cost [$]	1,766,400	2,035,200 (1,920,000)	1,420,800
Duration increase related to "Ideal World" [%]	92	65 (65)	28
Effort increase related to "Ideal World" [%]	52	37 (40)	18
Cost increase related to "Ideal World" [%]	53	37 (40)	18

Table 8.3: Results for scenario "Design Error Detection".

For the agile methodology we developed one systems dynamics model to simulate scenario "Code Error Detection" and "Design Error Detection" (see Chapter 7.4). Consequently only one systems dynamics model covers both scenarios. For that reason the results of the agile model listed in Tables 8.2 and 8.3 are identical.

For *scenario "Design Error Detection"* the duration for the agile type project takes the shortest duration, least effort and cost. The introduction of design rework increases the results for a waterfall type development most compared to the initial values of scenario "Ideal World". The spiral type model takes the longest duration, effort and cost. It seems that the agile methodology can most easily "swallow" errors.

Comparing Scenario "Requirements Creep"

Table 8.4 lists the results for scenario "Requirements Creep".

	Waterfall Model	Spiral Model	Agile Model
"Most" Product Completed			
Duration [months]	31	36 (36)	30
Effort [person months]	155	182 (170)	150
Cost [$]	1,488,000	1,747,200 (1,632,000)	1,440,000
Duration increase related to "Ideal World" [%]	29	16 (16)	20
Effort increase related to "Ideal World" [%]	29	17 (19)	20
Cost increase related to "Ideal World" [%]	29	17 (19)	20
Total Product Completed			
Duration [months]	47	52 (52)	36
Effort [person months]	187	213 (201)	162
Cost [$]	1,795,200	2,044,800 (1,929,600)	1,555,200
Duration increase related to "Ideal World" [%]	96	68 (68)	44
Effort increase related to "Ideal World" [%]	56	37 (41)	30
Cost increase related to "Ideal World" [%]	56	37 (41)	30

Table 8.4: Results for scenario "Requirements Creep".

For *scenario "Requirements Creep"* the results look very similar to the results for scenario "Design Error Detection" for a waterfall type model and a spiral type model.

The duration, effort and cost for the agile type model increased significant by introducing requirements creep. It appears that adding and removing requirements could be a suitable tool to keep the scope in line with the requirements. For the simulation of this scenario we add more requirements than we remove from the scope of this project. Consequently more requirements take more iterations (Sprints) to be implemented which results in a longer project duration for scenario "Requirements Creep". As we showed in Chapter 7.6 it is crucial to pay attention to requirements creep when using an agile model (see Table 7.3).

Comparing Lines of Code

As a result of introducing defects and rework more code is developed throughout the duration of a project. Table 8.5 lists the amount of code that was developed for each scenario for a waterfall type, a spiral type and an agile type methodology.

Scenario	Waterfall Model	Spiral Model	Agile Model
Ideal World	100,000 LoC	100,000 LoC	100,000 LoC
Code Error Detection	100,000 LoC	100,000 LoC	100,000 LoC
Design Error Detection	103,000 LoC	102,000 LoC	100,000 LoC
Requirements Creep	106,000 LoC	102,300 LoC	107,000 LoC

Table 8.5: Code creation of all scenarios.

For the spiral model requirements are clarified before the product is implemented. Consequently we assumed that less new requirements or requirements changes are identified. The results for a spiral type model show the least increase in lines of code. A waterfall or agile type model show similar results.

Chapter 9: Conclusion and Outlook

In Chapter 2 of this thesis we explained the basics of project management. We defined the relationship between three key processes of product development: the product development life cycle, the project life cycle and the software methodology in Chapter 3. We mapped these processes one to another to illustrate how they interact and showed the key role the project life cycle plays. If the project life cycle is not or only insufficiently defined the project cannot be managed properly. As a result projects can experience one or more of the impacts listed below:

- Major delays
- Scope Creep
- Cost overrun
- High turn-over
- Lack of project and/or product direction

Therefore the project life cycle has to be defined by the organization and adapted to organizational changes.

In order to explore the impact of a software methodology on a software project we defined systems dynamics models for each methodology (waterfall: Chapter 5, spiral: Chapter 6, agile: Chapter 7). The results are discussed in Chapter 8.

Below we describe what conclusions we can draw from the results of this thesis and how these conclusions support the claims we identified in Chapter 1.

We made the following claims at the beginning of this thesis:

- ***Claim 1:*** *Alignment of the relationship between product, project and software development life cycle can be done in an organization*
- ***Claim 2:*** *The software development method determines at what key points of a project and in what form information becomes available.*
- ***Claim 3:*** *Different software methodologies generate different project durations and effort.*

9.1 Conclusions from Process Mapping

By identifying the need for reviews of a software project in Chapter 2 we provided the foundation for mapping the product development life cycle, the project life cycle and the software methodology one to another. We acknowledged the need for management reviews and project reviews as part of Chapter 2 and 3. We aligned the management reviews with the product development life cycle (see Figure 3.1) and concluded that these management reviews are major decision points for the direction of a product or software solution in an organization. We recognized that each milestone takes place at the end of a phase of the product development life cycle.

The concept of process mapping turned out to be very helpful. In a concise form it shows to the project manager at what points the processes for project, product and software methodology interact and when information is transferred between these processes. Based on the results of process mapping project communication plans can be created.

By mapping the product development lifecycle to the project life cycle and further to the software methodology we found out that the proposed arrangement of the project reviews are well aligned with the project life cycle and the software methodology. The project reviews support the management decision process of the product development life cycle.

By applying the practice of process mapping we could demonstrate that there is a strong relationship between product, project and software development life cycle and conclude that these three life cycles can be aligned (Claim 1 in Chapter 1). As a result we showed that the project life cycle builds a link between the product development life cycle and the software methodology. The relationship between these life cycles is illustrated for the waterfall, spiral and agile type methodologies, respectively in Figure 3.4, 3.7 and 3.11.

The alignment of project life cycle and software methodology build the foundation for the exchange of information between all three life cycles. Figure 3.5, 3.8 and 3.12 demonstrate the timely availability of the project information (see Claim 2 in Chapter1). For each methodology we showed what information can be available at what phase of the product development life cycle. The process mapping helps to identify when different kinds of project and product information becomes available during the product development. Management can identify for each phase of the project and software development phase what deliverables need to be available.

Based on the process mappings we concluded that most of the needed product information is identified during the product development phase of the product development life cycle. During this phase the software project is initiated, planned and carried out. We aligned the software methodology with the project life cycle and identified the project review milestones as well as the information that is exchanged between these processes.

By identifying the project review milestones we discovered that the software methodology influences significantly the timing of the project reviews.
Table 9.1 shows a summary of the project review milestones for a waterfall type, a spiral type and an agile type methodology.

Methodology	*Project Review Milestones*			
	Project Life Cycle			
	Initiation	Planning	Executing	Closing
Waterfall	Initiation	Requirement Planning	Design Implementation Alpha Review, Beta Review	Release Readiness
Spiral	Cycle Reviews	Cycle Reviews Planning	Detailed Design Implementation Alpha, Beta	Release Readiness
Agile				Product increment Review

Table 9.1: Key characteristics of project review milestones.

The time between the project reviews can vary for a waterfall type model and a spiral type model. We used the agile methodology Scrum [Schwaber- Beedle, 2002] [Schwaber, 2004]. Iterations are called Sprints in Scrum. It is suggested that they last 30 days. For Scrum all iterations, also called Sprints, have the same duration (30 days). Consequently the reviews take place at the end of each iteration. The number of reviews is highly related to the duration of the overall project for an agile project and not necessarily for a waterfall or a spiral type development.

The reviews for a project applying a waterfall or spiral type methodology are defined by the phases of these software methods and therefore have variable time intervals.

Specifically the duration between the planning and the alpha review milestone of a *waterfall* type development is critical for the project. During this time the implementation of the product takes place. Throughout this phase the progress of the project can be closely monitored. The product will be verified during the alpha phase for the first time. Therefore the longer the duration of the implementation phase, the higher the risk for the project to miss the market requirements and / or market window.

The *spiral* model has reviews at the end of each cycle during its initial iterative part. At these reviews the plans for the next cycle are approved. During each cycle requirements and design of the product are specified in increasing level of detail. During the product implementation of the spiral type model the same milestones apply as for the waterfall type model. As more emphasize is placed on the requirements definition the implementation phase will be more focused and (hopefully) require less rework.

The *agile* type methodology has regular reviews to present and formally accept the created product increment of each iteration. In case of Scrum a project review takes place at the end of every Sprint (30days). We can conclude that agile type methodologies provide the tightest level of control from all three software methodologies (waterfall, spiral and agile) over the output of the project.

As a consequence we can conclude that claim #1 and claim #2 (see Chapter 1) of this thesis have been proven. Table 9.2 summarizes the conclusions for the process mapping part of this thesis.

Conclusions	Claim #1: *Alignment of the relationship between product, project and software development life cycle can be done*	Claim #2: *The software development method determines at what key points of a project and in what form information becomes available.*
1) Management reviews are decision points for the direction of a product	X	
2) Project reviews are aligned with the project life cycle and the software methodology	X	
3) The project life cycle builds a link between the product development life cycle and the software methodology	X	
4) Most of the product information is identified during the product development phase of the product development life cycle	X	X
5) The software methodology influences significantly at what point the project reviews need to take place		X
6) Agile type methodologies provide the tighest control from all three software methodologies (waterfall, spiral and agile) over the output of the project.		X

Table 9.2: Summary of conclusions for the process mapping part of the thesis.

9.2 Conclusions from Systems Dynamics Models

In the previous section we could show how we support claim #1 and claim #2 of this thesis. Claim #3 states that different software methodologies generate different project durations and efforts.

In order to support claim# 3 we created systems dynamics models for a waterfall, a spiral and an agile type model. We showed how systems dynamics models for software development methodologies can be build und used. We developed these models based on values derived from [Jones, 1996] and the author's experience in the software industry. These models provide for the selected values reasonable results. Applying more statistical representative data would lead to more objective results.

We built these systems dynamics models based on four scenarios for each software methodology:

- *Scenario "Ideal World":* No errors occur during the implementation of the product.

212

- *Scenario "Code Error Detection"*: Defects are detected that require code fixes.
- *Scenario "Design Error Detection"*: Defects require fixes in code and changes in design.
- *Scenario "Requirements Creep"*: In addition to defects detected during testing also new requirements and requirements changes are identified which are triggered by testing.

We simulated each scenario for each software development based on a number of common assumptions (Chapter 4.6.2): We assumed a project with 100 requirements that creates a software product with about 100,000 LoC. Based on this size of application we assigned five Engineers [Jones, 1998] to this project who were spread across the development activities. This is consistent with data provided by [Jones, 1998]. We assumed that all Engineers would be assigned to the project until the product reaches the so called "most product completion point", where it has "good enough" quality to be released to the market (see Chapter 4.6.2 and Figure 4.10).

We also assumed a change rate of thirty percent of tested code for scenario "Requirements Creep".

By creating the systems dynamics models we were able to assess the behavior of each methodology over time. The results of our simulations support claim #3. We can conclude that each selected approach created a different project duration and effort for similar project conditions. Further we also identified that the application of each software methodology can be optimized.

The key results for simulating all four scenarios are summarized in Table 9.3.

Results	Waterfall	Spiral	Agile	Unit
Scenario "Ideal World"				
Product Size	100,000	100,000	100,000	LoC
Project Duration	24	31	25	Months
Effort	120	155	125	Person Months
Scenario "Code Error Detection"				
Product Size	100,000	100,000	100,000	LoC
Project Duration	45	51	32	Months
Effort	179	210	148	Person

Results	Waterfall	Spiral	Agile	Unit
				Months
Scenario "Design Error Detection"				
Product Size	103,000	102,000	100,000	LoC
Project Duration	46	51	32	Months
Effort	182	212	148	Person Months
Scenario "Requirements Creep"				
Product Size	106,000	102,300	107,000	LoC
Project Duration	47	52	36	Months
Effort	187	213	162	Person Months

Table 9.3: Summary of key results for all scenarios of each methodology.

Table 9.3 shows that the agile methodology takes the shortest duration based and the least effort to complete the simulated project. The waterfall model comes second and then the spiral model. We assumed in our model for the spiral type methodology that all cycles of a spiral type development take the same duration. As a result the iterative part of the spiral model has a high influence on the project duration. In our simulations we also assumed that for a waterfall type development the code cannot be processed in the same speed as requirements and design documents are created. Consequently a backlog of errors accumulates over the duration of the development and is addressed after most of the product has been implemented. The combination of the effect of the backlog of errors and the assumption that each spiral cycle takes the same duration leads to the result that the spiral type model takes the longest duration.

The waterfall model often experiences rework that leads to a higher error backlog and therefore takes a long duration. In comparison using Scrum rework is added to the product backlog list at the end of each iteration (Sprint). These errors can be addressed as part of ongoing development activities. Prioritising and removing requirements on the product backlog list helps to manage the scope of the project. In our simulations we balance the requirements creep. As a result the project applying the agile (Scrum) methodology finishes earlier than the projects using spiral or waterfall type methodologies.

The product size seems to increase the most for an agile model under the condition of "Requirements Creep".

These simulations are based on similar conditions. We assume that when the conditions vary the results are likely to vary too.

Based on the results listed in Table 9.3 we can conclude that different software development methodologies generate different project durations and efforts "(Claim 3).

Further we evaluated for each methodology how to reduce or optimize the duration of a development. In order to optimize the conditions for the waterfall (Chapter 5.7) and the spiral (Chapter 6.7) methodologies we assumed we can:

- Reduce the scope creep
- Implement quality best practices to reduce the defect rate.
- Improve the process time of development
- Assign appropriate resources to development activities

Based on these assumptions we doubled the number of requirements processed per time unit and the design documents that were progressed per time unit. In addition we also doubled the speed of code implementation and test. At the same time we decreased the amount of defects and changes by five percent from 30 percent to 25 percent (Table 5.3 and 6.4). Table 9.4 lists the key results for the optimized simulation of the waterfall and spiral type model comparing to the results of the agile type model.

Optimized Result	Waterfall	Spiral	Agile	Unit
Product Size	104,000	101,600	107,000	LoC
Project Duration	32	39	36	Months
Effort	93	123	162	Person Months

Table 9.4: Comparison of optimized simulations of waterfall and spiral model with agile type model.

Based on the results presented in Table 9.4 we can conclude that in theory the duration of waterfall and a spiral type model can be optimized to improve project duration and efforts. Not only the selected methodology influences the duration of the project but also the management of the project plays a key role how well the methodology is applied for

215

the project and delivers the expected results. Management can decrease the amount of rework by implementing so called software best practices to improve the quality of software development. Also resources can be assigned in a way to improve the process time of development. One key aspect in the optimized case is that testing can be processed in the speed code becomes available.

We also evaluated the impact of requirements creep on agile type models. Our assessment in Chapter 7.6 concluded that agile methodologies only work well when adding to the scope is kept in balance with reducing the scope. If changes result in an inflated scope, agile methodologies can turn a project from user oriented into uncontrollable.

9.3 Outlook

In today's world project management has an increasing role in how business is conducted. Due to globalization project management wins on importance. Projects are no longer limited to take place within one organization in one location. Specifically software development has experienced significant changes within the last decade. Project management processes and their alignment to other organizational processes such as product development processes and software methodologies have to be understood and working before more complexity such as larger projects, distributed teams, multiple location and cultural differences can be introduced.

In this thesis we explained the basics of project management and how it relates to product processes and software methodologies. We focused our view and assessment on the project management processes and how they fit into an organization that produces software products. We demonstrated how the project life cycle can be mapped to a product life cycle and a software methodology.

These process mappings can be used as templates for organizations that try to identify and utilize the relationship of their life cycles. They can also be used as reference or baseline to define an organizational product development process.

We also used simulations of systems dynamics models to show how the behavior of software methodologies can be evaluated. Both the process mappings as well as the systems dynamics models for waterfall, spiral and agile type models provide a baseline that can be used and expanded on for further study.

The systems dynamics models can be used to simulate the behavior of a software methodology with changing parameters. As these models are based on the essentials of each methodology they can be expanded to add other aspects that influence a project such as cultural differences or outsourcing.
Influencing factor such as time delay caused by distributed teams that work on different locations can be added to assess its effect on the project.

Project management processes have to be understood within an organization first, before more complexity can be added. Process mapping and systems dynamics modeling can help to assess the complexity before implementing it to a new or existing organization or project.

References:

[Abrahamsson, O. Salo, 2002], P. Abrahamsson, O. Salo, J. Ronkainen and J. Warsta, (2002), "Agile software development methods , Review and Analysis", ESPOO 2002 VTT Publications 478; retrieved from http://www.inf.vtt.fi/pdf/publications/2002/P478.pdf.

[ACM, 2006], ACM Job Migration Task Force,"Globalization and Offshoring of Software" retrieved from http://www.acm.org/globalizationreport/ on April 10th, USA 2006.

[AgileAlliance, 2001], Agile Alliance, "The Agile Manifesto", retrieved from http://agilemanifesto.org/, Agile Gathering, Utah, United States, 2001.

[Anderson-Johnson, 1997], V. Anderson and L. Johnson, "Systems Thinking Basics, from Concepts to Causal Loops", Pegasus Communications, USA, 1997.

[Bahn-Naumann, 1997], D. L. Bahn and J. D. Naumann, "Evolution versus Construction, Distinguishing user review of software prototypes from conventional review of software specification", Proceedings of the 1997 ACM SIGCPR conference on Computer personnel research, pp. 240-245, San Francisco, California, United States, 1997.

[Baker, 1992], S.Baker and K.Baker, "On Time/On Budget" A Step-by-Step Guide for ManagingbAny Project", Prentice-Hall, New Jersey, 1992.

[Beck, 2000], K.Beck, "Extreme Programming Explained", Addison-Wesley, New Jersey 2000.

[Bentley, 1997], C. Bentley, "Prince2, A Practical Handbook", Butterworth-Heinemann, Great Britain 1997.

[Bertalanffy, 1976], L. Bertalanffy., "General System Theory: Foundations, Development, Applications", George Braziller, New York, USA.

[Boehm, 1988], B. Boehm "A Spiral Model of Software, Development and Enhancement", Computer, pp.61-72, May 1988.

[Boehm-Brown, 2000], B. Boehm., A. Brown, C. Abts., "Software Cost Estimation with COCOMO II",Prentice Hall PTR, New Jersey, 2000

[Boehm- Egyed, 1998], B. Boehm B., A. Egyed., J. Kwan., D. Port, A. Shah, "Using the WinWin Spiral Model: A Case Study", IEEE Computer, July 1998.

[Boehm-Gruenbacher, 2001], B. Boehm, P. Gruenbacher., "Developing Groupware for Requirements Negotiation: Lessons Learned", IEEE Software, May/June 2001.

[Boehm-Ross, 1989], B. Boehm and R. Ross, "Theory-W Software Project Management: Principles and Examples", IEEE Trans. Software Engr., July 1989.

[Boehm-Bose, 1994], B. Boehm and P. Bose, "A Collaborative Spiral Software Process Model Based on Theory W", Third International Conference on the Software Process, Proceedings, pp: 59 -68, 1994.

[Boehm-Turner, 2005], B. Boehm and R. Turner, "Balancing Agility and Discipline", Addison-Wesley, Pearson Education, Boston, MA, 2005.

[Bosch, 2000], Bosch: "Design & Use of Software Architectures", Addison-Wesley Professional; 1st edition (May 19, 2000), 2000.

[Brooks, 1995], F. Brooks, "The Mthical Man-Months", Addison Wesley Longman, pp.25, 1995

[Cavaleri-Obloj, 1993], S. Cavaleri and K.Obloj, "Management Systems, A Global Perspective", Wadsworth, CA, USA, 1993.

[Caupin, 1999], G.Caupin, H. Knöpfel, P. Morris, E. Motzel and O. Pannenbäcker , "IPMA Competency Baseline", Monmouth, United Kingdom: International Project Management Association, 1999.

[Chroust, 1992], G.Chroust, "Modelle der Software- Entwicklung", Oldenbourg, pp.111, Muenchen, 1992

[Chroust, 1996], G.Chroust, "What is a software process?", Journal of Systems Architecture 42(1996) 591-600, Elsevier Science B.V, 1996.

[Chroust-Lexen, 1999], G.Chroust and H.Lexen, "Software inspections-theory, new approaches and an experiment", EUROMICRO Conference, 1999. Proceedings. 25th, pp. 286 - 293 vol.2, 1999

[Chroust, 2002], G.Chroust, "System Properties under Composition", European Meeting on Cybernetics and Systems Research pp. 203-208, Vienna, April 2002.

[Chroust, 2006], Conversation with G.Chroust in Dissertation Privatissimum on 12/09/06, Austria, 2006.

[Chroust-Koppensteiner, 2006], G. Chroust and S. Koppensteiner, "Aspects of Software Project Management", SEA Publications of the Institute for Systems Engineering and Automation, J.Kepler Unoiversity Linz, 2006.

[Clements., 2002], Clements et al.: "Software Product Lines - Patterns and practices", Addison Wesley Professional, The SEI Series in Software Engineering., 2002.

[CMMI Product Team, 2001], CMMI Product Team, Capability Maturity Model® Integration (CMMI[SM]), Version 1.1, CMMI[SM] for Systems Engineering, Software Engineering, and Integrated Product and Process Development (CMMI-SE/SW/IPPD, V1.1), Carnegie Mellon SEI, December 2001.

[Coombs, 2003], P. Coombs, "IT Project Estimation, a practical guide to the costing of software", Cambridge University Press, Cambridge UK, 2003.

[Davis-Bersoff-Comer, 1988], A. Davis, E. Bersoff and E. Comer, "A Strategy for Comparing Alternative Software Development Life Cycle Models", , IEEE Transactions on Software Engineering, pp: 1453 -1461, 1988.

[DeMarco, 1997], T.DeMarco, "The Deadline", Dorset House, pp.247-260, New York 1997

[DeMarco, 2002], T. DeMarco, "Slack- Getting past Burnout, Busywork, and the Myth of Total Efficiency", Broadway Books, pp.45-53, New York 2002.

[Deutscher Normenausschuß, 1983], Deutscher Normenausschuß, DIN 69900, Netzplantechnik Deutscher Normenausschuß, Franfurt 1983.

[Doerner, 2003], D.Doerner, "Die Logik des Misslingens, Strategisches Denken in komplexen Situationen", Rohwohlt Taschenbuch Verlag, pp.62-63, Hamburg, 1989, 2003.

[Donohoe, 2006], P. Donohoe, "Introduction to Software Product Lines", 10th International Software Product Line Conference, Baltimore, USA, 2006.

[Ehrlich-Stampfel, 1990], W. Ehrlich, J. Stampfel, J. Wu., "Application of Software Reliability Modeling to Product Quality and Test Process", 12th International Conference on Software Engineering, proceedings pg.108-116,IEEE 1990.

[Eschelbeck, 2006], G. Eschelbeck, Private conversation with Gerhard Eschelbeck on 08/03/06, USA, 2006.

[Farlex, 2007], Keyword "Review", http://www.thefreedictionary.com , 2007.

[Fischermanns, 2006], G. Fischermanns, "Praxishandbuch Prozessmanagement", Band 9, Verlag Dr. Goetz Schmidt, Deutschland, 2006.

[Goldratt, 1997], E. Goldratt., "Critical Chain", The North River Press Publishing Corporation, Great Barrington MA, 1997.

[Gray-Larsen, 2006], C. Gray, E. Larson, "Projekt Management, the managerial process", McGraw-Hill Irwin, New York, 2006.

[Hanakawa-Morisaki, 1998], N. Hanakawa., S. Morisaki., K. Matsumoto, "A Learning Curve Based Simulation Model for Software Development",Proceedings of the 1998 (20th) International Conference on Software Engineering, pg.350-359, 1998.

[Heinrich-Roithmayr, 2004], L.Heinrich, A.Heinzl and F.Roithmayr, "Wirtschaftsinformatiklexikon", Oldenburg Verlag, Muenchen, 2004.

[Hoyer, 2007], C. Hoyer, "ProLISA, An Approach to the Specification of Product Line Software Architectures", Dissertation at Institute for Systems Engineering and Automation, Austria, 2007.

[Hsia-Hsu-Kung;1999], P. Hsia, C. Hsu and D. Kung, "Brooks' Law Revisited: A System Dynamics Approach", COMPSAC '99 Proceedings, pp370-375, 1999

[Hughes, 1996], R. Hughes, "Expert judgment as an estimating method", Information and Soft Technology, pp.67-75, 1996.

[Humphrey, 1989], W. Humphrey, "Managing the software process", SEI Series in Software Engineering, Addison Wesley, USA, 1989.

[Hunger, 2005], M. Hunger, "Erfahrungssicherung in IT- Projekten", DUV, Wiesbaden, Germany, 2005.

[IPMA, 2005], IPMA, IPMA website http://www.ipma.ch/?page=65517,2005.

[ISO 15288, 2002], ISO/IEC 15288: Information Technology-Life Cycle Management System- System Life Cycle Processes, Int. Org. for Standardization, ISO 15288, 2002

[ISO 15504, 1998], ISO/IEC 15504: Software Process Improvement and Capability Determination SPICE, Int. Org. for Standardization, ISO 15504, 1998.

[Jones, 1996], T Jones, Computer Volume 29, Issue 6, Pages: 92 – 94, USA, June 1996.

[Jones, 1998], T Capers Jones, "Estimating Software Costs", McGraw-Hill, New York, 1998.

[Koppensteiner-Udo, 2004], S.Koppensteiner and N.Udo, "How Agile Software Methodologies Influence the Role of the Project Manager", 19th IPMA conference ,June 2004.

[Krull, 2000],R. Krull, "Is More Beta Better?", Professional Communication Conference, 2000. Proceedings of 2000 Joint IEEE International and 18th Annual Conference on Computer Documentation (IPCC/SIGDOC 2000), pg:301 – 308, 2000.

[Lakhotia, 1999], A. Lakhotia, "Collate software maintenance statistics", website: http://www.cacs.louisiana.edu/~arun/projects/archive/maintenance-statistics.html, retrieved November 2006.

[Larman, 2004], C.Larman, "Agile & Iterative Development",Addison Wesley, USA, 2004.

[Litke, 1995], H. Litke, "Projekt Management, Methoden, Techniken, Verhaltensweisen", 3.Auflage, Carl Hanser Verlag –München, Wien, 1995.

[Litke, 1996], H. Litke, "DV-Projekt-management, Zeit und Kosten richtig einschätzen", Carl Hanser Verlag –München, Wien, 1996.

[Mendes-Counsell, 2000], E. Mendes and S. Counsell. "Web Development Effort Estimation using Analogy", Australian Software Engineering Conference, pg: 203 – 212, 2000.

[Mockus-Weiss, 2003], A. Mockus, D. Weiss and P. Zhang, "Understanding and Predicting Effort in Software Projects", 25th International Conference on Software Engineering, pg:274 – 284, 2003.

[Montana-Charnov, 2000], P. Montana and B. Charnov, "Management", Barron's Educational Series Inc., New York, USA, 2000.

[Muranko-Drechsler, 2006], B. Muranko and R. Drechsler, "Technical Documentation of Software and Hardware in Embedded Systems", 14th IFIP International Conference on Very Large Scale Integration VLSI-SoC, Nice France, 2006.

[Ning, 1997], J. Ning, „Component- Based Software Engineering", Fifth International Symposium on Assessment of Software Tools and Techniques, Pittsburgh, USA, 1997.

[Ossimitz, 2000], G. Ossimitz, "Entwicklung systemischen Denkens", Profil Verlag GmbH, Germany, 2000.

[Parnas, 1976], Parnas," On The Design and Development of Program Families", IEEE Transactions on Software Engineering, vol. SE-2, No.1 (March 1976), 1976.

[PDMA, 2006], Product development and management association, Terms from glossary for new product development retrieved from http://www.pdma.org/library/glossary.html, United States, 2006.

[Pennypacker-Dye, 1999], J. Pennypacker and L. Dye.," Project Portfolio Management", Center for Business Practices, 1999.

[Perreault-McCarthy, 1997], W. Perreault and E. McCarthy, "Essentials of Marketing, A Global Managerial Approach", pp.224-226 ,IRWIN, 1997.

[Philips-Bothell, 2002], J.J. Phillips, T. Bothell, G. Snead, "The project management score card", pp.3-11, Butterworth-Heinemann, 2002.

[PMI 2000], Project Management Institute, "A guide to the project management body of knowledge (PMBOK® Guide) ,Newtown Square, PA, 2000.

[PMI 2002], Project Management Institute, "Practice Standard for Work Breakdown Structures", PMI,2002.

[PMI 2004], Project Management Institute, "A guide to the project management body of knowledge (PMBOK® Guide) ,Newtown Square, PA, 2004.

[PMI 2005], PMI, PMI-website, http://www.pmi.org/info/AP_IntroOverview.asp?nav=0201, 2005.

[Raccoon, 1997], B. Raccoon, "Fifty Years of Progress in Software Engineering", ACM SIGSOFT Software Engineering Notes vol 22 no 1 Page 88, USA, January 1997.

[Royce, 1987], W. Royce, "Managing the development of large software systems", Proceedings of the 9th international conference on software engineering, pp.328-338, Monterey, California, United States, 1987.

[Saliu -Ahmed, 2004], M. Saliu., M. Ahmed and J. AlGhamdi, "Towards Adaptive Soft Computing Based Software Effort Prediction", IEEE Annual Meeting of the Fuzzy Information,pg.16-21,Volume 1, 2004.

[SearchSMB, 2003], SearchSMB.com, "Definition for timeline", retrieved from http://searchsmb.techtarget.com/sDefinition/0,,sid44_gci214199,00.html, 2003.

[Senge, 1994], P. Senge, "The Fifth Discipline, The Art & Practice of the Learning Organization", Currency and Doubleday, New York, USA, 1994.

[Sterman, 2000], J. Sterman, "Business Dynamics, Systems Thinking and Modeling for a Complex World", McGraw-Hill, 2000.

[Schwaber- Beedle, 2002], K. Schwaber and M. Beedle, "Agile Software Development with Scrum", Prentice Hall, pp TBD, New Jersey 2002.

[Schwaber, 2004], K. Schwaber, "Agile Project Management with Scrum", Microsoft Press, USA, 2004.

[SoftwareMag, 2004], Software Mag.com, "Standish: Project Success Rates Improved Over 10 Years", website. http://www.softwaremag.com/L.cfm?Doc=newsletter/2004-01-15/Standish, 2004.

[Softwareproductlines, 2007], Softwareproductlines.com, website:: www.softwareproductlines.com , 2007.

[Standish, 1994],Standish Group, "The Standish Group Report", website, http://www.projectsmart.co.uk/docs/chaos_report.pdf, 1994.

[Standish, 2001], Standish Group, "Extreme Chaos", website, http://www.standishgroup.com/sample_research/PDFpages/extreme_chaos.pdf , 2001.

[Standish, 2004], Standish Group, "2004 Third Quarter Research Report", website, http://www.standishgroup.com/sample_research/PDFpages/q3-spotlight.pdf, 2004.

[Tadayon, 2005], N. Tadayon, "Neural Network Approach for Software Cost Estimation", International Conference on Coding and Computing,Volume 2, pg: 815 – 818, 2005

[Tan-Mookerjee, 2005], Y. Tan. and V. Mookerjee., "Comparing uniform and flexible policies for software maintenance and replacement", Software Engineering, IEEE Transactions Volume 31, Issue 3, March 2005 pg:238 – 255, 2005.

[The Spire Partner, 2000], The Spire Partner, The European Community, "The SPIRE Handbook, Better, Faster, Cheaper Software Development in Small Organizations", version 2, Centre for Software Engineering Ltd, Ireland, 2000.

[Udo-Koppensteiner, 2003], N. Udo and S. Koppensteiner, "Will Agile Development change the Way we manage Software Projects, Agile from a PMBOK Guide Perspective", 2003 PMI Global Congress, Baltimore 2003.

[Vensim, 2004], Ventana Systems, Inc., "Vensim ®Version 5 Documentation", USA, 1989-2004.

[Verzuh, 1999], E. Verzuh., "The Fast Forward MBA in Project Management", Wiley & sons, Canada, 1999.

[Wikipedia:prototype, 2006], Key word "Prototype", website:http://en.wikipedia.org/wiki/, 2006.

[Wikipedia:time, 2006], Keyword "Time", website:http://en.wikipedia.org/wiki/, 2006.

[Wikipedia:revenue, 2006], Keyword "Revenue", website:http://en.wikipedia.org/wiki/, 2006.

[Wikipedia:router, 2006] Keyword "Router", website:http://en.wikipedia.org/wiki/, 2006.

[Wikipedia:world wide web, 2006] Keyword "World Wide Web", website:http://en.wikipedia.org/wiki/, 2006.

[Wilson, 2001], L. Wilson, „Software Development Industry Standard", SBTDC, from www.sbtdc.org/pdf/software.pdf, retrieved on 12/15/06, 2001.

223

Appendix A: Systems Dynamics Model for a Waterfall Model

A1: Stock and Flow Diagrams

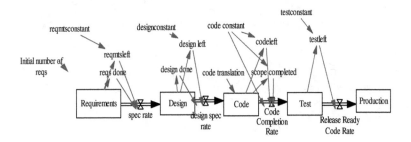

Figure A1.1: Systems dynamics model for a waterfall type model for scenario "Ideal World".

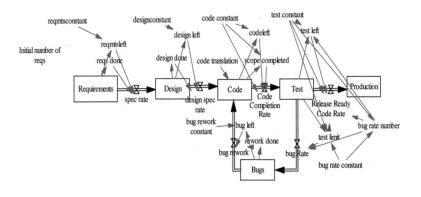

Figure A1.2: Systems dynamics model for a waterfall type model for scenario "Code Error Detection".

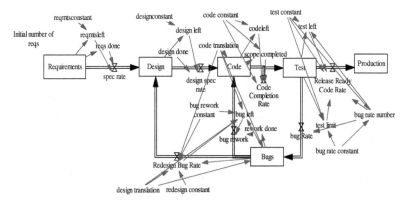

Figure A1.3: Systems dynamics model for a waterfall type model for scenario "Design Error Detection".

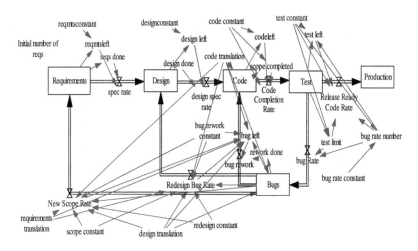

Figure A1.4: Systems dynamics model for a waterfall type model for scenario "Requirements Creep".

A2: Source Code for a Systems Dynamics Model for a Waterfall Type Model

Figures A2.1 to A2.4 list the code that was generated by Vensim [Vensim, 2004], a simulation software tool for systems dynamics models. Vensim uses a graphical interface were the stock and flow parameters are defined and the formulas are edited through a dialog box. When simulating a systems dynamics model, Vensim generates the code. In Chapter 5 we focus our explanations on how these models simulate the software methodologies. We focus on the parameter used to create and influence the behavior of the software model. Other auxiliary variables are needed to make these models work. Consequently there are some variables listed in the code and shown in the Figures A1.1 to A1.4 that were defined to create positive results of the simulations. As an example all stock variables have to stay positive as there are no negative requirements, design, code or test existing in the real world.

As we proceeded with our simulations we discovered that we used non-descriptive names for some parameters. Table 5.1 (page 105) lists the descriptive names and the non-descriptive names that were used for the systems dynamics models.

We developed these models in steps. We started with the basic model representing the most idealistic scenario "Ideal World" and successive developed the next more complex model for the scenarios "Code Error Detection", "Design Error Detection", and "Requirements Creep". Consequently the code listed in this chapter becomes more complex and increases in size with each scenario.

Figure A2.1 lists the code for the systems dynamic model that we created for the scenario "Ideal World".

```
Waterfall, Scenario "Ideal World"
(01)   Code= INTEG ((design spec rate* code
       translation) - Code Completion Rate ,0)
       Units: LoC [0,?]
(02)   Code Completion Rate=IF THEN
       ELSE(scope completed, code constant,
       codeleft)
       Units: LoC/Week [0,3000]
(03)   code constant=1500
       Units: LoC
(04)   code translation=1000
       Units: LoC/Documents [0,10000]
(05)   codeleft=IF THEN ELSE(Code<code
       constant, Code , code constant)
       Units: LoC
(06)   Design= INTEG (spec rate-design spec
       rate,0)
       Units: Documents [0,?]
(07)   design done=
       IF THEN ELSE(Design<= 0, 1 , 0)
       Units: Dmnl
(08)   design left=IF THEN
       ELSE(Design<designconstant, Design ,
       designconstant)
       Units: Documents
(09)   design spec rate=IF THEN ELSE(design
       done, 0 , design left)
       Units: Documents/Week
(10)   designconstant=2
       Units: Documents
(11)   FINAL TIME  = 200
       Units: Week
       The final time for the simulation.
(12)   Initial number of reqs=100
       Units: Documents
(13)   INITIAL TIME  = 0
       Units: Week
       The initial time for the simulation.
(14)   Production= INTEG (Release Ready Code
       Rate, 0)
       Units: LoC
(15)   Release Ready Code Rate= testleft
       Units: LoC/Week

(16)   reqmtsconstant=4
       Units: Documents
(17)   reqmtsleft=IF THEN
       ELSE(Requirements<reqmtsconstant,
       Requirements , reqmtsconstant)
       Units: Documents
(18)   reqs done=
       IF THEN ELSE(Requirements<= 0, 1 , 0)
       Units: Dmnl
(19)   Requirements= INTEG (
       -spec rate , Initial number of reqs)
       Units: Documents [0,100,1]
(20)   SAVEPER  =
            TIME STEP
       Units: Week [0,?]
       The frequency with which output is
       stored.
(21)   scope completed=
       IF THEN ELSE(Code >=code constant,
       1,0)
       Units: Dmnl
(22)   spec rate=
       IF THEN ELSE(reqs done, 0 ,reqmtsleft)
       Units: Documents/Week
(23)   Test= INTEG (
       Code Completion Rate-Release Ready
       Code Rate ,0)
       Units: LoC
(24)   testconstant=1030
       Units: LoC
(25)   testleft=IF THEN
       ELSE(Test>=testconstant, testconstant,
       Test)
       Units: LoC
(26)   TIME STEP  = 1
       Units: Week [0,?]
       The time step for the simulation.
```

Figure A2.1: Source code of a systems dynamics model for a waterfall type model for scenario "Ideal World".

Figure A2.2 lists the code for the systems dynamic model that we created for the scenario "Code Error Detection".

Waterfall: Scenario "Code Error Detection"

(01) bug left=IF THEN ELSE(Bugs<bug rework constant, Bugs , bug rework constant)
Units: LoC

(02) bug Rate=IF THEN ELSE(test limit, bug rate number, 0)
Units: LoC

(03) bug rate constant=0.3
Units: Percentage

(04) bug rate number=bug rate constant*test constant
Units: LoC

(05) bug rework=IF THEN ELSE(rework done, 0, bug left)
Units: LoC

(06) bug rework constant=200
Units: LoC

(07) Bugs= INTEG ((bug Rate-bug rework),0)
Units: Bugs

(08) Code= INTEG ((design spec rate* code translation) - Code Completion Rate + bug rework,0)
Units: LoC [0,?]

(09) Code Completion Rate=IF THEN ELSE(scope completed, code constant, codeleft)
Units: LoC/Week [0,3000]

(10) code constant=1500
Units: LoC

(11) code translation=1000
Units: LoC/Documents [0,10000]

(12) codeleft=IF THEN ELSE(Code<code constant, Code , code constant)
Units: LoC

(13) Design= INTEG (spec rate-design spec rate,0)
Units: Documents [0,?]

(14) design done=IF THEN ELSE(Design<= 0, 1 , 0)
Units: Dmnl

(15) design left=IF THEN ELSE(Design<designconstant, Design , designconstant)
Units: Documents

(16) design spec rate=
IF THEN ELSE(design done, 0 , design left)
Units: Documents/Week

(17) designconstant=2
Units: Documents

(18) FINAL TIME = 200
Units: Week
The final time for the simulation.

(19) Initial number of reqs=100
Units: Documents

(20) INITIAL TIME = 0
Units: Week
The initial time for the simulation.

(21) Production= INTEG (Release Ready Code Rate,0)
Units: **undefined**

(22) Release Ready Code Rate=IF THEN ELSE(test limit, test constant-bug rate number, test left)
Units: LoC/Week

(23) reqmtsconstant=4
Units: **undefined**

(24) reqmtsleft=IF THEN ELSE(Requirements<reqmtsconstant, Requirements , reqmtsconstant)
Units: Documents

(25) reqs done=
IF THEN ELSE(Requirements<= 0, 1 , 0)
Units: Dmnl

(26) Requirements= INTEG (-spec rate , Initial number of reqs)
Units: Documents [0,100,1]

(27) rework done=
IF THEN ELSE((Bugs)<=0, 1 , 0)
Units: Dmnl

(28) SAVEPER =
        TIME STEP
Units: Week [0,?]
The frequency with which output is stored.

(29) scope completed=IF THEN ELSE(Code >=code constant, 1,0)
Units: Dmnl

(30) spec rate=IF THEN ELSE(reqs done, 0 ,reqmtsleft)
Units: Documents/Week

(31) Test= INTEG (Code Completion Rate-Release Ready Code Rate -bug Rate,0)
Units: LoC

(32) test constant=1030
Units: LoC

(33) test left=IF THEN ELSE(Test>=test constant, test constant-bug rate number,Test)
Units: LoC

(34) test limit=IF THEN ELSE(Test <(test constant), 0,1)
Units: Dmnl

(35) TIME STEP = 1
Units: Week [0,?]
The time step for the simulation.

Figure A2.2: Source code of a systems dynamics model for a waterfall type model for scenario "Code Error Detection".

Figure A2.3lists the code for the systems dynamic model that we created for the scenario "Design Error Detection".

```
Waterfall, Scenario "Design Error Detection"
(01)    bug left=
        IF THEN ELSE(Bugs<bug rework constant-
        Redesign Bug Rate*code translation/
        design translation, Bugs-Redesign Bug Rate*code
        translation/design translation, bug rework constant-
        Redesign Bug Rate*code translation/design
        translation)
        Units: LoC
(02)    bug Rate=
        IF THEN ELSE(test limit, bug rate number, 0)
        Units: LoC
(03)    bug rate constant=0.3
        Units: Percentage
(04)    bug rate number=
        bug rate constant*test constant
        Units: LoC
(05)    bug rework=
        IF THEN ELSE(rework done, 0, bug left)
        Units: LoC
(06)    bug rework constant=200
        Units: LoC
(07)    Bugs= INTEG ((bug Rate-bug rework-Redesign
        Bug Rate*code translation/design translation),0)
        Units: Bugs
(08)    Code= INTEG (
        (design spec rate* code translation) - Code
        Completion Rate + bug rework,0)
        Units: LoC [0,?]
(09)    Code Completion Rate=
        IF THEN ELSE(scope completed, code constant,
        codeleft)
        Units: LoC/Week [0,3000]
(10)    code constant=1500
        Units: LoC
(11)    code translation=1000
        Units: LoC/Documents [0,10000]
(12)    codeleft=
        IF THEN ELSE(Code<code constant, Code , code
        constant)
        Units: LoC
(13)    Design= INTEG (spec rate-design spec
        rate+Redesign Bug Rate,0)
        Units: Documents [0,?]
(14)    design done=IF THEN ELSE(Design<= 0, 1 ,
0)
        Units: Dmnl
(15)    design left=IF THEN
        ELSE(Design<designconstant, Design
        designconstant)
        Units: Documents
(16)    design spec rate=IF THEN ELSE(design done, 0 ,
        design left)
        Units: Documents/Week
(17)    design translation=10
        Units: LoC
(18)    designconstant=2
        Units: Documents
(19)    FINAL TIME  = 250
        Units: Week
        The final time for the simulation.
(20)    Initial number of reqs=100
        Units: Documents
(21)    INITIAL TIME  = 0
        Units: Week
        The initial time for the simulation.
(22)    Production= INTEG (Release Ready Code
        Rate,0)
        Units: **undefined**
(23)    Redesign Bug Rate=IF THEN ELSE(
        Bugs>bug rework constant, redesign
        constant*bug rework constant*design
        translation/code translation, 0)
        Units: **undefined**
(24)    redesign constant=0.05
        Units: **undefined**
(25)    Release Ready Code Rate=
        IF THEN ELSE(test limit, test constant-bug
rate number, test left)
        Units: LoC/Week
(26)    reqmtsconstant=4
        Units: **undefined**
(27)    reqmtsleft=IF THEN
        ELSE(Requirements<reqmtsconstant,
        Requirements , reqmtsconstant)
        Units: Documents
(28)    reqs done=IF THEN ELSE(Requirements<= 0, 1
, 0)
        Units: Dmnl
(29)    Requirements= INTEG (-spec rate ,Initial number
        of reqs)
        Units: Documents [0,100,1]
(30)    rework done=IF THEN ELSE(Bugs<=0, 1 , 0
)
        Units: Dmnl
(31)    SAVEPER  =         TIME STEP
        Units: Week [0,?]
        The frequency with which output is stored.
(32)    scope completed=IF THEN ELSE(Code >=code
        constant, 1 , 0)
        Units: Dmnl
(33)    spec rate=IF THEN ELSE(reqs done, 0
        ,reqmtsleft)
        Units: Documents/Week
(34)    Test= INTEG (Code Completion Rate-Release
        Ready Code Rate -bug Rate,0)
        Units: LoC
(35)    test constant=1030
        Units: LoC
(36)    test left=IF THEN ELSE(Test>=test constant,
        test constant-bug rate number,Test)
        Units: LoC
(37)    test limit=
        IF THEN ELSE(Test < (test constant), 0,1)
        Units: Dmnl
(38)    TIME STEP  = 1
        Units: Week [0,?]
        The time step for the simulation.
```

Figure A2.3: Source code of a systems dynamics model for a waterfall type model for scenario "Design Error Detection".

229

Figure A2.4 lists the code for the systems dynamic model that we created for the scenario "Requirements Creep".

Waterfall, Scenario "Requirements Creep"

(01) bug left=IF THEN ELSE(Bugs<bug rework constant-
(Redesign Bug Rate*code translation
/design translation)-(New Scope Rate*code
translation
/requirements translation), Bugs, bug rework constant-
(Redesign Bug Rate*code translation/design translation)
-(New Scope Rate*code translation/requirements
translation))
Units: LoC

(02) bug Rate=
IF THEN ELSE(test limit, bug rate number, 0)
Units: LoC

(03) bug rate constant=0.3
Units: Percentage

(04) bug rate number=bug rate constant*test constant
Units: LoC

(05) bug rework=IF THEN ELSE(rework done, 0, bug
left)
Units: LoC

(06) bug rework constant=200
Units: LoC

(07) Bugs= INTEG (bug Rate-bug rework-(Redesign Bug
Rate*code translation/design translation)-(New Scope
Rate*code translation/design translation),0)
Units: Bugs

(08) Code= INTEG ((design spec rate* code translation) -
Code Completion Rate + bug rework,0)
Units: LoC [0,?]

(09) Code Completion Rate=IF THEN ELSE(scope
completed, code constant, codeleft)
Units: LoC/Week [0,3000]

(10) code constant=1500
Units: LoC

(11) code translation=1000
Units: LoC/Documents [0,10000]

(12) codeleft=IF THEN ELSE(Code<code constant, Code ,
code constant)
Units: LoC

(13) Design= INTEG (spec rate-design spec rate+Redesign
Bug Rate,0)
Units: Documents [0,?]

(14) design done=IF THEN ELSE(Design<= 0, 1 , 0)
Units: Dmnl

(15) design left=IF THEN ELSE(Design<designconstant,
Design , designconstant)
Units: Documents

(16) design spec rate=IF THEN ELSE(design done, 0 ,
design left)
Units: Documents/Week

(17) design translation=10
Units: LoC

(18) designconstant=2
Units: Documents

(19) FINAL TIME = 300
Units: Week
The final time for the simulation.

(20) Initial number of reqs=100
Units: Documents

(21) INITIAL TIME = 0
Units: Week
The initial time for the simulation.

(22) New Scope Rate=IF THEN ELSE(Bugs >= bug rework
constant, scope constant*bug rework
constant*requirements translation/code translation,0)
Units: **undefined**
Units: **undefined**

(23) Production= INTEG (
Release Ready Code Rate,0)
Units: **undefined**

(24) Redesign Bug Rate=IF THEN ELSE(
Bugs>=bug rework constant, redesign
constant*bug rework constant
*design translation/code translation , 0)

(25) redesign constant=0.05
Units: **undefined**

(26) Release Ready Code Rate=I
F THEN ELSE(test limit, test constant-bug rate
number, test left)
Units: LoC/Week

(27) reqmtsconstant=4
Units: **undefined**

(28) reqmtsleft=IF THEN
ELSE(Requirements<reqmtsconstant,
Requirements , reqmtsconstant)
Units: Documents

(29) reqs done=IF THEN ELSE(Requirements<= 0,
1 , 0)
Units: Dmnl

(30) Requirements= INTEG (-spec rate+New Scope
Rate,
Initial number of reqs)
Units: Documents [0,100,1]

(31) requirements translation=10
Units: **undefined**

(32) rework done=
IF THEN ELSE(Bugs<=0, 1 , 0)
Units: Dmnl

(33) SAVEPER =   TIME STEP
Units: Week [0,?]
The frequency with which output is stored.

(34) scope completed=
IF THEN ELSE(Code >=code constant, 1,0)
Units: Dmnl

(35) scope constant=0.05
Units: **undefined**

(36) spec rate=
IF THEN ELSE(reqs done, 0 ,reqmtsleft)
Units: Documents/Week

(37) Test= INTEG (Code Completion Rate-Release
Ready Code Rate -bug Rate,0)
Units: LoC

(38) test constant=1030
Units: LoC

(39) test left=IF THEN ELSE(Test>=test constant,
test constant-bug rate number,Test)
Units: LoC

(40) test limit=
IF THEN ELSE(Test < (test constant), 0,1)
Units: Dmnl

(41) TIME STEP = 1
Units: Week [0,?]
The time step for the simulation.

Figure A2.4: Source code of a systems dynamics model for a waterfall type model for scenario "Requirements Creep".

A3: Simulations Variations

In theory all the parameters listed in Table 5.1 (page 105) can be modified to run simulations with these models. In order to identify the influence of key variables on the outcome of our models we use the values stated as in Table 5.1 (page 105) and modify one key parameter at a time.

We use the systems dynamics model we developed for the most realistic scenario "Requirements Creep" for our simulations.

Variations of Design Rework

We change the *percentage of design bugs* ("Redesign Portion") to evaluate what impact it has on Production. Table A3.1 lists the results for these simulations. Figure A3.1 shows the result for the stock variable "Production".

Redesign Portion [Percent]	5	10	15
Duration [months]	47	48	48.3
Effort [person months]	187	190	192
Cost [$]	1,795,200	1,824,000	1,843,200
Size of end product [LoC]	106,000	109,000	112,000

Table A3.1: Results for variations of "Redesign Portion".

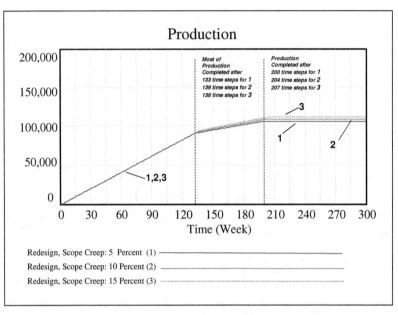

Figure A3.1: Results for variations of "Redesign Portion" and "Scope Creep Portion".

Variations of Requirements

We vary the amount of requirements that are added to the original scope ("Scope Creep Portion".

Scope Creep Portion [Percent]	5	10	15
Duration [months]	47	48	48.3
Effort [person months]	187	190	192
Cost [$]	1,795,200	1,824,000	1,843,200
Size of end product [LoC]	106,000	109,000	112,000

Table A3.2: Results for variations of "Redesign Portion".

Changes of "Scope Creep Portion" influence the outcome in the same way as the changes for "Redesign Portion" and produce identical results. Figure A3.1 represents also the results for the simulations of "Scope Creep Portion".

Variations of Code

Next we vary the value for the speed of code creation ("Code Generation Speed").The results are listed in Table A3.3.

Code Generation Speed [LoC]	1000	1500	3000
Duration [months]	47	47	47
Effort [person months]	187	187	187
Cost [$]	1,795,200	1,795,200	1,795,200
Size of end product [LoC]	106,000	106,000	106,000

Table A3.3: Results for variations of "Code Generation Speed".

All three simulation runs show the same results. As long as testing is processing slower or at the same speed as implementation an increase in coding has no influence on decreasing the project duration. The results are identical to the results of scenario "Requirements Creep" (see Figure 5. 30 in Chapter 5.6).

Variations of Test

We vary the value for the speed of testing ("Test Generation Speed").The results are listed in Table A3.4. Figure A3.2 shows the results in graphical format.

Test Generation Speed [LoC]	750	1000	1500
Duration [months]	52	47	43
Effort [person months]	240	187	143
Cost [$]	2,304,000	1,795,200	1,372,800
Size of end product [LoC]	106,300	106,000	105,000

Table A3.4: Results for variations of "Test Generation Speed".

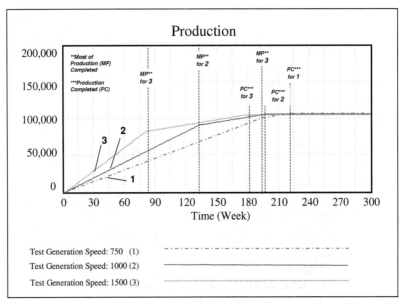

Figure A3.2: Results for variations of "Test Generation Speed".

Testing has a direct influence on the outcome of the project. When more code is tested per time step the project can complete earlier. Only code that has been developed can be tested. Increasing the test speed beyond the coding speed will result in testing resources that wait for code to be completed.

Variations of Change

We vary the value for the bug rate that is detected during development ("Bug Rate Portion").The results are listed in Table A3.5. Figure A3.3 shows the results in graphical format.

Bug Rate Portion [Percent]	25	30	35
Duration [months]	39	47	54
Effort [person months]	171	187	201
Cost [$]	1,641,600	1,795,200	1,929,000
Size of end product [LoC]	105,000	106,000	107,000

Table A3.5: Results for variations of "Bug Rate Portion".

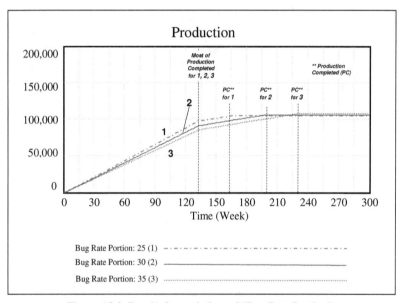

Figure A3.3: Results for variations of "Bug Rate Portion".

The results in Table A3.5 show that an increase in defect rate has a high influence on when the product will be available.

Variations of Bug Rework

We vary the value for how much code can be fixed per time step ("Bug Rework Portion").The results are listed in Table A3.5. Figure A3.4 shows the results in graphical format.

235

Bug Rework Portion [Percent]	150	200	300
Duration [months]	58	47	37
Effort [person months]	203	187	184
Cost [$]	1,948,800	1,795,200	1,766,400
Size of end product [LoC]	105,000	106,000	107,000

Table A3.6: Results for variations of "Bug Rework Portion".

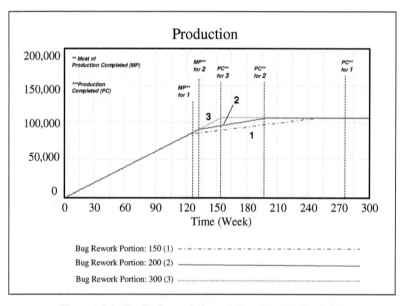

Figure A3.4: Results for variations of "Bug Rework Portion".

The results in Table A3.6 show that increasing the amount of code fixes helps to reduce the project duration. As a side effect more code errors might be introduced as more code is fixed at a given time step. This could lead to an increase in the amount of code for the end product.

236

Appendix B: Systems Dynamics Model for a Spiral Type Model

B1: Stock and Flow Diagrams

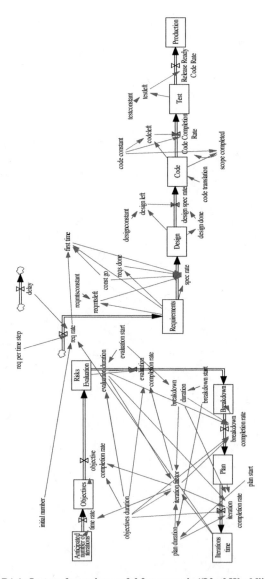

Figure B1.1: System dynamics model for scenario "Ideal World" of a spiral type.

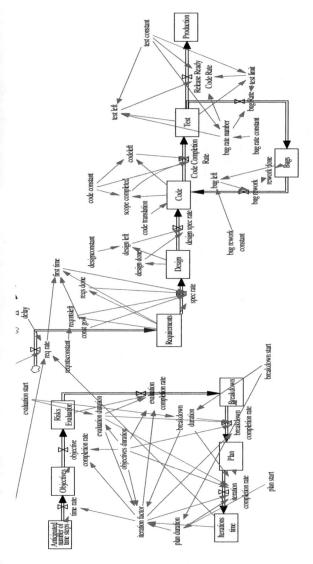

Figure B1.2: System dynamics model for scenario "Code Error Detection" of a spiral type model.

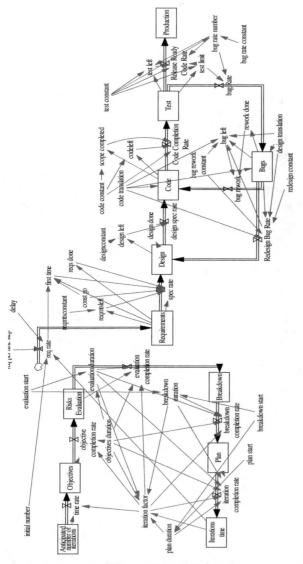

Figure B1.3: System dynamics model for scenario "Design Error Detection" of a spiral type model.

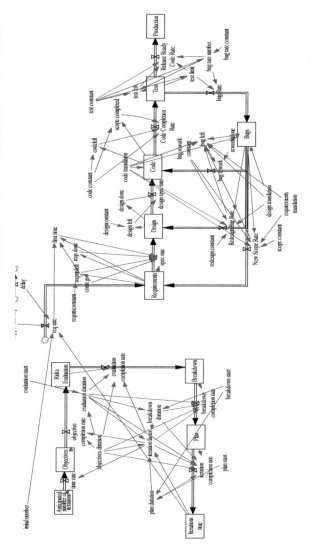

Figure B1.4: System dynamics model for scenario "Requirements Creep" of a spiral.

B2: Source Code for a Systems Dynamics Model for a Spiral Type Model

Figures B2.1 to B2.4 list the code that was generated by Vensim [Vensim, 2004], a simulation software tool for systems dynamics models. Vensim uses a graphical interface were the stock and flow parameters are defined and the formulas are edited through a dialog box. When simulating a systems dynamics model, Vensim generates the code. In Chapter 6 we focus our explanations on how these models simulate the software methodologies. We focus on the parameter used to create and influence the behavior of the software model. Other variables are needed to make these models work. Consequently there are some variables listed in the code and shown in the Figures B1.1 to B1.4 that were defined to create positive results of the simulations. As an example all stock variables have to stay positive as there are no negative requirements, design, code or test existing in the real world.

As we proceeded with our simulations we discovered that we used non-descriptive names for some parameters. Table 6.1 (page 145) lists the descriptive names and the non-descriptive names that were used for the systems dynamics models.

We developed these models in steps. We started with the basic model representing the most idealistic scenario "Ideal World" and successive developed the next more complex model for the scenarios "Code Error Detection", "Design Error Detection", and "Requirements Creep". Consequently the code listed in this chapter becomes more complex and increases in size with each scenario.

Figure B2.1 lists the code for the systems dynamic model that we created for the scenario "Ideal World".

```
Spiral, Scenario "Ideal World"
(01)    Anticipated number of iterations= INTEG (
        -time rate,initial number)
        Units: **undefined**
(02)    Breakdown= INTEG (
        +evaluation completion rate-breakdown
        completion rate, 0)
        Units: **undefined**
(03)    breakdown completion rate=
        IF THEN ELSE(Breakdown>0,
        PULSE(iteration factor+objectives
        duration+evaluation duration
        +breakdown duration, 1) , 0 )
        Units: **undefined**
(04)    breakdown duration=
        breakdown start-evaluation start
        Units: **undefined**
(05)    breakdown start=8
        Units: **undefined**
(06)    Code= INTEG (
        (design spec rate* code translation) - Code
        Completion Rate , 0)
        Units: LoC [0,?]
(07)    Code Completion Rate=
        IF THEN ELSE(scope completed, code
        constant, codeleft)
        Units: LoC/Week [0,3000]
(08)    code constant=1500
        Units: LoC
(09)    code translation=1000
        Units: LoC/Documents [0,10000]
(10)    codeleft= IF THEN ELSE(Code<code
        constant, Code , code constant)
        Units: LoC
(11)    const go=100
        Units: **undefined**
(12)    delay=PULSE(0, 1 )
        Units: **undefined**
(13)    Design = INTEG (
        spec rate -design spec rate,0)
        Units: Documents [0,?]
(14)    design done=
        IF THEN ELSE(Design<= 0, 1 , 0)
        Units: Dmnl
(15)    design left= IF THEN
        ELSE(Design<designconstant, Design ,
        designconstant)
        Units: Documents
(16)    design spec rate=
        IF THEN ELSE(design done, 0 , design left)
        Units: Documents/Week

((17)   designconstant=4
        Units: Documents
(18)    evaluation completion rate=
        IF THEN ELSE(Risks Evaluation>0,
        PULSE(iteration factor+objectives
        duration+evaluation duration, 1), 0 )
        Units: **undefined**
(19)    evaluation duration=
        evaluation start-objectives duration
        Units: **undefined**
(20)    evaluation start=5
        Units: **undefined**
(21)    FINAL TIME  = 200
        Units: Week
        The final time for the simulation.
(22)    first time=
        IF THEN ELSE(Requirements>const
        go:OR:(req rate=0:AND:Requirements>0
        ),const go, 0)
        Units: Documents
(23)    initial number=5
        Units: **undefined**
(24)    INITIAL TIME  = 0
        Units: Week
        The initial time for the simulation.
(25)    iteration completion rate=
        IF THEN ELSE(Plan>0, PULSE(iteration
        factor+objectives duration+evaluation
        duration+breakdown duration+plan
        duration, 1 ) , 0 )
        Units: **undefined**
(26)    iteration factor=
        Iterations time*(objectives
        duration+evaluation duration+breakdown
        duration+plan duration)
        Units: **undefined**
(27)    Iterations time= INTEG (
        iteration completion rate,0)
        Units: **undefined**
(28)    objective completion rate=
        IF THEN ELSE(Objectives>0,
        PULSE(objectives duration+iteration
        factor, 1) , 0)
        Units: **undefined**
(29)    Objectives= INTEG (
        -objective completion rate+time rate,0)
        Units: **undefined**
(30)    objectives duration=2
        Units: **undefined**
```

(31) Plan= INTEG (breakdown completion rate-
iteration completion rate, 0)
Units: **undefined**
(32) plan duration= plan start-breakdown start
Units: **undefined**
(33) plan start=10
Units: **undefined**
(34) Production= INTEG (Release Ready Code
Rate, 0)
Units: LoC
(35) Release Ready Code Rate=testleft
Units: LoC/Week
(36) req per time step=2
Units: **undefined**
(37) req rate= IF THEN ELSE(Iterations
time<initial number:AND:delay=0, req per
time step,0)
Units: **undefined**
(38) reqmtsconstant=6
Units: **undefined**
(39) reqmtsleft=IF THEN
ELSE(Requirements<reqmtsconstant,
Requirements , reqmtsconstant)
Units: Documents
(40) reqs done= IF THEN
ELSE(Requirements<= 0, 1 , 0)
Units: Dmnl
(41) Requirements= INTEG (
req rate -spec rate,0)
Units: **undefined**
(42) Risks Evaluation= INTEG (+objective
completion rate-evaluation completion rate,
0)
Units: **undefined**
(43) SAVEPER = TIME STEP
Units: Week [0,?]
The frequency with which output is stored.
(44) scope completed= IF THEN ELSE(Code
>=code constant, 1,0)
Units: Dmnl
(45) spec rate= IF THEN
ELSE(Requirements>const go
:OR:(Requirements<=const go :AND: :NOT:
reqs done:AND:first time=const go)
,reqmtsleft, 0)
Units: **undefined**
(46) Test= INTEG (Code Completion Rate-
Release Ready Code Rate ,0)
Units: LoC
(47) testconstant=1030
Units: LoC

(48) testleft= IF THEN
ELSE(Test>=testconstant, testconstant,
Test)
Units: LoC
(49) time rate= IF THEN ELSE(Anticipated
number of iterations>0, PULSE(iteration
factor+1
, 1) , 0)
Units: **undefined**
(50) TIME STEP = 1
Units: Week [0,?]
The time step for the simulation.

Figure B2.1: Source code of a systems dynamics model for a spiral type model for scenario "Ideal World".

Figure B2.2 lists the code for the systems dynamic model that we created for the scenario "Code Error Detection".

Spiral, Scenario "Code Error Detection"

(01) Anticipated number of time steps= INTEG (
-time rate,initial number)
Units: **undefined**

(02) Breakdown= INTEG (+evaluation
completion rate-breakdown completion rate,
0)
Units: **undefined**

(03) breakdown completion rate=IF THEN
ELSE(Breakdown>0, PULSE(iteration
factor+objectives duration+evaluation
duration+breakdown duration, 1) , 0)
Units: **undefined**

(04) breakdown duration=breakdown start-
evaluation start
Units: **undefined**

(05) breakdown start=8
Units: **undefined**

(06) bug left=IF THEN ELSE(Bugs<bug rework
constant, Bugs , bug rework constant)
Units: LoC

(07) bug Rate= IF THEN ELSE(test limit, bug
rate number, 0)
Units: LoC

(08) bug rate constant=0.3
Units: Percentage

(09) bug rate number= bug rate constant*test
constant
Units: LoC

(10) bug rework=IF THEN ELSE(rework done, 0,
bug left)
Units: LoC

(11) bug rework constant=200
Units: LoC

(12) Bugs= INTEG ((bug Rate-bug rework),0)
Units: Bugs

(13) Code = INTEG ((design spec rate* code
translation) - Code Completion Rate + bug
rework,0)
Units: LoC [0,?]

(14) Code Completion Rate =
IF THEN ELSE(scope completed, code
constant, codeleft)
Units: LoC/Week [0,3000]

(15) code constant=1500
Units: LoC

(16) code translation =1000
Units: LoC/Documents [0,10000]

(17) codeleft =IF THEN ELSE(Code<code
constant, Code , code constant)
Units: LoC

(18) const go=100

(19) delay=PULSE(0, 1)
Units: **undefined**

(20) Design= INTEG (spec rate -design spec
rate, 0)
Units: Documents [0,?]

(21) design done =IF THEN ELSE(Design<=
0, 1 , 0)
Units: Dmnl

(22) design left =
IF THEN ELSE(Design<designconstant,
Design , designconstant)
Units: Documents

(23) design spec rate =
IF THEN ELSE(design done, 0 , design
left)
Units: Documents/Week

(24) designconstant=4
Units: Documents

(25) evaluation completion rate=
IF THEN ELSE(Risks Evaluation>0,
PULSE(iteration factor+objectives
duration
+evaluation duration, 1), 0)
Units: **undefined**

(26) evaluation duration=
evaluation start-objectives duration
Units: **undefined**

(27) evaluation start=5
Units: **undefined**

(28) FINAL TIME = 300
Units: Week
The final time for the simulation.

(29) first time=
IF THEN ELSE(Requirements>const
go:OR:(req rate=0:AND:Requirements>0
),const go, 0)
Units: Documents

(30) initial number=5
Units: **undefined**

(31) INITIAL TIME = 0
Units: Week
The initial time for the simulation.

(32) iteration completion rate=
IF THEN ELSE(Plan>0, PULSE(iteration
factor+objectives duration+evaluation
duration+breakdown duration+plan
duration, 1) , 0)
Units: **undefined**

(33) iteration factor=Iterations time*(objectives duration+evaluation duration+breakdown duration+plan duration)
Units: **undefined**

(34) Iterations time= INTEG (iteration completion rate, 0)
Units: **undefined**

(35) objective completion rate=
IF THEN ELSE(Objectives>0, PULSE(objectives duration+iteration factor, 1), 0)
Units: **undefined**

(36) Objectives= INTEG (
-objective completion rate+time rate, 0)
Units: **undefined**

(37) objectives duration=2
Units: **undefined**

(38) Plan= INTEG (
breakdown completion rate-iteration completion rate,0)
Units: **undefined**

(39) plan duration=
plan start-breakdown start
Units: **undefined**

(40) plan start=10
Units: **undefined**

(41) Production = INTEG (
Release Ready Code Rate,0)
Units: **undefined**

(42) Release Ready Code Rate =
IF THEN ELSE(test limit, test constant-bug rate number, test left)
Units: LoC/Week

(43) req per time step=2
Units: **undefined**

(44) req rate=IF THEN ELSE(Iterations time<initial number:AND:delay=0, req per time step ,0)
Units: **undefined**

(45) reqmtsconstant=6
Units: **undefined**

(46) reqmtsleft= IF THEN ELSE(Requirements<reqmtsconstant, Requirements , reqmtsconstant)
Units: Documents

(47) reqs done= IF THEN ELSE(Requirements<= 0, 1 , 0)
Units: Dmnl

(48) Requirements= INTEG (
req rate -spec rate,0)
Units: **undefined**

(49) rework done=
IF THEN ELSE((Bugs)<=0, 1 , 0)
Units: Dmnl

(50) Risks Evaluation= INTEG (
+objective completion rate-evaluation completion rate, 0)
Units: **undefined**

(51) SAVEPER = TIME STEP
Units: Week [0,?]
The frequency with which output is stored.

(52) scope completed =
IF THEN ELSE(Code >=code constant, 1,0)
Units: Dmnl

(53) spec rate=
IF THEN ELSE(Requirements>=const go :OR:(Requirements<=const go :AND: :NOT:reqs done:AND:first time=const go) ,reqmtsleft, 0)
Units: **undefined**

(54) Test = INTEG (
Code Completion Rate-Release Ready Code Rate -bug Rate, 0)
Units: LoC

(55) test constant=1030
Units: LoC

(56) test left=
IF THEN ELSE(Test>=test constant, test constant-bug rate number,Test)
Units: LoC

(57) test limit=
IF THEN ELSE(Test <test constant, 0,1)
Units: Dmnl

(58) time rate=
IF THEN ELSE(Anticipated number of time steps>0, PULSE(iteration factor+1, 1) , 0)
Units: **undefined**

(59) TIME STEP = 1
Units: Week [0,?]
The time step for the simulation.

Figure B2.2: Source code of a systems dynamics model for a spiral type model for scenario "Code Error Detection".

Figure B2.3 lists the code for the systems dynamic model that we created for the scenario "Design Error Detection".

Spiral, Scenario "Design Error Detection"

(01) Anticipated number of iterations= INTEG (
-time rate,initial number)
Units: **undefined**

(02) Breakdown= INTEG (+evaluation
completion rate-breakdown completion
rate,0)
Units: **undefined**

(03) breakdown completion rate=
IF THEN ELSE(Breakdown>0,
PULSE(iteration factor+objectives
duration+evaluation duration+breakdown
duration, 1) , 0)
Units: **undefined**

(04) breakdown duration=
breakdown start-evaluation start
Units: **undefined**

(05) breakdown start=8
Units: **undefined**

(06) bug left=IF THEN ELSE(Bugs<bug rework
constant-Redesign Bug Rate*code
translation/design translation, Bugs-
Redesign Bug Rate*code translation/design
translation , bug rework constant-Redesign
Bug Rate*code translation/design
translation)
Units: LoC

(07) bug Rate=IF THEN ELSE(test limit, bug rate
number, 0)
Units: LoC

(08) bug rate constant=0.3
Units: Percentage

(09) bug rate number=
bug rate constant*test constant
Units: LoC

(10) bug rework=
IF THEN ELSE(rework done, 0, bug left)
Units: LoC

(11) bug rework constant=200
Units: LoC

(12) Bugs= INTEG (
(bug Rate-bug rework-Redesign Bug
Rate*code translation/design translation), 0)
Units: Bugs

(13) Code = INTEG (
(design spec rate* code translation) - Code
Completion Rate + bug rework,0)
Units: LoC [0,?]

(14) Code Completion Rate =
IF THEN ELSE(scope completed, code
constant, codeleft)
Units: LoC/Week [0,3000]

(15) code constant=1500
Units: LoC

(16) code translation =1000
Units: LoC/Documents [0,10000]

(17) codeleft =
IF THEN ELSE(Code<code constant, Code
, code constant)
Units: LoC

(18) const go=100
Units: **undefined**

(19) delay=PULSE(0, 1)
Units: **undefined**

(20) Design = INTEG (
spec rate-design spec rate+Redesign
Bug Rate,0)
Units: Documents [0,?]

(21) design done =
IF THEN ELSE(Design<= 0, 1 , 0)
Units: Dmnl

(22) design left =
IF THEN ELSE(Design<designconstant,
Design , designconstant)
Units: Documents

(23) design spec rate =
IF THEN ELSE(design done, 0 , design
left)
Units: Documents/Week

(24) design translation=10
Units: LoC

(25) designconstant=4
Units: Documents

(26) evaluation completion rate=
IF THEN ELSE(Risks Evaluation>0,
PULSE(iteration factor+objectives
duration+evaluation duration, 1), 0)
Units: **undefined**

(27) evaluation duration=
evaluation start-objectives duration
Units: **undefined**

(28) evaluation start=5
Units: **undefined**

(29) FINAL TIME = 300
Units: Week
The final time for the simulation.

(30) first time=
IF THEN ELSE(Requirements>const
go:OR:(req rate=0:AND:Requirements>0
), const go, 0)
Units: Documents

(31) initial number=5
Units: **undefined**

(32) INITIAL TIME = 0
Units: Week
The initial time for the simulation.

(33) iteration completion rate=
IF THEN ELSE(Plan>0, PULSE(iteration
factor+objectives duration+evaluation
duration+breakdown duration+plan
duration, 1) , 0)
Units: **undefined**

(34) iteration factor= Iterations
time*(objectives duration+evaluation
duration+breakdown duration
+plan duration)
Units: **undefined**

(35) Iterations time= INTEG (
iteration completion rate,0)
Units: **undefined**

(36) objective completion rate=
IF THEN ELSE(Objectives>0,
PULSE(objectives duration+iteration factor,
1) , 0)
Units: **undefined**

(37) Objectives= INTEG (
-objective completion rate+time rate,0)
Units: **undefined**

(38) objectives duration=2
Units: **undefined**

(39) Plan= INTEG (breakdown completion rate-
iteration completion rate,0)
Units: **undefined**

(40) plan duration=plan start-breakdown start
Units: **undefined**

(41) plan start=10
Units: **undefined**

(42) Production = INTEG (Release Ready Code
Rate, 0)
Units: **undefined**

(43) Redesign Bug Rate=
IF THEN ELSE(Bugs>bug rework constant,
redesign constant*bug rework constant
*design translation/code translation, 0)
Units: **undefined**

(44) redesign constant=0.03
Units: **undefined**

(45) Release Ready Code Rate =
IF THEN ELSE(test limit, test constant-bug
rate number, test left)
Units: LoC/Week

(46) req per time step=2
Units: **undefined**

(47) req rate=
IF THEN ELSE(Iterations time<initial
number:AND:delay=0, req per time step, 0)
Units: **undefined**

(48) reqmtsconstant=6
Units: **undefined**

(49) reqmtsleft=IF THEN ELSE (Requirements<
reqmtsconstant, Requirements ,
reqmtsconstant)
Units: Documents

(50) reqs done=
IF THEN ELSE(Requirements<= 0, 1 , 0)
Units: Dmnl

(51) Requirements= INTEG (
req rate -spec rate,0)
Units: **undefined**

(52) rework done=
IF THEN ELSE(Bugs<=0, 1 , 0)
Units: Dmnl

(53) Risks Evaluation= INTEG (
+objective completion rate-evaluation
completion rate, 0)
Units: **undefined**

(54) SAVEPER = TIME STEP
Units: Week [0,?]
The frequency with which output is
stored.

(55) scope completed =
IF THEN ELSE(Code >=code constant, 1
, 0)
Units: Dmnl

(56) spec rate=
IF THEN ELSE(Requirements>const go
:OR:(Requirements<=const go :AND:
:NOT:reqs done:AND:first time=const go)
,reqmtsleft, 0)
Units: **undefined**

(57) Test = INTEG (
Code Completion Rate-Release Ready
Code Rate -bug Rate, 0)
Units: LoC

(58) test constant=1030
Units: LoC

(59) test left=
IF THEN ELSE(Test>=test constant, test
constant-bug rate number,Test)
Units: LoC

(60) test limit=
IF THEN ELSE(Test < (test constant),
0,1)
Units: Dmnl

(61) time rate=
IF THEN ELSE(Anticipated number of
iterations>0, PULSE(iteration factor+1, 1)
, 0)
Units: **undefined**

(62) TIME STEP = 1
Units: Week [0,?]
The time step for the simulation.

**Figure B2.3: Source code of a systems dynamics model for a spiral type model for
scenario "Design Error Detection".**

Figure B2.4 lists the code for the systems dynamic model that we created for the scenario "Requirements Creep".

```
Spiral, Scenario "Requirements Creep"

(01)    Anticipated number of iterations= INTEG (
        time rate,initial number)
        Units: **undefined**
(02)    Breakdown= INTEG (
        +evaluation completion rate-breakdown
        completion rate,0)
        Units: **undefined**
(03)    breakdown completion rate=
        IF THEN ELSE(Breakdown>0,
        PULSE(iteration factor+objectives
        duration+evaluation duration
        +breakdown duration, 1) , 0 )
        Units: **undefined**
(04)    breakdown duration=
        breakdown start-evaluation start
        Units: **undefined**
(05)    breakdown start=4
        Units: **undefined**
(06)    bug left=
        IF THEN ELSE(Bugs<bug rework constant-
        (Redesign Bug Rate*code translation
        /design translation)-(New Scope Rate*code
        translation/requirements translation)
        , Bugs, bug rework constant-(Redesign Bug
        Rate*code translation/design translation) -
        (New Scope Rate*code
        translation/requirements translation))
        Units: LoC
(07)    bug Rate=
        IF THEN ELSE(test limit, bug rate
        .number,0)
        Units: LoC
(08)    bug rate constant=0.3
        Units: Percentage
(09)    bug rate number=
        bug rate constant*test constant
        Units: LoC
(10)    bug rework=
        IF THEN ELSE(rework done, 0, bug left)
        Units: LoC
(11)    bug rework constant=200
        Units: LoC
(12)    Bugs= INTEG (
        bug Rate-bug rework-(Redesign Bug
        Rate*code translation/design translation)-
        (New Scope Rate*code translation/design
        translation),0)
        Units: Bugs
(13)    Code = INTEG (
        (design spec rate* code translation) - Code
        Completion Rate + bug rework, 0)
        Units: LoC [0,?]
(14)    Code Completion Rate =
        IF THEN ELSE(scope completed, code
        constant, codeleft)
        Units: LoC/Week [0,3000]

(15)    code constant=1500
        Units: LoC
(16)    code translation =1000
        Units: LoC/Documents [0,10000]
(17)    codeleft =
        IF THEN ELSE(Code<code constant,
        Code , code constant)
        Units: LoC
(18)    const go=100
        Units: **undefined**
(19)    delay=PULSE(0, 1 )
        Units: **undefined**
(20)    Design= INTEG (
        spec rate -design spec rate+Redesign
        Bug Rate, 0)
        Units: Documents [0,?]
(21)    design done =
        IF THEN ELSE(Design<= 0, 1 , 0)
        Units: Dmnl
(22)    design left =
        IF THEN ELSE(Design<designconstant,
        Design , designconstant)
        Units: Documents
(23)    IF THEN ELSE(design done, 0 , design
        left)
        Units: Documents/Week
(24)    design translation=10
        Units: LoC
(25)    designconstant=4
        Units: Documents
(26)    evaluation completion rate=
        IF THEN ELSE(Risks Evaluation>0,
        PULSE(iteration factor+objectives
        duration+evaluation duration, 1), 0 )
        Units: **undefined**
27)     evaluation duration=
        evaluation start-objectives duration
        Units: **undefined**
(28)    evaluation start=3
        Units: **undefined**
(29)    FINAL TIME  = 300
        Units: Week
        The final time for the simulation.
(30)    first time=
        IF THEN ELSE(Requirements>const
        go:OR:(req rate=0:AND:Requirements>0
        ), const go, 0)
        Units: Documents
(31)    initial number=5
        Units: **undefined**
(32)    INITIAL TIME  = 0
        Units: Week
        The initial time for the simulation.
```

(33) iteration completion rate=
IF THEN ELSE(Plan>0, PULSE(iteration
factor+objectives duration+evaluation
duration +breakdown duration+plan
duration, 1) , 0)
Units: **undefined**

(34) iteration factor=
Iterations time*(objectives
duration+evaluation duration+breakdown
duration+plan duration)
Units: **undefined**

(35) Iterations time= INTEG (
iteration completion rate,0)
Units: **undefined**

(36) New Scope Rate=
IF THEN ELSE(Bugs >= bug rework
constant, scope constant*bug rework
constant*requirements translation/code
translation,0)
Units: **undefined**

(37) objective completion rate=
IF THEN ELSE(Objectives>0,
PULSE(objectives duration+iteration factor,
1), 0)
Units: **undefined**

(38) Objectives= INTEG (
-objective completion rate+time rate,0)
Units: **undefined**

(39) objectives duration=2
Units: **undefined**

(40) Plan= INTEG (
breakdown completion rate-iteration
completion rate, 0)
Units: **undefined**

(41) plan duration=
plan start-breakdown start
Units: **undefined**

(42) plan start=5
Units: **undefined**

(43) Production = INTEG (
Release Ready Code Rate,0)
Units: **undefined**

(44) Redesign Bug Rate=
IF THEN ELSE(Bugs>=bug rework
constant, redesign constant*bug rework
constant*design translation/code translation
, 0)
Units: **undefined**

(45) redesign constant=0.03
Units: **undefined**

(46) Release Ready Code Rate =
IF THEN ELSE(test limit, test constant-bug
rate number, test left)
Units: LoC/Week

(47) req per time step=4
Units: **undefined**

(48) req rate=
IF THEN ELSE(Iterations time<initial
number:AND:delay=0, req per time step,
0)
Units: **undefined**

(49) reqmtsconstant=6
Units: **undefined**

(50) reqmtsleft=
IF THEN
ELSE(Requirements<reqmtsconstant,
Requirements , reqmtsconstant)
Units: Documents

(51) reqs done=
IF THEN ELSE(Requirements<= 0, 1 , 0)
Units: Dmnl

(52) Requirements= INTEG (
req rate -spec rate+New Scope Rate,0)
Units: **undefined**

(53) requirements translation=10
Units: **undefiued**

(54) rework done=
IF THEN ELSE(Bugs<=0, 1 , 0)
Units: Dmnl

(55) Risks Evaluation= INTEG (
+objective completion rate-evaluation
completion rate,0)
Units: **undefined**

(56) SAVEPER = TIME STEP
Units: Week [0,?]
The frequency with which output is
stored.

(57) scope completed =
IF THEN ELSE(Code >=code
constant, 1,0)
Units: Dmnl

(58) scope constant=0.01
Units: **undefined**

(59) spec rate=
IF THEN ELSE(Requirements>const go
:OR:(Requirements<=const go :AND:
:NOT:reqs done:AND:first time=const go)
,reqmtsleft, 0)
Units: **undefined**

(60) Test = INTEG (Code Completion Rate-
Release Ready Code Rate -bug Rate,0)
Units: LoC

(61) test constant=1030
Units: LoC

(62) test left= IF THEN ELSE(Test>=test
constant, test constant-bug rate
number,Test)
Units: LoC

(63) test limit=IF THEN ELSE(Test < (test
constant), 0,1)
Units: Dmnl

(64) time rate=IF THEN ELSE(Anticipated
number of iterations>0, PULSE(iteration
factor+1
, 1) , 0)
Units: **undefined**

**Figure B2.4: Source code of a systems dynamics model for a spiral type model for
scenario "Requirements Creep".**

250

B3: Simulations Variations

In theory the parameters listed in Table 6.1 (page 145) can be modified to run simulations with these models. We like to show how some key variables influence the outcome of our models. We showed the influence of key variables of a waterfall model in Appendix A3. We use the systems dynamics model of the waterfall model for the waterfall part of the spiral model. Consequently the waterfall part of a spiral model and its parameters show the same behavior.

We show variations of simulations for the iterative part of the spiral model. We use the systems dynamics model we developed for scenario "Requirements Creep" for these simulations.

Variations of the Cycle Duration

We vary the duration of the cycles of the iterative part of the spiral model by varying the number of "Plan Duration". The results are listed in Table B3.1. Figure B3.1 shows the results in graphical format.

Plan Duration [weeks]	1	2	3
Cycle Duration [Weeks]	5	6	7
Duration [months]	52	53	54
Effort [person months]	213	218	225
Cost [$]	2,044,800	2,092,800	2,160,000
Size of end product [LoC]	102,000	102,000	102,000

Table B3.1: Results for variations of Cycle Duration.

251

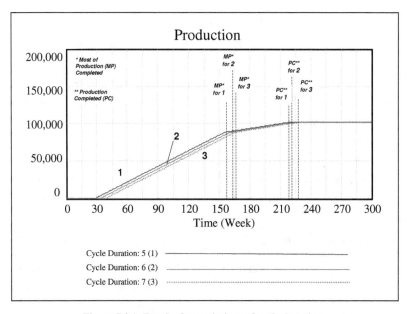

Figure B3.1: Results for variations of cycle duration.

The results in Table B3.1 show that an increase in cycle duration increases the project duration.

Variations of the Number of Iterations

We vary the number of iterations of the spiral model. The results are listed in Table B3.2. Figure B3.2 shows the results in graphical format.

Number of iterations [iterations]	3	5	7
Duration [months]	50	52	54
Effort [person months]	201	213	225
Cost [$]	1,929,600	2,044,800	2,160,000
Size of end product [LoC]	102,000	102,000	102,000

Table B3.2: Results for variations of number of iterations.

252

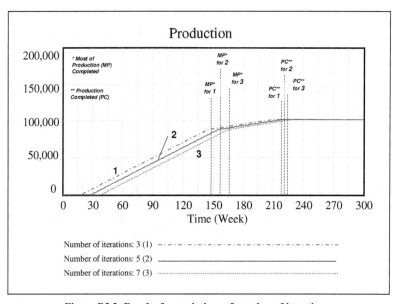

Figure B3.2: Results for variations of number of iterations.

The results in Table B3.2 show that an increase in number of iterations increases the project duration.

Appendix C: Systems Dynamics Model for a Spiral Type Model

C1: Stock and Flow Diagrams

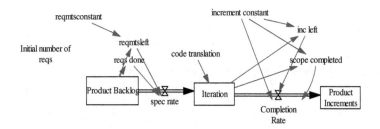

Figure C1.1: System dynamics model for scenario "Ideal World' of an agile type model.

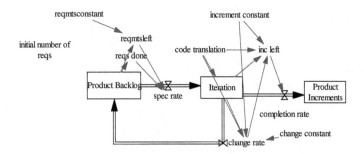

Figure C1.2: System dynamics model for scenario "Code Error Detection"' and scenario "Design Error Detection"' of an agile type model.

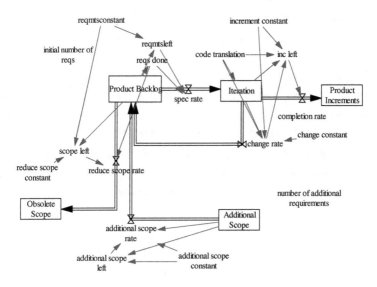

Figure C1.3: System dynamics model for scenario "Requirements Creep"' of an agile type model.

C2: Source Code for a Systems Dynamics Model for a Spiral Type Model

Figures C2.1 to C2.3 list the code that was generated by Vensim [Vensim, 2004], a simulation software tool for systems dynamics models. Vensim uses a graphical interface were the stock and flow parameters are defined and the formulas are edited through a dialog box. When simulating a systems dynamics model, Vensim generates the code. In Chapter 7 we focus our explanations on how these models simulate the software methodologies. We focus on the parameters used to create and influence the behavior of the software model. Other auxiliary variables are needed to make these models work. Consequently there are some variables listed in the code and shown in the Figures C1.1 to C1.3 that were defined to create positive results of the simulations. As an example all stock variables have to stay positive as there are no negative iterations existing in the real world.

As we proceeded with our simulations we discovered that we used non-descriptive names for some parameters. Table 7.1 (page 179) lists the descriptive names and the non-descriptive names that were used for the systems dynamics models.

We developed these models in steps. We started with the basic model representing the most idealistic scenario "Ideal World" and successive developed the next more complex model for the scenarios "Code Error Detection", "Design Error Detection", and "Requirements Creep". Consequently the code listed in this chapter becomes more complex and increases in size with each scenario.

Figure C2.1 lists the code for the systems dynamic model that we created for the scenario "Ideal World".

```
Agile, Scenario "Ideal World"
(01)    code translation=1000
        Units: LoC/Requirement [0,10000]
(02)    Completion Rate=
        IF THEN ELSE(scope completed, increment
        constant, inc left)
        Units: LoC/Iteration [0,3000]
(03)    FINAL TIME  = 100
        Units: Month
        The final time for the simulation.
(04)    inc left=
        IF THEN ELSE(Iteration<increment
        constant, Iteration , increment constant)
        Units: LoC
(05)    increment constant=4120
        Units: LoC
(06)    Initial number of reqs=100
        Units: Documents
(07)    INITIAL TIME  = 0
        Units: Month
        The initial time for the simulation.
(08)    Iteration= INTEG (
        (spec rate* code translation) - Completion
        Rate,0)
        Units: LoC [0,?]
(09)    Product Backlog= INTEG (
        -spec rate,Initial number of reqs)
        Units: Documents [0,100,1]
(10)    Product Increments= INTEG (
        Completion Rate,0)
        Units: LoC
(11)    reqmtsconstant=4
        Units: Documents
(12)    reqmtsleft=
        IF THEN ELSE(Product
        Backlog<reqmtsconstant, Product Backlog ,
        reqmtsconstant)
        Units: Documents
(13)    reqs done=
        IF THEN ELSE(Product Backlog<= 0, 1 , 0)
        Units: Dmnl

(14)    SAVEPER =        TIME STEP
        Units: Month [0,?]
                The frequency with which
        output is stored.
(15)    scope completed=
        IF THEN ELSE(Iteration >=increment
        constant, 1,0)
        Units: Dmnl
(16)    spec rate=
        IF THEN ELSE(reqs done, 0 ,reqmtsleft)
        Units: Requirements/Iteration
(17)    TIME STEP  = 1
        Units: Month [0,?]
        The time step for the simulation.
```

Figure C2.1: Source code of a systems dynamics model for an agile type model for scenario "Ideal World'.

Figure C2.2 lists the code for the systems dynamic model that we created for the scenario "Code Error Detection" and "Design Error Detection".

```
Agile, Scenario "Code Error Detection" &
"Design Error Detection"
(01)    change constant=0.2
        Units: **undefined**
(02)    change rate=
        IF THEN ELSE(Iteration>=increment
        constant, increment constant*change
        constant/code translation , 0 )
        Units: LoC
(03)    code translation=1000
        Units: LoC/Requirement [0,10000]
(04)    completion rate=inc left
        Units: LoC/Iteration [0,3000]
(05)    FINAL TIME  = 100
        Units: Month
        The final time for the simulation.
(06)    inc left=IF THEN ELSE((Iteration>=
        increment constant+change rate*code
        translation), increment constant, Iteration-
        (change rate*code translation))
        Units: LoC
(07)    increment constant=4000
        Units: LoC
(08)    initial number of reqs=100
        Units: Documents
(09)    INITIAL TIME  = 0
        Units: Month
        The initial time for the simulation.
(10)    Iteration= INTEG (
        (spec rate* code translation) - completion
        rate - (change rate*code translation),0)
        Units: LoC [0,?]
(11)    Product Backlog= INTEG (
        -spec rate+change rate,initial number of
        reqs)
        Units: Documents [0,100,1]
(12)    Product Increments= INTEG (
        completion rate,0)
        Units: LoC
(13)    reqmtsconstant=4
        Units: Documents

(14)    reqmtsleft=
        IF THEN ELSE(ProductBacklog<
        reqmtsconstant, Product Backlog ,
        reqmtsconstant)
        Units: Documents
(15)    reqs done=
        IF THEN ELSE(Product Backlog<= 0, 1 0)
        Units: Dmnl
(16)    SAVEPER =        TIME STEP
        Units: Month [0,?]
        The frequency with which output is
        stored.
(17)    spec rate=
        IF THEN ELSE(reqs done, 0 ,reqmtsleft)
        Units: Requirements/Iteration
(18)    TIME STEP  = 1
        Units: Month [0,?]
        The time step for the simulation.
```

Figure C2.2: Source code of a systems dynamics model for an agile type model for scenario "Code Error Detection"' and scenario "Design Error Detection"'.

Figure C2.3 lists the code for the systems dynamic model that we created for the scenario "Requirements Creep".

```
Agile, Scenario "Requirements Creep"
(01)    Additional Scope= INTEG (
        -additional scope rate,number of additional
        requirements)
        Units: **undefined**
(02)    additional scope constant=0.3
        Units: **undefined**
(03)    additional scope left=
        IF THEN ELSE(Additional Scope<additional
        scope constant:AND:Additional Scope
        >0, Additional Scope, 0)
        Units: **undefined**
(04)    additional scope rate=
        IF THEN ELSE(Additional
        Scope>=additional scope constant,
        additional scope constant
        , additional scope left)
        Units: **undefined**
(05)    change constant=0.2
        Units: **undefined**
(06)    change rate=
        IF THEN ELSE(Iteration>=increment
        constant, increment constant*change
        constant/code translation , 0 )
        Units: LoC
(07)    code translation=1000
        Units: LoC/Requirement [0,10000]
(08)    completion rate=inc left
        Units: LoC/Iteration [0,3000]
(09)    FINAL TIME  = 100
        Units: Month
        The final time for the simulation.
(10)    inc left=
        IF THEN ELSE(Iteration>= increment
        constant+change rate*code translation,
         increment constant, Iteration-(change
        rate*code translation))
        Units: LoC
(11)    increment constant=4000
        Units: LoC
(12)    initial number of reqs=100
        Units: Documents
(13)    INITIAL TIME  = 0
        Units: Month
        The initial time for the simulation.
(14)    Iteration= INTEG (
        (spec rate* code translation) - completion
        rate - (change rate*code translation),0)
        Units: LoC [0,?]
(15)    number of additional requirements=10
        Units: new requirements per development

(16)    Obsolete Scope= INTEG (
        reduce scope rate,0)
        Units: **undefined**
(17)    Product Backlog= INTEG (
        -spec rate+change rate-reduce scope
        rate+additional scope rate,initial number
        of reqs)
        Units: Documents [0,100,1]
(18)    Product Increments= INTEG (completion
        rate, 0)
        Units: LoC
(19)    reduce scope constant=0.1
        Units: **undefined**
(20)    reduce scope rate=
        IF THEN ELSE(reqs done, 0, scope left)
        Units: **undefined**
(21)    reqmtsconstant= 4
        Units: Documents
(22)    reqmtsleft=
        IF THEN ELSE(Product
        Backlog<reqmtsconstant, Product
        Backlog , reqmtsconstant)
        Units: Documents
(23)    reqs done=
        IF THEN ELSE(Product Backlog<= 0, 1 0)
        Units: Dmnl
(24)    SAVEPER  =        TIME STEP
        Units: Month [0,?]
        The frequency with which output is
        stored.
(25)    scope left=
        IF THEN ELSE(Product
        Backlog<reqmtsconstant, 0 , reduce
        scope constant)
        Units: **undefined**
(26)    spec rate=
        IF THEN ELSE(reqs done, 0 ,reqmtsleft)
        Units: Requirements/Iteration
(27)    TIME STEP  = 1
        Units: Month [0,?]
        The time step for the simulation.
```

Figure C2.3: Source code of a systems dynamics model for an agile type model for scenario "Requirements Creep".

259

C3: Simulations Variations

In theory all the parameters listed in Table 7.1 (page 179) can be modified to run simulations with these models. In order to identify the influence of key variables on the outcome of our models we use the values stated as in Table 7.1 (page 179) and modify one key parameter at a time.

We use the systems dynamics model we developed for scenario "Requirements Creep" for our simulations.

Variations of Requirements Speed

We vary the value for how many requirements become available for each iteration ("Requirements Generation Speed"). The results are listed in Table C3.1. Figure C3.1 shows the results in graphical format.

Requirements Generation Speed [Documents]	3	4	5
Duration [months]	37	36	36
Effort [person months]	169	162	162
Cost [$]	1,622,400	1,555,200	1,555,200
Size of end product [LoC]	106,500	106,800	107,600

Table C3.1: Results for variations of "Requirements Generation Speed".

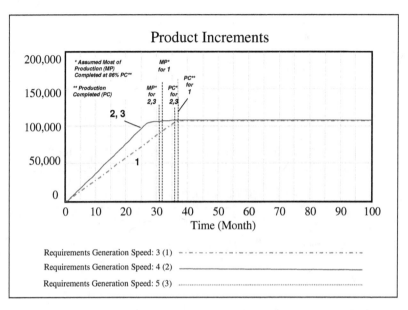

Figure C3.1: Results for variations of "Requirements Generation Speed".

Each iteration generates a product increment up to a maximum size. Each requirement generates 1000 LoC, An increase of requirements has only influence on the duration of the project until the maximum number of LoC for the product increment is reached.

Variations of Increment Speed

We vary the maximum value of code that can become available for each iteration ("Increment Generation Speed").The results are listed in Table C3.2. Figure C3.2 shows the results in graphical format.

Increment Generation Speed [LoC]	2000	3000	4000
Duration [months]	56	38	36
Effort [person months]	256	173	162
Cost [$]	2,457,600	1,660,800	1,555,200
Size of end product [LoC]	107,100	107,000	106,800

Table C3.2: Results for variations of "Increment Generation Speed".

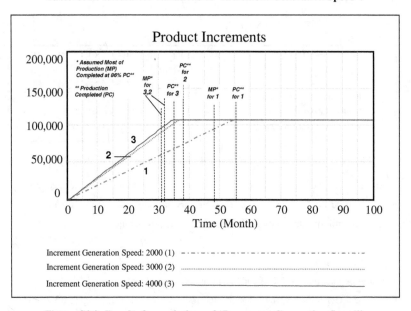

Figure C3.2: Results for variations of "Increment Generation Speed".

The project duration decreases with increasing size of the product increment.

Variations of Change Rate

We vary the percentage of code and design defects that are identified at the review at the end of each iteration ("Change Portion").The results are listed in Table C3.3. Figure C3.3 shows the results in graphical format.

Change Portion [Percentage]	0.2	0.3	0.4
Duration [months]	36	40	45
Effort [person months]	162	182	207
Cost [$]	1,555,200	1,747,200	1,987,200
Size of end product [LoC]	106,800	106,300	105,800

Table C3.3: Results for variations of "Change Portion".

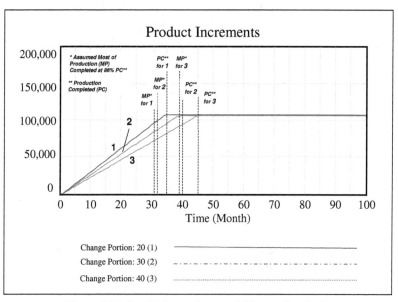

Figure C3.3: Results for variations of "Change Portion".

Table C3.2 and Figure C3.3 show that an increase in defects increases the project duration.

Variation of Requirements Creep

The influence of requirements creep has been assed in Chapter 7.6 (see Table 7.3 and Figure 7.20).